The book of foxhunting

the book of foxhunting

J. N. P. WATSON

ARCO PUBLISHING COMPANY, INC.
NEW YORK

Published 1978 by Arco Publishing Company, Inc.
219 Park Avenue South, New York, N.Y. 10003

Printed in Great Britain

Library of Congress Cataloging in Publication Data

Watson, J   N   P
    The book of foxhunting.

    Bibliography: p. 215
    1. Foxhunting. I. Title.
SK285.W33   799.2′59′74442   77-8511
ISBN 0-668-04356-3

CONTENTS

List of Illustrations 9

Acknowledgments 11

Introduction 12

Chapter 1 **The History of Foxhunting** 15
Britain
The United States *Alexander Mackay Smith*

Chapter 2 **The Fox** 36

Chapter 3 **Scent** 41

Chapter 4 **The Foxhound** 47
Britain
The United States *Alexander Mackay Smith*

Chapter 5 **Five Unique Packs** 65
The Curre
The College Valley
The Cotley
The Dumfriesshire
The Scarteen

Chapter 6 **Kennels and Welfare** 77

Chapter 7 **Ethics, Organization and Appointments** 88

Chapter 8 **Hunting the Fox** 96

Chapter 9 **The Hunter** 109

Chapter 10 **Riding to Hounds** 117
Britain
The United States *Alexander Mackay Smith*

Chapter 11 **Accidents and First Aid in the Hunting Field** *Michael W.
Gibson*, BVMS, MRCVS 128

Chapter 12 **Following on Foot** 133

Chapter 13 **Hunting on the Fells of Lakeland** 137

Chapter 14 **The Irish Scene** 146

Chapter 15 **An American Foxhunting Tour** 155

Chapter 16 **Foxhunting Around the World** 166
Australia *Heather B. Ronald*
Canada *Lt-Col. A. Britton Smith*, MC, QC, *Master of the Frontenac
Hunt*
Italy *Count Cigala Fulgosi, Master of the Rome Hunt*
Portugal

Chapter 17 **Point-to-Point Racing** *G. B. Fairbairn, Sometime Chairman of the
Point-to-Point Secretaries' Association* 183

Chapter 18 **The Future of Foxhunting in Britain** 188

Chapter 19 **The Literature of the Sport** 195
British Literature
American Foxhunting Bibliography

Appendixes

The Locations of the American Hunts   217

Foxhunting Terms   220

A Simple Guide for Hunter Trials   *British Horse Society*   227

Dedication

To all those kind, hospitable people who have had my wife and me to stay during our numerous hunting visits at home and abroad

List of Illustrations

(Illustrations 1–19 appear between pages 80 and 81)

1 Peter Beckford (1740–1809)
2 Hugo Meynell (1753–1800)
3 Thomas Assheton Smith (1776–1858)
4 Charles James Apperley, 'Nimrod' (1778–1843)
5 'Taking a Toss with a Variety of Effects', Henry Alken
6 'The Death Postponed', designed by Gill, 1822
7 'The Cheshire Hounds', by Goodwin Kilburne
8 The Pytchley Hunt Meet near Northampton
9 Lady Zia Wernher, Joint Master of Fernie's
10 A Welsh hound
11 The Duke of Beaufort's pontiff in 1972
12 Foxhounds of Hugo Meynell's day
13 Dumfriesshire Dancer
14 Cotley Songstress
15 Curre
16 Scarteen Acrobat
17 Blencathra Trueman
18 College Valley Poacher
19 A litter of six hound puppies

(Illustrations 20–30 appear between pages 144 and 145)

20 Quorn hounds at exercise
21 Judging at Peterborough Royal Foxhound Show
22 Pembrokeshire hounds at post-hunt feeding time
23 Bitches of the Galway Blazers
24 The Crawley and Horsham at Shipley
25 Master and Huntsman of the Heythrop with his hounds
26 Enfield Chase Hunt Meet
27 Hounds crossing Ford Brook, Vale of Aylesbury Hunt

28 The North Shropshire Hunt Secretary collecting caps
29 A Cottesmore gate-shutter
30 The Melbourne Hunt

(Illustrations 31 to 46 appear between pages 192 and 193)

31 The Rome hounds near Pantano Borghese
32 Equipagem de Santo Huberto, Portugal
33 Snake-rail fence, a typical Canadian obstacle
34 A characteristic fence, Virginia, USA
35 A grey fox, USA
36 Jumping a fence, Battle Creek Hunt, Michigan
37 Mr Robert Irwin's five-year-old hunter 'Kit-Chin'
38 Cotswold followers near Chedworth, Gloucestershire
39 Meynell Hunt
40 Mr Tom Oldfield & Mr Keith Preston with the Sinnington terriers
41 The Adjacent Hunts Moderate Race
42 Quorn Hunter Trials in Leicestershire
43 Opening meet of the Ullswater at Dockray, Cumberland
44 John Nicholson with Lunesdale hounds
45 Three-year-old Linda Savage with Chiddingfold Farmers Hunt
46 Octogenarian Mr Joe Bond out with the Stevenstone

Acknowledgments

I AM MOST GRATEFUL to the Editor of *Country Life* whose employment has enabled me to gather much of the information contained in these pages and for his permission to reproduce the sections on Portugal and on the American Tour. I would also like to thank Mr Mackay-Smith, Editor of America's *Chronicle of the Horse*, Count Cigala Fulgosi, M.F.H., Lt-Col. A. Britton Smith, M.F.H., and Mrs Heather B. Ronald, for descriptions of foxhunting in the United States, Italy, Canada and Australia, respectively; Mr George Fairbairn and Mr Michael Gibson for their contributions on point-to-point racing and first aid; and The British Horse Society for permitting *A Simple Guide for Hunter Trials* to be reproduced as an appendix. I am also grateful to the following who between them read my type-script and offered many helpful suggestions: Capt. C. G. E. Barclay, M.F.H.; Baron Frederic de Beck, Master of Portugal's Equipagem de Santo Huberto; Mr Michael Berry; Major Sir Rupert Buchanan-Jardine Bt, M.F.H.; Capt. S. T. Clarke, M.F.H.; Lt-Col. R. F. P. Eames, M.F.H.; Capt. E. Hartley Edwards; Mr Gerald W. Evans, Secretary of the Hunters' Improvement and National Light Horse Breeding Society; Sir Alfred Goodson Bt, M.F.H.; Mr Ben H. Hardaway III, M.F.H.; Col. Albert P. Hinckley, M.F.H.; the late Major Robert Hoare, M.F.H.; Col. John L. Hornor Jr, M.F.H.; Major J. J. Mann, M.F.H.; Mr. J. O'M. Meade, M.F.H.; Mr Richard Russell, Secretary of the Irish M.F.H.A.; Mr T. F. Ryan, M.F.H.; Major David Style, formerly Secretary of the Central Committee of Fell Hunts; and to my wife for her considerable help and support throughout.

I would also express my thanks to the following people and organizations for permission to reproduce copyright photographs: Robert Chapman for fig 45; *Country Life* for figs 3, 4, 7; Foto Mariani, Rome for fig 31; Foxphotos Ltd for fig 44; A. Mackay-Smith for figs 34-6; Jim Meads for figs 11, 18, 20-3, 25-9, 38-43; Mrs Heather Ronald for fig 30; Sport and General Press Agency Ltd for fig 9; John Tarlton for the frontispiece, and figs 19, 24 and 37; Topical Press Agency for fig 8.

Introduction

LIKE MANY other enterprises started by the English, foxhunting is not only enjoyed by the sportsmen of several other countries but is still conducted in those countries in the English manner. Whether the fox is hunted over the American or Canadian prairies, with snake-fences to jump, across Ireland's vivid pasture, with its banks and doubles, over Australia's timbered creeks and sandy ridges, across Italy's *marrane* and *spallete* scrub wilderness, or through the cork, olive and eucalyptus groves of Portugal, fundamentally the methods used, and the spirit in which the sport is conducted, are the same as that which prevailed in Hugo Meynell's Leicestershire two centuries ago; and, wherever the fox is hunted, the lines upon which hounds are bred, the dress, and even the language are still essentially English.

So, although descriptions of the hunting scenes in all those countries are given here, it is from the English viewpoint that it is written.

I am not sure the book is internationally exhaustive. *Baily's Directory* lists a foxhunt in Mexico, but, despite several attempts, I have not been able to contact the Master. I am told the fox is hunted in Belgium and France, but, since those countries became afflicted with rabies, I have discovered no one in either who will admit it. I only hope that those not represented in Chapter 16 will send in a portrait of the sport in their part of the world, for inclusion, perhaps, in our second edition.

It may be wondered why I have described the present (1977) situation in each of the Irish hunts but not in the foxhunting countries of England, Scotland and Wales. The answer is simply that the length and scope of the book allowed for the one and not the other. There is a chapter devoted to those who, in Britain, follow hounds by foot and other means. They probably amount to at least as many as the mounted enthusiasts, perhaps more, counting the Lakeland Fells and the dismounted packs of Scotland and Wales. Because, in Britain, there is a measure of opposition to hunting with hounds (as distinct from shooting, trapping, gassing or poisoning), it is most important for the name of the sport that as many as possible are encouraged to participate and enjoy it.

It is not unnatural for townsmen who are aware that foxes are pursued with the intention of killing them, who know nothing else about it, who have heard distantly, like Oscar Wilde, of 'the pursuit of the uneatable by the unmentionable', will oppose the sport on moral grounds. For who, without a knowledge of how foxes live and die; who, if they had not experienced the magic of the sport, the 'charisma of the chase', would condone it? There is, indeed, a great deal of misunderstanding about the methods, motives and virtues of field sports, especially hunting with hounds, but one rarely, if ever, hears of anyone objecting to it once they have genuinely, intelligently and open-mindedly taken part in the sport.

In Britain, foxhunting is part of the countryman's way of life. If it is an anachronism, it is one that gives healthy pleasure to a host of people from every walk of life; and those who have indulged in it and have learned its mysteries know that, if it is 'cruel', it saves a thousand other cruelties. If this book encourages more people to 'go foxhunting', and that proudly, then it will not have been written in vain.

J. N. P. WATSON
PANNETT'S,
SHIPLEY,
WEST SUSSEX
1977

Chapter 1
The history of Foxhunting

BRITAIN

THE SCIENCE of foxhunting as we know it today, the most sophisticated branch of venery ever devised, was born in England two centuries ago. It is a legacy from those eighteenth-century squires who, in an age demanding greater speed and excitement, found in the fox, a then rather scarce villain of the countryside, a more adventurous quarry than the hare, but of course the spirit of hunting came down to those Georgian squires by a long, long road.

From earliest times man hunted that he might live. His own primate antecedents had shared that way of life with their fellow-animal predators. Hunting remained primitive man's first skill and his first adventure: tracking and stalking and subsequently assaulting his quarry with stone and spear, sharing hardship and danger and excitement with his comrades, being a part of nature's chain of predator–prey relationships; next to love it was the happiest thing on earth.

Ever in search of power early man observed how wolves hunted in packs and wished he could tame such packs for his own employment. He brought home the puppies of wolves and wild dogs for his children to play with, and these became watch and guard dogs. The ancient civilizations improved upon this: they tracked their quarry through the scenting power of two or more hounds; they practised venery. The Assyrians and Babylonians bred magnificent-looking hounds, and used them in combination with bow and arrow. The Egyptians, from whom so much of our western culture derives, were probably the first to breed for nose. Yet they too kept their hounds to catch meat rather than to make sport, and they followed them by chariot and foot more than from the back of a horse.

It was from the Egyptians that the Hellenic Greeks learned the basic principles of venery and of riding to hounds. What was the development of the equine beast up to this time? We know that the wild Asiatic horse was tamed towards the end of the Stone Age, but at the beginning of this domestication horses were too small to ride in battle or out hunting. The Libyans and Egyptians put them in harness and drove them to the two-wheeled chariot. Then they bred up their bone and stature and began to ride them; they passed on their art to the Greeks, who refined it.

Alexander the Great commanded Aristotle to write his *Treatise on the Chase*, and there are many other works about venery in Greek literature. However,

Xenophon, the contemporary of Euclid and Plato, pupil of Socrates and hero of the Persian wars, was the first expert on hunting and equitation to record his theories and experiences. Xenophon's works are among the great ancient classics. As many soldiers have done in every age since his time, he spent his retirement engrossed with hunting and horses and farming. He was a prolific writer. In his book on hunting he mentions two hounds: the Castorian, said to have been founded by the god Castor, and the Fulpine, a 'cross between a dog and a fox'.

Few would disagree with the gist of Xenophon's teachings. Here is an example:

'Hounds that run forward and frequently examine the discoveries of the others when they are casting about and hunting have no confidence in themselves, while those that will not let their cleverer mates go forward, but fuss and keep them back, are confident to a fault. Others will drive ahead, eagerly following false lines and getting wildly excited over anything that turns up. . . . '

Xenophon's contemporaries shared his judgments on the virtue of hunting; judgments like this:

'The first pursuit that a young man just out of boyhood should take up is hunting, and afterwards he should go on to other branches of education . . . hunting makes the body healthy, improves the sight and the hearing and keeps men from growing old. It affords the best training for war. For men who are sound in mind and body stand always on the threshold of success. . . . '

Here is Plato on the subject:

'There can be no more important kind of information than the exact know-ledge of a man's own country; and for this as well as for more general reasons of pleasure and advantage, hunting with hounds and other kinds of sport should be pursued by the young.'

In the ancient world the young military leaders were chosen from those who showed initiative, resourcefulness and courage out hunting. War and the chase, with their varied and mutual skills and demands upon the human character, have always been closely linked.

The Romans improved upon the breeds of horses and hounds, deriving their knowledge as much from the peoples they conquered as from the Greeks. 'Give up the use of nets', the consul Arrian urged his fellow-countrymen, 'and hunt the hare with hounds according to the practice of Gaul. . . . ' 'How excellent were the hounds of Gaul,' Arrian remembers at the end of his life, 'much faster than contemporary Greek hounds, some being called Sergusii, but the Vertragi were the fastest. . . . ' Julius Caesar mentioned that the Gauls 'coursed for sport rather than what they got'. Many of the roots of modern venery go back to ancient France.

Caesar's officers found horses and hounds well developed when they came to Britain too. 'You would not admire any hounds', Gratius insisted, 'so much as

the British dog.' Oppian, the Greek poet and huntsman of Second Century
A.D. commented:

> 'There is a strong breed of dog in this case used for tracking purposes ... which
> the wild tribes of painted Britons are accustomed to breed called Agassaei. ...
> In power of scent they are easily superior to all other hounds and the very best
> in the world for hunting, since they are very clever at finding the trail of those
> creatures that walk the earth, but are also able to indicate with accuracy even
> the scent which is carried through the air.'

The Norman hunting tradition stemmed from the fresh spirit of the eighth and
ninth centuries, from Charlemagne, the Christian revivalist and Emperor of the
West, who built a new order and civilization out of the chaos of the Dark Ages,
and founded the 'age of chivalry'. Charlemagne welded Europe in the first
instance by the sword. He regarded the hunting field as the primary training
ground for battle. His knights were imbued with the soldier's sense of duty and
straight living. They had to be accomplished horsemen and skilled *veneurs*. In
Carolignian Europe the cavalry leader and the hunter, with his new code of
honour and chivalry, was the *beau idéal*; and, because the chase was the training
pursuit and forerunner of battle, it was given a military ceremonial: the hunting
man acquired a glamour, striking styles of dress, precedences and etiquette. As
for the hunting horn it required an artistic as well as a practical sense, an ear for
music as well as a facility for straight aural communication. The stag, which was
then, as it is now, the continental man's most prized beast of the chase, became
sacrosanct. So when William the Conqueror, who inherited Charlemagne's
traditions and who 'loved the high game as though he had been their father',
defeated the Anglo-Saxons and occupied their island, he changed the character
of British hunting.

'I will that every man be entitled to his hunting in wood and in field of his
own possession', Canute had said half a century earlier, 'and let everyone forego
my hunting.' But William of Normandy thought this arrangement too *laissez-
faire*, too free-for-all. He saw that, without strict limits and discipline, game would
be in danger of extinction, and 'game' meant deer. For, in the days before man
learned to overwinter his cattle, venison was at a premium. Not only did William
insist that 'every man eschew my hunting' and tighten up the existing laws,
Canute's *constitutes de foresta*, but throughout the land he stipulated men's rights,
according to their property and income, to hunt at all. He created the New
Forest as his own domain. The Forest Laws were severe; the Normans and
Plantagenets imposed them remorselessly: the cruelties of the feudal bureaucracy
were rarely more terrible than when perpetrated upon 'offenders against the
king's game'.

However, the image of hunting England had become at once more studious,
more business-like and more elegant. With the Normans came the principal
ancestors of our modern foxhounds: the blue-mottled Gascons and the blood-

B

hounds, which came to be known in Britain as Talbots, their lines returning to the long-backed, heavy St Hubert, which was bred originally in the seventh century by the Bishop of Liége, founder of the monastery of St Hubert in the Ardennes. Occasionally the Talbot was crossed with the British hound which had been so admired by the Romans. From these hybrid Talbots emerged the Southern hound, the ancestor of the modern foxhound. By present-day standards all of them were very slow, but then so were the horses, which were litter palfreys or the heavy-boned military-charger type, bred to carry the mailed knight. So there was as yet no swift and hectic body of followers crashing on the hounds' heels. The Normans did, however, use a certain amount of Spanish blood to improve their hunting horses. During the Crusades, the Plantagenets, Richard Coeur de Lion and his brother John, went one better: they imported Arab stallions. The English learned many lessons in the art of venery from these Mediterranean campaigns, and, increasingly, hunting became a matter of sport as much as of flesh-gathering. Early in the fourteenth century Philip V of France encouraged his noblemen to hunt their big game 'by force and cunning'. Nets and spears and arrows were dispensed with, and hounds made all the going from drag and find through to the death. This was *la vénerie française*. It was the English model, too.

The fourteenth century was a fertile era for hunting literature, and in it we see the fox faintly emerging as a beast of chase. About 1340 Guillaume Twici, huntsman to the English king Edward II, produced his *Treatise on the Craft of Hunting*, and in it he gives the fox a high place in the order of precedence of beasts of the chase:

> '*And for to set young hunterys in the way*
> *To venery I cast me first to go:*
> *Of which four beasts be, that is to say,*
> *The hare, the herte, the wulf and the wild boar.*
> *And there ben other beasts five of the chase;*
> *The buck the first, the second is the do;*
> *The fox the third which hath ever hard grace;*
> *The fourth the martyn, and the last the roe.*'

In the 1380s Gaston Phoebus, Comte de Foix, a relation of the Plantagenets, wrote *Le Livre de Chasse*. This was translated into English by another Plantagenet, Edward, Duke of York, Edward III's grandson, the prince who was master of hart hounds to his cousin, Henry IV (and who died leading the vanguard at Agincourt, when his horse rolled over on him). Writing during his imprisonment in Pevensey Castle on a treason charge, Edward added several chapters of his own and called his book *The Master of Game*. This seems to be the most authoritative reference work on hunting until Peter Beckford's *Thoughts upon Hunting* appeared nearly 400 years later. As with the Carolignian and Norman princes and knights, so with the Plantagenets: they loved their hunting, and none

more than John of Gaunt, Duke of Lancaster, from whom the hunting Somersets
are descended, in particular Britain's twentieth-century doyen of the chase, the
Duke of Beaufort.

Le Livre de Chasse and *The Master of Game* show a significant difference
emerging between hunting in England and hunting in France. For Gaston de
Foix, 'the hart comes before all beasts', whereas Edward of York insisted, 'the
hare is the king of all venery . . . for all fair terms of hunting cometh of the seeking and hunting of the hare'. Of foxhunting Edward has this to say:

> 'When men seek in cover for a fox and the hounds happen to find him, then
> the hunter rejoicest for the exploit of his hounds, and also because it is vermin
> they run to. . . . If the hounds put up a fox while drawing for a hare, a warning
> note must be blown that there is a thief in the wood. . . . '

In those days Reynard was not simply a rogue but there was a premium on his
pelt as well.

Yet our tutors, the French, were never really attracted to the fox as a beast of
chase. Why did they remain faithful to deer hunting, and why did the English
abandon it? France was—and is, by comparison—a country in which woodlands
predominated, whereas the English forests were separated by broad expanses of
downland, punctuated by scrub. So it was natural that Englishmen should be
enticed into the open by Edward of York's 'king of all venery', the hare. *The
Short Treatise on Hunting* by Sir Thomas Cockayne (the first master, so it is
claimed, to hunt fox deliberately) was written towards the end of the sixteenth
century; and it shows that hunting bucks in summer and hunting hares—with
wild cats, martens and foxes as equal second favourites—in winter were then the
leading pursuits of the English country gentleman. The hounds they used were
the two types descended from the Gascon and Talbot strains: the short-legged
Southern hound, heavy and slow, with a deep sonorous cry and powerful nose;
and the speedier slighter Northern hound, that is the Talbot crossed with pointer
and greyhound, of which the distinguished horse breeder Gervase Markham
(1560–1637) wrote:

> 'He has a head more slender [than the Southern hound], with a longer nose;
> ears and flews more shallow, broad back, belly gaunt, joints long, tail small,
> and his general form is more slender and greyhound-like; but the virtues of
> these Yorkshire hounds I can praise no further than for scent or swiftness, for
> with respect to mouth they have only a little shrill sweetness, but no depth of
> tone or solemn music.'

In fact this faster northern-bred hound was, by modern standards, also seriously
deficient in both nose and drive.

For royal parties in sixteenth- and seventeenth-century England, the 'noble
stag' was still the glittering prize of venery. Weapons were developing as well as

hounds, and a rather degenerate pastime was enjoyed by the Tudors. The deer were hunted around strongly enclosed parks for the sportsmen to shoot with the deadly crossbow, from hides and vantage points. This *battue*-style hunting, which was a favourite pursuit of Elizabeth I, was promoted by the fashion of formal landscaping and emparkment, by which huge deer-ranch areas near the noble-man's house were fashioned, surrounded by wooden pales, banks and ditches. It was from these artificial hunting confines that the ornamental parks of the eighteenth century evolved.

James I, with his French upbringing, abhorred this coarse slaughter by the Tudors and, when he came to the throne in 1603, promptly borrowed Louis XIII's top *veneur*, the Marquis de Vitry, to re-educate the English in *la vénerie française*, but deer hunting in this country really was on the wane. The First Duke of Buckingham bred a level pack for James I, who was grateful for 'so fyne a kennell of young houndes. All of them run together in a lumpe, both of scent and veue. . . . ' These hounds were entered to hare and fox but not to deer.

The shape of the English countryside was changing: the oak forests, suppliers of timber for successive fleets, were dwindling, while here and there across the landscape, to feed a growing population, more and more woodland and marsh and heath were reclaimed for pasture and arable. Under the Protectorship the Forest Laws fell into abeyance, interest in hunting was frowned upon; it declined, and throughout the 1650s vagabonds and bands of hungry soldiers, discharged after the Civil War, roamed the forests and poached the parks and killed all the game they could lay their hands on. 'Nothing remains', mourned a cavalier, 'except rabbits and Roundheads.' The days of William the Conqueror's sacro-sanct stags were over for ever. Then with the Restoration's march of trade and agriculture, the squirearchy was expanded and enriched, and more and more landowners kept hounds. The heyday of the hare ensued.

At this point, since foxhunting implies riding to hounds, it is necessary to go back a century and to resume the progress in the equine world. British horseflesh gained a startling facelift under Queen Elizabeth. At the time of the Armada threat she took one disgusted look at the horse-soldiers who might have met the beautifully mounted Spanish cavalry and bade her generals set to and breed a decent warhorse. With the increasing power of military weapons, particularly field artillery and the musket, tactics demanded greater speed and flexibility. Faster, hardier horses were bred. Under the Stuarts Englishmen learned much from the great continental riding-schools and from their own leading horse-master, the Duke of Newcastle, courtier and general to Charles I and tutor to Charles II. The Stuarts laid the foundation of the modern bloodhorse; with the infusion of the Darley Arabian pace improved; point-to-point racing began under Charles II; and in the reign of Queen Anne, who gave the turf her active patronage, hunter plates were introduced. Sportsmen saw what excitement the horse could provide. Already under the Stuarts there was an urge to make horses 'fly' over long distances, across the new stretches of grassland provided by the growing movement of land reclamation; but the hare, the so-called 'king of all venery', was too parochial, too meandering, too short-distance a quarry for the young bloods brought up in this new open country.

If at the close of the seventeenth century the hare was still the favoured beast of venery, the fox was giving a greater sense of mission. He was verminous, the rascal of legend and folklore. By now some hunting men pursued whichever quarry was found first, hare or fox. The Second Duke of Buckingham, of Yorkshire foxhunting fame, died of a fever one wet evening in 1687 waiting for a fox to be dug out of a Yorkshire covert. By this time the Charlton Hunt, near Chichester in Sussex, was famous for its foxhunts, through the names of the Duke of Monmouth and Lord Grey of Werke; between 1690 and 1700, in Hampshire and Wiltshire, Lord Arundell was hunting fox only. (His hounds, incidentally, were eventually sold to Thomas Boothby, the first Master of the Quorn, and their descendants went on to Hugo Meynell, the co-pioneer of scientific foxhound breeding.) Many followed Lord Arundel's example: Thomas Fownes, in Dorset, was one of them. In the early eighteenth century great aristocrats spent much of their winter on the move, pursuing the foxes inhabiting their empires from staging points. Lord Berkeley's stretch was from Bristol to Kensington Gardens, Sir Richard Puleston's from Flintshire to Leicestershire and Lord Darlington's from Raby Castle, Durham, all the way down to Doncaster. The Dukes of Grafton hunted in Surrey, Norfolk and Northamptonshire; in the 1740s the Second Duke of Grafton had a bill pushed through Parliament for the building of London Bridge when his patience with the Croydon ferry ran out. The Brocklesby, a hunt that was to play a famous part in the story of the modern hound, was recognized as a pack of foxhounds by 1713.

During the eighteenth century many owners of hounds turned from deer or hare in favour of fox by chance, as recorded by the sporting writer, 'Cecil':

'The Fifth Duke of Beaufort, then still a minor, while passing Silkwood on his way home after a poor day's sport in 1762, threw his hounds into covert; a fox was found, which gallantly faced the open; a capital run was the result, which so delighted the young sportsmen that the Badminton hounds were forthwith steadied from deer and encouraged to fox. . . .'

The Duke of Rutland's hounds were turned from stag to fox the same year. The more foxes these men found, the more they wanted, but the changeover was slow to become universal. The conservative squire, with less exotic ideas of sport, preferred what he called 'cunning hunting'; he condemned 'racing down the quarry with fast packs'; for him the hare was still 'king of all venery'.

Not that the new sport of foxhunting had acquired much dash yet. The foxhunters set out as nonchalantly as their harrier friends—at dawn. They followed their quarry's overnight drag to the kennel where he slept off his meal; then they slowly pursued the glutted victim, all day very often. It was said that 'they walked their fox to death'. As often as not they hunted him to ground and then dug him

out. By the middle of the eighteenth century the huge majority of Britain was
still unhunted, but, as the science of hunting became a primary hobby (for some
almost a religion) among the squires, more foxhunting packs were formed, more
areas resounded to the music of hounds. Later in the century every self-respecting
squire came to know his Peter Beckford and William Somerville. Beckford's
Thoughts upon Hunting soon became the classic on hunting both hare and fox.
Scholar, linguist and connoisseur, it was said of the author:

> 'Never had fox or hare the honour of being chased to death by so accomplished
> a huntsman; never was huntsman's table graced by such urbanity and wit. He
> could bag a fox in Greek, find a hare in Latin, inspect his kennels in Italian and
> direct the economy of his stables in excellent French. . . .'

Beckford understood that, to hunt a fox in earnest, a hound with an ideal combination of stamina, speed, nose and cry must be bred. He advocated a hound of
the middle size. 'I believe', he said, 'all animals of that description are the strongest
and best able to endure fatigue.' Beckford echoed his contemporary, Somerville,
'the poet laureate of the chase' and himself a Master of Foxhounds:

> *'Of such compose thy pack: but here a mean*
> *Observe nor the large hounds prefer, of size*
> *Gigantick; he in the thick-woven covert*
> *Painfully tugs, or in the thorny brake*
> *Torn and embarrass'd bleeds; but if too small*
> *The pigmy brood in every furrow swims;*
> *Moiled in flogging clay, panting they lag*
> *Behind inglorious; or else shivering creep*
> *Benumbed and faint, beneath the shelt'ring thorn.*
> *For hounds of middle size, active and strong*
> *Will better answer all thy various ends*
> *And crown thy pleasing labours with success.'*

Nor would the modern pundits of Peterborough argue much with that, but
Beckford and Somerville were cast in the 'hunt a drag at dawn' mould. Elsewhere
pace was becoming the thing. Hugo Meynell, who succeeded his grandfather-in-
law, Thomas Boothby, in the Mastership of the Quorn in 1753, John Smith-
Barry in Cheshire, John Musters in Lincolnshire and Nottinghamshire and John
Warde in Northamptonshire started to hunt their foxes, fresh and alert in the
middle of the morning, and to make them 'fly or die'; but their hounds were too
slow to catch them in any great numbers.

Hugo Meynell, appreciating that a hound cannot be swifter than its scenting
power, knew that the best way to get on even terms with these midday foxes,
the only way to better sport and less digging, was to breed for drive, to produce
a hound not only with a new turn of speed but with nose to match it. He took

the best of the pack of light-boned Northern hounds, which he inherited from Thomas Boothby, and crossed them with a draft of the ponderous deep-voiced Southern hounds, which he bought from Lord Arundell, Master of the hunt that would become the South and West Wilts. Meynell then carried out a rigorous programme of selective breeding, and with his 'Stormer 1791', as the prototype and most-used sire, his pack set the seal of conformation and character on the modern foxhound. Close behind Meynell in these breeding experiments followed his friend, the First Lord Yarborough, Master of the Brocklesby, whose hounds exercised, perhaps, equal influence, and, Englishmen being pre-eminent as breeders of animals, it was not long before ambitious foxhunters all over the country emulated the trials and endeavours in the kennels at Quorn and Brocklesby.

Hunting by horse was concurrently established in Scotland and Ireland. It may also be mentioned here that, in the hills of Wales and the Lake District, foxes were hunted on foot long before this time.

Coincidentally, while foxhounds were getting faster, the patchwork face of the English landscape became less open and more productive and complex. Under the feudal system of the 'common field', each countryman had the right to graze so many animals on the common pasture, proportionate to the amount of ploughland he possessed or rented near his village. In the face of the rapidly expanding population (and, in George III's reign, of the Napoleonic blockades) a system producing greater agricultural yield was required. Better drainage for richer grazing meant crisper, more resilient turf. Wider acreages were put under the plough and were divided into plots, and, largely as a result of Robert Bakewell's experiments in breeding, cattle and sheep were properly penned. To effect these measures a further heavy programme of enclosure was ordered. It was indeed the influence of the Enclosure Acts, producing big thorn fences, often protected by palisades of timber, so beloved by British foxhunters, which were to contribute so much to the thrill of the chase.

For the sporting community a combination of faster, more agile and enduring horses, hounds with drive as well as speed and a country with better drainage and criss-crossed with hedges and ditches and post-and-rail fences could only result in one desire: to fly across the country, steeplechase fashion. A Mr Childe of Kinlet Hall, Shropshire, was said to be the first to keep up with hounds by galloping and 'flying' his fences. To Mr Meynell's great disgust, Childe persisted in this habit in Leicestershire: 'I have not had a day's happiness since I heard of it', mourned the genius of the Quorn. The bucks, however, were soon on the heels of 'the Flying Child'. Meynell responded by charging subscriptions. Pressed by the thrusters, he was prompted to breed hounds with still greater drive. The quarry ran far, the quarry ran straight and all jockeyed for position to be first at the kill: there was nothing to beat foxhunting. Soon the sport would develop its own very special *esprit de corps* and bond of fraternity, with a glamour and pageantry inherited from the ancient traditions of the French *véneurs* and of the

English monarchs and princes, that would make it the most beautiful and viva-cious activity of the English countryside.

Modern foxhunting was born, too, just as the Industrial Revolution was getting under way. Rural industry and craftsmanship were being transplanted wholesale to the urban areas. The towns mushroomed and boomed: during the next century the population of London would double, and half the people of England would be town dwellers. In the late eighteenth century and early nineteenth century the nation suffered a division from which it never really recovered, a division between town and country. In the urban districts no common interests linked the social strata, but in the rural areas, because healthy common denominators in both work and leisure existed, all classes mixed happily together: countrymen shared love of the land and field sports, with foxhunting as the greatest leveller of all; whereas townsmen of different backgrounds had no mutual interest except money. For them the ways of the countrymen were alien; that is why, funda-mentally, most city folk never came to terms with hunting. They lacked any grasp of the virtues of the hunting instinct; they failed to see that the foxhunters (albeit unwittingly) had substituted the wolf as the fox's natural predator for their highly-bred hound; and, since these townsmen never understood foxhunting's huge appeal and following, they were jealous.

One anti-hunting landowner was the Earl of Essex. In 1809 he sued his brother, the Rev. the Hon. William Capel, for taking hounds across his land, adding that 'the destruction of a noxious animal was not the real reason for the trespass'. The case went against Capel. Thereafter no one could hunt across another's land without permission, and hunt boundaries began to take shape. From this time forward, too, farmers were shown increasing respect.

1820 to 1890—this was the 'golden age' of foxhunting: the era after the Napo-leonic wars, when macadamization of roads and the application of advanced land drainage were introduced, and before the age of barbed wire, motor cars and patent manures. John Loudon Macadam's new metalled roads enabled followers to stage and drive over long distances: by 1840 there were 22,000 miles of turn-pike highway in England, and Regency coaches made comfortable 'covert hacks'. With the Industrial Revolution came hundreds of miles, first of canals, then of railways. Many believed these massive new lines of communication would sound the death-knell of hunting. 'The Grand Union Canal', complained Dick Knight, huntsman to Lord Althorp, 'has ruined the country.' Also the widely acclaimed sporting writer, Delmé Radcliffe, on railways commented, 'The effect of the railway bills will be to drain to the source the very springs of hunting's existence, to dry up the fountains by which it is supported . . . they will transform the rural soil into one vast gridiron.' However, foxhunters soon came to realize what a boon trains were. Putting the words into the mouth of his cari-cature of a Cockney master, John Jorrocks, R. S. Surtees sums up the situation well, 'My offices in Great Coram Street are close to the two best covert hacks—the Great Northern and Euston Stations.' The railways made hunting accessible to all sorts of people who would otherwise never have followed hounds. Trains meant, above all, that foxhunters could venture away from their more mundane provinces and enjoy hunting's Mecca: Leicestershire and Rutland.

But sportsmen were making long expeditions to the Shires many years before the railways came in. For those counties, having more or less escaped the strictures of the Corn Laws, were a paradise of grass, with first-class scenting conditions. Leicestershire had the tradition of the great Hugo Meynell and the level hard-driving hounds he had bred, and of the Duke of Rutland's and the Cottesmore. Money fairly poured into the county, and by the early 1800s Melton Mowbray had become the capital of foxhunting. This is how Charles James Apperley, that highly gifted and experienced—albeit affected and snobbish— hunting correspondent and horseman, who wrote under the pseudonym of Nimrod, describes the Melton style in about 1820:

'At rather an early hour are to be seen groups of hunters, the finest in the world, setting out in different directions to meet different packs of hounds. Each sportsman sends forward two. On one is mounted a very light, but extremely well-dressed, lad who returns home on his master's cover hack, or in the dickey of his carriage, if he has happened to be carried to cover in the more luxurious fashion. . . . About an hour and a half after the servants have gone forward with the hunters, a change of scene is to be observed at Melton. Carriages and four appear at some doors; at others very clever, and, most commonly, thorough-bred hacks, led gently in hand, ready for their owners to mount. The by-roads of this country being bad for wheels, the hack is often the better conveyance of the two—always, indeed, unless the fixture be at a place on, or not far from, a turnpike road; and twelve or fourteen miles are performed by him in the hour. . . . The style of your Meltonian foxhunter has long distinguished him above his brethren of what he calls the *provincial* chase. When turned out of the hands of his valet, he presents the very *beau idéal* of his caste. The exact Stultz-like fit of his coat, his superlatively well-cleaned breeches and boots, and the generally apparent high breeding of the man, can seldom be matched elsewhere. . . .'

The Alkens put it as well on canvas.

Out with the eighteenth century went the tricorne-hatted frock-coated squire on his ambling nag; in with the nineteenth century came the blade, dressed in top hat, white leather breeches and scarlet swallowtails, sitting astride his glistening bloodhorse, with what became known as the 'English hunting seat', which had prompted the folding over at the top of the thigh boot, thus evolving into his close-fitting mahogany-topped boot.

Participation was now *de rigueur* in England: by the end of the Napoleonic wars, to be a mere patron of sport, a Corinthian, was a mean thing. The degeneracy of the Regency had come to be regarded with ridicule and contempt. Everywhere countrymen praised the Duke of Wellington's officers, fresh from the Peninsular and Waterloo, 'returning to England to bring out a second edition of cavalry charges over the pastures of the Shires', where John Warde and Lord Althorp had made the Pytchley famous, where the Duke of Rutland was at the Belvoir's helm, where the First Lord Lonsdale offered dashing runs with the Cottesmore and where Squire Osbaldeston—another celebrated breeder of hounds and hunting field genius—offered famous days with the Quorn. This happened in Shropshire, too, where the crazy young squire, John Mytton, epitomized the recklessness of the 'bloods', and in Cheshire where Tom Cholmondeley was another who welcomed the young victors over the French. Foxhunting had become the great activity in which men were accepted for what they did and achieved rather than who they were. The man who rode well to hounds acquired a special radiance in society as a whole. In rural Britain in those days it was said that, for many, 'foxhunting is next to holiness'. In all corners of the kingdom notices of the meets were nailed to church doors. To be a Master of Hounds was an ultimate in ambition: 'If I were as rich as Mr Darcy', says Master Lucas in *Pride and Prejudice*, 'I would keep a pack of foxhounds and drink a bottle of wine every day.'

By now Brocklesby and Belvoir, the two tap-roots of English foxhound blood, were famous, and Osbaldeston Furrier and Brocklesby Rallywood were acknowledged as being the foundation-stones of the kennel stud book. As for the horses, no fashionable foxhunter rode anything less than a thoroughbred. 'The soundness of the pastures', noted Lord Willoughby de Broke, looking back on the mid-nineteenth century, 'and the general advance in the science of horsemanship, made riding over the country more delightful than ever.'

Roads, railways, enclosure, drainage and canals were not the only physical innovations to influence nineteenth-century hunting. The shotgun improved, and the 'pheasant versus foxhunting' controversy began early. It was reckoned that over 2,000 pheasants a season fell to Squire Mytton's breech-loader years before Waterloo was fought, while a little later, Lord Stamford, Master of the Quorn, was disappointed if he and his guests failed to bag 1,750 a day. Even in those days there were a few non-hunting squires who refused to let hounds across their land before the New Year. Albeit foxes were scarcer, the gamekeepers' antipathy for them was stronger than it is today. From the hunting man's point of view, foxes were too scarce, but 'bagmen' could be bought at Leadenhall market where there was a turnover of several thousands every year. The standard rate was 2s. 6d. a fox. The best specimens were English, but most came from France, where they were a good deal more numerous.

Squire Osbaldeston's regular orders were always accompanied by this stricture, 'old English foxes, if you please, no damned French dunghills'. Beckford, with his regular instinct for truth, had written of bagmen, 'The scent of them is too good and makes hounds idle; besides, in the manner in which they are generally turned out, it makes hounds very wild.' Nimrod put the morals of it in a nutshell, 'To hunt any animal whom you have had in your hand is not sport.'

However, Masters were sometimes desperate to keep their hounds in blood and this usually meant to resort to a 'bagman'.

Besides Leadenhall, earths were remorselessly dug up, and cubs were sold to the best payers in neighbouring countries. This deplorable practice continued only until about the middle of the century, by which time there were enough foxes for all. To increase the fox population, enlightened Masters concentrated on improving their coverts, while all across the country fresh coverts were planted, especially with gorse, which seemed to be the best fox refuge of them all. With its density and prickliness, gorse was also a good deterrent to cub thieves. Things went further in favour of the huntsman and his hound when the Game Laws were relaxed in 1831 and were finally abolished under Gladstone. Hitherto no one other than a privileged minority were permitted to take rabbits or hares, let alone game-birds; consequently the country teemed with small game, and hound riot was a real problem. When more or less anyone could obtain a permit for snaring and shooting, there was a great deal less to distract the foxhound's nose and eye, while there was still plenty of small game left for the fox's larder.

Foxhunting was never a cheap pursuit. Henry Hall Dixon ('The Druid') recorded that early in the nineteenth century the Hertfordshire could be hunted seven days a fortnight with 12 horses and 50 couple of hounds for £2,000 a year, while the Quorn on the same scale would be £4,000—very substantial amounts a century and a half ago. As costs rose (and fortunes frequently diminished) Masters were less willing to carry the burden single-handed. By the end of Victoria's reign few private packs remained: nearly all had gone subscription. On this issue most foxhunters concurred with Surtees:

'Subscription packs are productive of more energy and less cavilling than private packs; every man feels his interest at stake both summer and winter and will look to things all the year round, instead of lounging carelessly out during the season, leaving the breeding and protection of foxes, the propitiation of farmers and other etceteras to the private owner of the hounds, who in all probability leaves it to the huntsman, who deputes it to the earth stopper, who leaves it to the assistant, who leaves it undone. A subscription pack makes every man put his shoulder to the wheel, not only to keep down expense, but to promote sport. . . . '

Arrogant masters of private packs could be unwelcoming, rude and dictatorial and often arrived very late for meets or cancelled them on personal whim. With subscriptions many more sportsmen were inclined to turn out, even women. In spite of the dashing example of Lady Salisbury, who hunted her own pack from Hatfield in the eighteenth century, very few women appeared out hunting till the second half of the nineteenth century. It was considered too risky; they were afraid of getting their faces scratched. It was also considered indecorous; it smacked of the adventuress: 'Ladies are more in their element in the drawing-room or in Kensington Gardens than in the kennel or in the field', wrote Col. Cook in his *Observations on Hunting*. But, by the time the lovely Skittles, Miss Walters, the ex-circus-girl-turned-courtesan, was banished from the Quorn by a sad Lord Stamford at the request of a jealous Lady Stamford, women had a fairly firm toehold in the hunting field. That elegant horsewoman and generous and tragic soul, Empress of Austria, who visited England in the 1870s and early 1880s and was piloted over some of the best hunting country of England and Ireland—in turn by Capt. Bay Middleton, J. O. Trotter and Col. Charles Rivers Bulkeley—did as much as any other single woman to make Dianas fashionable. In the wake of the women came the children.

One asset that remained indispensable from the beginning was the farmers' support. It is a misconception to think that landowners rode over the crops of their own tenants or of other people's tenants, that they left gates open or that they were, generally, anything but polite and considerate. It was said of the great Hugo Meynell that 'he would wait 20 minutes at a covertside for a farmer, but 10 minutes was all the law he would allow for a duke', and in 1821 Sir Bellingham Graham was obliged to give up the Pytchley after a single season because he could not carry the farmers with him. 'It is an axiom', wrote G. F. Underhill, 'that hunting depends upon the sufferance of the farmers.' 'You should endeavour to gain the goodwill of the farmers,' the veteran, Col. John Cook, urged potential masters, 'for if any respectable body of persons suffer from hunting is is them; and I think it is not only ungentlemanly but impolitic to treat them in the field or elsewhere, otherwise than with kindness and civility. . . . ' From the beginning farmers themselves hunted. They were, they have always been, the back-bone of the sport. The true foxhunter sees them as Will Ogilvie saw them:

> '*Looking back on the season that's ended,*
> *We blush for our track in the seeds,*
> *For the fences we left to be mended,*
> *And the damage we did in the swedes;*
> *And so, when we know there's no brooding*
> *And the mending is cheerfully done,*
> *Let us drink to the farmers; including*
> *The grandfather, father, and son!'*

As Victorian stability and rationality was felt in all spheres of life, people's attitude to riding to hounds grew more sober, more realistic: 'To ride your horse fairly,' said Lord Ribblesdale, Master of the Queen's buckhounds, near the turn of the twentieth century, 'to get to the end of many runs with few falls and to finish a season with a soundish stud is more the criterion of artistic riding to hounds, not the bravo-like adventures of the Mytton type which entitled the foxhunter to a place in the sporting anthologies of 60 years ago.'

But now the curtain had come down on the 'golden age'; Lord Willoughby de Broke wrote:

'For some years past, even before the war, life was becoming more complex, particularly for the agricultural landlords, who for many generations had directed the field sports of the British Isles. The agricultural depression, which began in the late 1870s, took away from many county families their hereditary privilege of being the chief financiers of foxhunting. . . . Railways produced a gradual effect; the change was hardly perceptible, but . . . cars came suddenly, and in hordes. They also marked a completely new era in the customs and indeed the manners of the nation. . . . '

Then, slicing heavily into Britain's youth and taking a heavy toll of the horses, came the Great War; and, in the post-war years, while the big estates were broken up, smallholders, many of them opposed to hunting, set the tone. Cars replaced horses, grooms became mechanics, and the social and economic revolution smeared the image of old Edwardian England to such an extent that many sportsmen, who regarded hunting as an integral portion of the old way of life, vowed it could never be revived.

But revived it was, and for a much broader strata of society. This oft-quoted truth written, 70 years before, by William Bromley-Davenport, all-round sportsman, poet and politician, echoed again, 'If hunting were based on exclusiveness, it would have perished long ago.' With a wider distribution of wealth and the advent of twentieth-century facility, more and more people wanted to ride to hounds and to send their children hunting; and the Prince of Wales, the world's most popular and adulated young man, by buying a stud and hunting regularly with his brothers from Melton Mowbray, gave the sport fresh impetus and a revived glamour.

Most sportsmen sensed that if hunting could surmount the holocaust of 1914–18, there was little reason why it should be trounced by Hitler's war. Those same jealous non-understanding townsmen of the kind who had always stood against hunting tried to effect what the most devastating war in history failed to effect: to break it. However, after the Second World War a government board, the Scott Henderson committee, 'enquiring into practices or activities which may involve cruelty to British wild mammals', judged that shooting, gassing, trapping and poisoning all entailed greater suffering and that hunting with hounds is at once the most effective and the most natural form of culling we have. Yet, with the passing of the 1930s went those regular and detailed hunting reports in *The Times* and *The Daily Telegraph*, which had demonstrated the old secure confidence in the sport. Foxhunting had become a nationally controversial subject. Feeling more sensitive about their image, most hunts phased out their displays of triumph in the death of the fox: the gathering round for the ritual of his 'breaking up', the 'blooding' of children and the taxidermists' mounting of masks and brushes and pads. The Masters of Foxhounds' Association revised a number of their rules to ensure the least possible suffering to the fox. Meanwhile, the British Field Sports Society worked, as they continue to work, with steady devotion and remarkable success to win more and more hearts to the cause of hunting.

In most parts of the country, the changing character of the land, intensive farming, the proliferation of roads and motor vehicles and the increased use of wire have, during the past half-century, made it more and more difficult for hounds to be with their fox. Bred to meet these hazards, the modern lighter hound with his improved scenting power, stamina and drive has made such names as the Duke of Beaufort, Ikey Bell, Peter Farquhar and R. E. Wallace famous in the history of the sport. Now, in the late twentieth century—in an era when the country is carved up by the impassable barrier of the motorway, when the railways have gone electric, when in most parts of England in the last 20 years the ratio of grass to arable has changed from 80% in favour of pasture to 80% in favour of plough, when the speedy expansion of industry and suburbia means a steady reduction in huntable areas, when the cost of employing a minimum staff and of maintaining a workable stable of hunt horses has become almost prohibitively expensive, when pheasant shoots are run increasingly on commercial lines, when the fox is often driven relentlessly from his habitat by overconscientious gamekeepers, when intensive manuring and herbicides obliterate scent—in an age that is inclined to be disdainful of pageantry and country traditions—in this era of man's grasping the last wild corners for his own amenity—the fox has never been pursued with more élan. Even now, each winter of the 'jet age', up to four days a week, 50,000 people turn out finely dressed and mounted, to insist, as their ancestors insisted, 'Be with them we will!' As many again, seeking something more than fresh air and exercise, yearning for a place next to nature, follow by car, by bicycle and on foot.

THE UNITED STATES. BY ALEXANDER MACKAY SMITH

Most settlers in what is now the continental United States—English, Dutch, Swedish, Spanish and French—brought dogs with them, many of them hounds. These were used as guard dogs, to warn of approaching Indians, bears, wolves and other 'varmints'. They were also used to hunt game destined for the larder, particularly the American rabbit (actually a small hare) and the white-tailed deer. Robert Brooke, who settled in Maryland about 1650, has sometimes been cited as having brought the first pack of foxhounds to North America, but it is far more probable that his hounds were kept for the above purposes rather than solely for the hunting of foxes. Virtually all the land, east of the Appalachian Mountains and lying along the Atlantic coast, was very heavily wooded, so, until this land had been cleared, riding to hounds for purposes of sport was impractical. By the 1720s and 1730s, however, travellers in the English colonies, particularly in Maryland and Virginia, began to note that hounds were being used for hunting foxes as they were in the 'mother country'.

The earliest surviving records of foxhunting in the modern manner—by what is now known as an organized hunt—maintained for the benefit of groups of foxhunters rather than for a single owner, are of the pack instituted by Thomas, Sixth Lord Fairfax, great-grandson of the famous parliamentary general. Fairfax had inherited from his grandfather, Lord Culpeper, the most magnificent estate in all the colonies, the Northern Neck of Virginia, granted by Charles II when in exile. This was his to give, since Virginia never acknowledged Oliver Cromwell, and therefore came to be known as 'The Old Dominion'. The Northern Neck lay between the Potomac and the Rappahannock Rivers. Since most of the eastern portion had already been granted at the time, Lord Fairfax inherited this estate; he moved to the Shenandoah Valley, to the west of which was the un-granted land and where the rich limestone soil was largely covered with natural prairie grass, undoubtedly the best section of his domain in which to ride to hounds. He even sent hounds ahead of him before his arrival—two dogs and a bitch from Sir Edward Filmore's pack of East Sutton, Kent, undoubtedly typical of the old Southern hound, particularly suitable for hunting the grey fox, the only species then to be found in the southern states, who normally runs a twisting, tortuous and circular line. In 1748 Fairfax employed, as one of the members of his various surveying crews, a 16-year-old named George Washington, who shared his employer's love of foxhunting. After Washington inherited the Mount Vernon plantation, a few miles south of the present city of Washington, and had married Martha Dandridge Custis, one of the richest widows of the colony, he established his own pack (1767), which he maintained until the outbreak of the American Revolution. After that conflict he re-established his pack, using, in part, French hounds sent over by his friend, the Marquis de Lafayette. Washington's diaries, which he kept meticulously, are full of items about foxhunting, by far the best surviving record of American foxhunting during the eighteenth century.

The earliest subscription pack was the Gloucester Foxhunting Club, founded by a group of Philadelphia gentlemen in 1766 and named after Gloucester County, New Jersey, directly across the Delaware River from the 'city of brotherly love'. There kennels were built and a 'rendezvous for foxhunting' was established at William Hugg's inn at Gloucester Point ferry. The history of the club, which flourished from 1766 to 1818, was written by William Milnor and was published by Judah Dobson at Philadelphia in 1830. With ample funds at its disposal, the Gloucester secured the best strains of hounds available both in America and in England, and showed great sport, not only on grey foxes but also on the red foxes, which appear to have been native to that part of New Jersey. Many of the notables visiting Philadelphia, then the metropolis of North America, hunted with the Gloucester, including, undoubtedly, His Excellency General George Washington, first President of the United States.

From 1800 until 1861, the date of the outbreak of the Civil War, a great majority of foxhunting packs in the United States were maintained privately by large plantation owners in the south. There were also subscription packs main-tained in such cities as Baltimore and Annapolis and also in Maryland and in Washington, D.C. The latter was particularly flourishing during the 1830s when the British Ambassador, Sir Charles Vaughan, served as President and when two members of his official staff served as whippers-in, namely Mr William Pitt Adams and Mr Andrew Buchanan, who later became the British Ambassador to Austria. Another *ante bellum* subscription pack was the Rose Tree Foxhunting Club whose headquarters was at the Rose Tree Inn, Media, Pennsylvania, not far from Philadelphia, a fine stone building constructed in 1796 which is still standing. Rose Tree continues to flourish and is currently the oldest subscription pack (1859) in the United States. The oldest existing private pack is the Piedmont, founded in 1840 by Richard Hunter Dulaney of 'Welbourne', Upperville, Virginia; this pack is now the property of eight proprietors living in the Piedmont country.

Before the Civil War, the major plantation owners had sufficient leisure to spend a considerable portion of it foxhunting, maintaining private packs. Most of them were ruined by the war, and their packs were scattered. Those able to retain ownership of their land were forced by circumstances to become their own overseers and to spend most of the daylight hours working. There thus grew up the practice of night-hunting, the established procedure being for a number of owners to bring their hounds at dusk to an area known to hold foxes, often mountainous. They built a fire on a ridge, where foxes are known to cross and from which hounds can be heard for long distances; then they turn hounds loose to find a fox on their own and listened to 'the race' as hounds drive their fox, usually in circles of several miles, which take them out of hearing and back again. The voice of each hound is perfectly familiar to its owner, who is thus able to determine, as hounds sweep by, whether his particular hound is at the head, at the tail or in the middle of the 'race'.

Out of night hunting developed the field trial. Pack-hunting hounds are bred and trained to hunt together as a team. In field trial hunting, on the other hand, hounds are bred and trained to excel as individuals, the best hound being considered the one which is able to run ahead of the others. Various local field trials were held informally, and during the middle of the nineteenth century, notably in Kentucky, where in 1864 a silver collar was offered by William Fleming for 'the fastest foxhound in the state', the annual trials were held for a few years in Madison County. The first organized foxhound field trial was actually instituted by the Brunswick Fur Club at Albany Hills, Maine, in November 1889, followed 5 years later by the National Foxhunters' Association trials at Olympia, Kentucky, trials which have been held annually ever since. There are now more than 200 such trials held annually in the United States and Canada. There are also, currently, three principal monthly magazines devoted to field trial hounds and field trials, each of which maintains its own stud book, *The Chase*, *The Red Ranger* and *The Hunter's Horn*. There is a good deal of betting on these field trials, and prices for top hounds are high. Actually, the number of field-trial registrations outnumber the pack-trial registrations of the Masters of Foxhounds' Association of America, by perhaps 100 to 1.

Riding to hounds after the Civil War was re-established largely by men who had hunted with the fashionable packs in the English shires, and who were anxious to establish this sport along similar lines in the United States. For example, Major Austin Wadsworth established the Genesee Valley Hunt in 1876 on the vast acreage in western New York State, which the Wadsworth family still owns and which the Genesee Valley still hunts in this part of the world, continuing to use English hounds. Another influential figure was Thomas Hitchcock, Sr, who was captain of the United States' first international polo team (1886) and father of the immortal Tommy Hitchcock, Jr, the greatest American polo player of his time. In 1880, while Mr Hitchcock, Sr, was attending Oxford, he helped Belmont Purdy to secure the draft of English hounds from Ireland, selected by J. Bourke Roche, with which the Meadow Brook Hunt was founded on Long Island.

Mr Hitchcock became Master of Meadow Brook in 1889 when he was 29 years old, resigning in 1893. He and Mrs Hitchcock, herself a brilliant horse-woman, had established themselves during the winters at Aiken, South Carolina. There, in December 1891, he founded his own pack and tried hunting the native foxes with some of the English hounds from Meadow Brook. Finding that they compared unfavourably with the local hounds, as far as hunting abilities were concerned, he turned to American foxhounds and in 1894 invited James M. Avent of Hickory Valley, Tennessee, to bring the latter's pack of American fox-hounds to Aiken where they showed great sport. In 1896, at the invitation of Major Wadsworth, Mr Hitchcock brought his American hounds to hunt the Genesee Valley country. One of the young men who followed these hounds this season was Harry Worcester Smith, who thereby acquired a lifelong enthusiasm for American hounds.

Mr Smith had also hunted from Melton Mowbray in England, in Ireland, with the Meadow Brook and with Mr Charles Mather's pack of English hounds, the Radnor, in Pennsylvania, so he had some basis for comparison. He was a friend of H. Rozier Dulany of Upperville, Virginia, whose cousin, Hal Dulany, main-tained the family pack, namely the Piedmont. After hunting with this pack Mr Smith became convinced that the northern Virginia counties constituted the greatest natural foxhunting section of the United States. He became joint-Master of the Piedmont and registered the boundaries of this country with the National Steeplechase and Hunt Association of New York City, which then recognized hunts for the purpose of determining the horses that were eligible for races restricted to 'horses regularly and fairly hunted'. At that time the greatest proponent of English hounds in North America was A. Henry Higginson who maintained the Middlesex pack near Boston.

Mr Higginson went permanently to live in England in 1931, becoming Master of the Cattistock. It should be remembered that, at this time the type of hound favoured at Peterborough, England's premier hound show, was the massive tricolour Belvoir type, with cat feet, often with a toe down, perfectly straight pasterns, knuckling over at the knee, with little or no cry, a type entirely suitable

C

for withstanding the charges of the immense number of horses and riders characteristic of the hunting fields of the English Midlands, but not at all suitable for the
cold-scenting countries with their immense woodlands, of the United States, into
which much wire had crept, so that the hunt staff and the field were necessarily
very dependent on cry for keeping with hounds.

In the course of a heated argument between Higginson and Smith, carried on
in the sporting periodicals, as to the relative merits of American and English
hounds, the latter challenged Mr Higginson to bring his hounds to the Piedmont
country in November of 1905, a challenge which was promptly accepted.
Hounds hunted on alternate days, six days a week for two weeks, at the end of
which the award was given to Mr Smith's American pack, largely stemming
from hounds acquired from Burrell Frank Bywaters, who hunted in nearby
Rappahannock and Madison Counties. The match was attended with a great deal
of publicity and was largely responsible for establishing northern Virginia as the
so-called 'Leicestershire of America', a status which it was to acquire during
succeeding decades. It also helped to establish the popularity of the American
hound, which now far outnumbers English hounds in the hunting countries of the
United States.

A group of foxhunters from Orange County, New York, during this same
period established themselves at The Plains in mid Fauquier County, hunting
territory within the map filed by Harry Worcester Smith with the National
Steeplechase and Hunt Association. When Smith protested this encroachment
and when the National Steeplechase and Hunt Association refused to take jurisdiction, Mr Smith called a meeting in 1907 at which was founded the Masters of
Foxhounds' Association of America, Major Wadsworth being elected president
and Henry Vaughan (Master of the Norfolk Hunt in Massachusetts) being elected
secretary. Major Wadsworth served one year as president, being succeeded by
Mr Thomas Hitchock, Sr, for 3 years and by Harry Worcester Smith for an
additional 3 years. Mr Higginson was then elected president and continued to
hold that office until he moved to England in 1931, when he was succeeded by
Henry G. Vaughan, the former secretary.

In 1933 Mr Vaughan succeeded in having transferred from the National
Steeplechase and Hunt Association to the Masters of Foxhounds' Association the
recognition of hunts and their boundaries. At the time of his death in 1939 there
were some 140 packs recognized by, or registered with, the association. Under
the editorship of Mr Higginson, the Masters of Foxhounds' Association of
America published four volumes of the *English Foxhound Kennel Stud Book*, the
last in 1927, restricted to hounds whose pedigrees traced in all lines to the British
stud book. In 1930, however, the title was changed to *The Foxhound Kennel Stud
Book of America*, which contained the pedigrees not only of English hounds but
of American hounds as well. To date, the association has published 12 volumes of
its stud book, the last covering the period 1969–72.

Harry Worcester Smith not only helped popularize the American foxhound but also persuaded the local hound-breeders of Rappahannock and Madison Counties to breed for conformation as well as for work, standing two of his own stud dogs in that section for the purpose. The fruits of this programme were gathered by Joseph B. Thomas, starting in 1912, who served as Master of the Piedmont from 1915 to 1919 and subsequently hunted a number of other countries, by invitation, until his pack was dispersed in 1933. Mr Thomas carried on hound breeding in the grand manner, sometimes having in his ownership, partly at his own kennels and partly with local hound breeders, as many as 500 couple of hounds! It was largely for this reason that the number of organized packs of hounds in the United States was able to make such a dramatic increase during the 1920s. Mr Thomas frequently supplied newly organized hunts with entire packs. As an advocate of the American hound, Mr Thomas founded in Middleburg, Virginia, in 1912, the American Foxhound Club which, ever since, has been the principal promoter of hound shows in the United States. These now include not only American hounds but English, cross-bred, Penn–Marydel, beagles and bassets.

In recent years, the club has undertaken a considerable publication programme, including two of my books, namely *The American Foxhound, 1747–1967* and *American Foxhunting, An Anthology*, published in 1968 and 1970 respectively.

The number of foxhound packs was considerably curtailed by the Second World War because of shortages of feed and labour. A further factor was the abolition of the United States Cavalry, together with a dozen packs of hounds connected with that arm of the service. A third factor has been that the requirements for recognition and registration are now much more rigorous than in the early days of the Masters of Foxhounds' Association. The enormous increase of interest in horses and riding, which has taken place during the past 10 years in the United States, however, during which our horse population has nearly doubled, has made itself felt in foxhunting circles, so that organized packs now number over 140 again. Though some packs in the suburbs of our larger cities have been forced by subdivisions either to cease or to move farther away, there is still an enormous amount of territory left suitable for foxhunting, particularly in the southern states, east of the Mississippi River, where the largest growth has taken place in recent years. Because the coyote leaves a scent far stronger than that of the fox, it has also been found possible to hunt it in the more arid sections west of the Mississippi. There seems little reason to doubt that foxhunting is currently in a very strong position, particularly since it is not catalogued as a 'blood sport', the object being the chase rather than the kill. We can confidently look forward to a very marked expansion of the sport during the rest of this century.

Chapter 2
The Fox

VULPES VULPES CRUCIGERA—that is the European fox's style; a member of the family Canidae, whose coat varies from grey-brown to bright russet, with black on the legs and ear-tips, white on the chest and sometimes a white tag on the end of his brush. His head and body are 2 feet long or more, with the brush adding another 2 feet to his total length. His height at the shoulder is about 14 inches; his weight is an average of 15 to 16 pounds. He is 'hare-footed' with four claws to each hindfoot and five to each forefoot, the fifth being a dew claw to help him climb and descend and surmount obstacles.

Highly adaptable, he is to be found in most parts of the world. Even in the British Isles he varies, being big and grey and rangy for the stone and heather uplands of Scotland, Wales and the Lake District and compact red-brown in the vale countries. True to his genus he has a dog-like shape and canine teeth in a sharp muzzle, but his ways are more the ways of a cat.

Vulpes vulpes . . . but from Greek and Roman legend on down the ages what mean and unflattering names he has been given. Chaucer, La Fontaine, Aesop, most of the fabulists and animal story-tellers have him in the role of the wily one, the successful deceiver. (As for his mate, which is the most trustworthy, a vixen or a shrew?) With his shiny red coat Reynard dazzles and beguiles, flaunting his thick brush—now used as a rudder, now as an indicator of emotion, now in sleep as a muff for his nose. Pricking his outsize ears, he glides effortlessly, noiselessly across the countryside. Through force of circumstances a creature of the night, his peregrinations and depredations are clothed in mystery. With crafty slanting eyes, whose elliptical daylight pupils open in darkness to a round bright yellow light, he steals out each evening, threading his way between the trees, through the brushwood, stalking, beguiling, pouncing, killing. Marauder of the henroost, terror of the lesser creatures, the heart and hand of mankind has nearly always been against him. It is his furtive cat-like character from which this reputation is derived: his litheness, his nocturnal activity, his stealthy prowling, his feline tread, one pad behind the other, always registering; his fastidiousness about dirt and wet, his cat's stalk and spring, the mewing cry of his vixen, his suffering in silence (so unlike a dog). The vulpine surely provides the link between the worlds of the canine and the feline. How formidable is he? Certainly he is a fierce animal and a brave one, but he is not particularly strong for his size: a determined terrier is more than a match for him.

As a rule he hunts at night, lies up by day. He is obliged by man in this habit. If he has favourite haunts, they are probably brushwood, gorse, bramble and other such thicket strongholds; but he really seems to be as happy around the ledges of the seacliffs, the rocky mountain summits, railway embankments, sheltered rubbish dumps and osier beds; or he may be found sunning himself in the bracken, the kale fields or the plough furrows. He does not live underground but only uses an earth as a haven in which to rear his young, as an occasional refuge from his enemies (man and dog) and as shelter from storms. Rarely is it originally his own earth; invariably he widens a rabbit warren or takes over a badger's set or occupies the drains supplied by man. Sometimes, in the breeding season, he moves into a complex of burrows, living with the badger and the rabbit as his neighbours.

It is because his diet is as omniverous as man's that he can make his home any-where. In Britain, after 1954, the year in which myxamatosis began in earnest, his diet became more varied than ever. Before that rabbits and hares formed 60% of the fox's diet, but, afterwards, evidence of rabbits and hares was found only in about one-fifth of the fox stomachs examined, and in those mainly hare. The fox takes game-birds and blackberries, weasels and earthworms, carrion and windfall apples, poultry and rats, frogs and voles, snails and small roosting birds. In the mountains of Scotland, quartering the moor like a pointer or setter, he will catch grouse and ptarmigan; in the city suburbs he will raid the dustbins, licking clean the spent cans, but his favourite food, especially where the rabbit is scarce, is the black beetle; a fox's droppings are often thick with their wing-cases. In the valleys and on the downs, when he and his vixen have a litter to feed, they will also occasionally take lambs, kids and fawns, swans and geese. In the hill countries they will slaughter any number of lambs, whose most succulent time probably coincides nicely with the period of the dependent fox cub's largest appetite. However, in most areas, now that the rabbit is back again, hunting is less of a problem for them.

Like the birds of prey the fox is a wonderful rodent-catcher and, along with the hawks and owls, is nature's exterminator of the poor specimens, the sick and the old. He will kill cats, too, whenever the opportunity occurs—not to eat them but because they are his natural enemies. He is also a famous creator of massacre around the chicken pens and domestic duck-ponds; he forgets his limit, leaving the enclosures littered with feathers and corpses, departing with a single bird, if any at all. It is mainly the parents of cubs and the maimed, lazy and old foxes that resort to man's domestic terrain for their food; by and large the healthy young fox is more interested in hunting in the wild.

As a hunter he lives well up to his wily reputation: like the stoat and the weasel he practises hypnosis; he gleans the pheasant coverts after the shooters have gone; he hunts along the wall-tops, gaining the advantage of tactical height for his pounces; he lies still as a statue in ambush, so that his scent, which grows strong or weakens according to his energy, movement and emotional output, will not give him away; he hunts the quick strong hare by patient ruse along the plough furrows or rolls the curled hedgehog into the water, making him expose his vulnerable head, then neatly turns the prickly skin inside out to devour him.

Not for choice does the fox travel far from home, perhaps 4 or 5 miles in search of a mate, and sometimes as far when food is scarce. Normally he clings to the familiar haunts within a radius of a mile or two of home. He learns the layout of this limited area of countryside in the most minute and detailed way. Nearly always he leaves his covert and returns to it by the same point for each expedition; he keeps to the 'green highways', the well-defined paths his race has used for generations, threading his way from point to point, recognizing a thousand landmarks en route, remembering practically every rock and twig he passes; but beyond his boundaries all will be strange to him.

He can hear the faintest rustle, feel the difference of every subtle texture, see the smallest movement; but the most important of his senses is smell. The meanest scent holds a message for him. His nose tells him not only where other foxes have stopped but also what they are up to; and from his own scent and urine, carefully deposited at intelligence posts, other foxes will know just how long ago he passed, upon what mission and in what mood.

Late December or January finds the fox with his vixen. Once mated he usually settles down and is faithful. Should he become a widower the strong mature dog fox is not much concerned with competition and generally finds a new mate in his own vicinity. It is the unmated 2-year-old tyro who must often travel far for a partner. He reconnoitres, he visits the 'post-boxes', the spots where other foxes leave their scent messages, and there deposits a sample of his own identity. He announces his presence by yapping and whining through the night, and the vixen replies with *miaows* and *clicketts* and weird screeches. Sometimes a particular vixen becomes a centre of attraction, every dog fox in the country comes to present his claims, and the sound can resemble that of a host of town cats on the moonlit roof-tops. Day and night in the mating season fierce and jealous duels are fought, and two dog foxes at battle will often be perfectly oblivious of man or beast standing within a few feet of them.

Soon after mating, the vixen begins to prepare for the arrival of her cubs. They are usually born at the base of an earth. Stub-bred litters do occur where earths are difficult to make, and stub-bred foxes do generally survive, but they are prone to many hazards, such as storms, other vixens who are jealous and roaming dogs. Unlike the young badger or rabbit, who enjoys a soft nest of leaves, grass and wool, the fox cub lies on the bare earth, or rock, of its underground lair. Four to five is the average size of the brood. They are usually born within a week or two of the middle of March, conveniently so, for they graduate from milk to other food after about 8 weeks, when the young rabbits and rats are innocent and tender. They are woolly and dark greyish-brown mouse-coloured in their infancy; their eyes are closed for the first fortnight, and they are toothless for the first three weeks of life, but they mature very quickly. After three months or so they will appear at the mouth of their burrow to play, and they are soon catching beetles, worms and grasshoppers and coping with the meat brought home by their parents. Hitherto their father has only brought food to his vixen; now he must work twice as hard to keep his cubs properly nourished, too. So this is when the domestic birds and animals are most in jeopardy.

Frequently at this stage the earth is so fouled that the vixen, picking the cubs up in her mouth, one by one by the scruff of their necks, conveys them to a new lair. She will almost inevitably so move them if her earth has been interfered with or if there is too much human scent in the vicinity, so that a single litter may well be transported, each cub in turn, to a number of different lairs. Either way, within five months the cubs are self-supporting, though their mothers usually keep a tender eye on them—at least through the following winter.

How do foxes die? Their age span is about 14 years, but they are lucky if they survive 4 years. It is estimated that in Britain each year 40,000–50,000 are destroyed by man. Of these some 9,000–12,000 are killed by packs of hounds. So about 25,000 suffer less natural deaths: they are run over; or they are shot, more often than not wounded, to die of gangrenous wounds; or they are trapped, often to die of shock, pain and starvation, if they do not wrench off the caught limb; or they are terrorized if they are caught in a caged trap; or they are gassed in their earths, which involves an excruciating end; or they are poisoned, which again means a slow and agonizing death; or they may die from an overdose of birds that are full of noxious seed dressings. However, in the case of hunting the fox is invariably snapped across the neck or back by one or two leading hounds, and death is instantaneous. With this death the fox feels little pain and no fear, until he knows he is going to die and that phase only lasts a few seconds. He minds so little about the cry of hounds behind him that he often behaves quite nonchalantly and will break off to hunt a rabbit or a bird if he passes one. An animal can only instinctively speculate, cannot look forward. Nor can he reflect but only looks back in so far as he registers certain details in order to fulfil his way of life. Briefly he can pine, but cannot feel remorse. In controlling our fox populations we must be sure, as far as possible, that they are spared pain. Hunting with hounds does this.

Up to 300 or 400 years ago the fox's natural enemy was the wolf. The wolf packs kept down the foxes, just as the foxes kept down the rats and mice, but, since man exterminated the wolf, it is fitting that he should replace the missing ecological link, fill in the gap caused in the predator–prey cycle, with his own dog packs—with foxhounds.

Moreover the hunts, to a great extent, protect foxes from the guns and traps and poisons of the farmers and shepherds, for hunting is a farmers' and shepherds' sport and against the gamekeepers' weapons, because foxhunting is a powerful rival to game shooting. By tradition, generally speaking, the shoot owners respect the interests of the foxhunters. In Britain the fox owes its existence to hunting. If hunting ended, man would exterminate the fox just as surely as he exterminated the wolf. Our country scene would thus be deprived of a very beautiful animal, and one which, if its stocks are right, fulfils a most important niche in the natural world.

Chapter 3

Scent

THE CONNECTING link of venery is that which holds the pack to the quarry—scent. The basic, if obvious, fact that there would be no foxhunting were it not that the fox leaves a scent-trail and that hounds are able to hunt the air that has come into contact with the scent particles is not always given the emphasis it deserves. Day by day it is upon scent conditions that sport depends, and in the long run it is according to the extent that scent is masked by man-made smells that the future of foxhunting partly depends.

There are three sources of a fox's scent: the anal glands, another gland a few inches from the root of the brush and smaller glands in the pads. The scent of the dog-fox is stronger than that of the vixen, a fact that enables the experienced huntsman to recognize the sex of his quarry. In the springtime, however, when vixens are breeding, their scent diminishes. This appears to be nature's way of protecting the pregnant or nursing mother. At this time of year only, the huntsman will probably be able to tell whether hounds are hunting a vixen, both by the way hounds hunt and by the way in which she runs.

Nature, with her peculiar reciprocity and scheme of endowment, gave foxes these glands for a variety of reasons: firstly, to assist them in their sex and family life and also, callous as it may seem, to help their similarly strong-nosed predators to find them, and so to kill and eat them. To achieve initial contact and dialogue and, indeed, prolonged relationships, the dog-fox seeks and finds his vixen primarily by scent, and they both leave their scent messages at visiting posts. They mark their territories with it. Their cubs, in their turn, if dispersed, find them by scent. What I said in Chapter 2 bears repeating here: just as the fox hunts, so nature deemed that he should be hunted—by the wolf and the wild dog, who were given keen noses to track him and by many other creatures, too—by the trail of that very scent that helped those creatures to procreate; and man, who domesticated the wild dog and destroyed the wolf, has bred the foxhound, thus filling the gap he caused in the prey–predator cycle.

What has man learnt of the nature of scent? From a study of comparative conditions on good and bad scenting days some of the early foxhunters made shrewd guesses. The eighteenth-century poet and Master of Foxhounds, William Somerville, wrote this:

> '*The panting chase grows warmer as he flies;*
> *And through the network of the skin perspires;*
> *Leaves a long, steaming trail behind, which by*
> *The cooler air condens'd, or rarefy'd*
> *By the meridian sun's intenser heat.*
> *To every shrub the warm effluvia cling,*
> *Hang on the grass, impregnate earth and skies.*
> *With nostril opening wide, o'er hill, o'er dale,*
> *The vigorous hounds pursue, with every breath*
> *Inhale the grateful steam. . . . '*

His friend and staunch admirer, Peter Beckford, seems to misinterpret Somerville when he writes this:

'I cannot agree with Mr Somerville in thinking scent depends upon air only. It depends also upon the soil. Without doubt the best scent is that occasioned by the effluvia, as he calls it, or particles of scent, which are constantly perspiring from the game as it runs and are strongest and most favourable to the hound when kept by the gravity of the air, to the height of his breast; for then it is neither above his reach, nor is it necessary that he should stoop for it. At such times scent is said to lie *breast high*. Experience tells us that difference of soil occasions difference of scent; and on the richness of soil and the moderate moisture of it does scent also depend, I think, as well as on the air. . . . Scent depends chiefly on two things, the condition the ground is in and the temperature of the air, both of which I apprehend should be moist without being wet. When both are in this condition, the scent is then perfect and vice versa; when the ground is hard and the air dry, there seldom will be any scent. It scarce ever lies with a north or an east wind: a southerly wind without rain and a westerly wind that is not too rough are the most favourable. . . . '

Both these eighteenth-century observers showed a shrewd understanding of the effects, if not the causes, of favourable and poor scenting conditions; and, although, later, Mr Smith* in his famous *Diary of a Huntsman* and Delmé Radcliffe in *The Noble Science* expressed their views on the subject forcibly enough, no one put their finger closer to the mark than Somerville and Beckford, until the 1930s, when H. M. Budgett (a joint-Master of the Bicester from 1925 to 1931 and author of *Hunting by Scent*) and Hugh B. C. Pollard, who wrote *The Mystery of Scent*, explained both the phenomenon and how climatic and physical conditions affected scent, in scientific terms. Though not precisely agreeing with each other, Budgett and Pollard proved that the animal's scent molecules, emanating by vapour action, settle on the ground in a surface layer one molecule thick, like drops of petrol spreading to an iridescent film on water. This scent diffusion is

---

*Thomas (otherwise known as 'Gentleman' or Craven) Smith, not to be confused with Thomas Assheton Smith, M.F.H. (1776–1858)

only possible by contact with the air, and, by using the water vapour moving into the air as balloons or lifts, the molecules then evaporate from earth or herbage into the air.

Pollard explains this:

'The greater the amount of water vapour molecules passing into the air the more scent vapour is dispersed and carried up, and, as the molecules are always in motion and collision, the best conditions prevail when this evaporation of water vapour (the upward movement of molecules of water vapour into the air) near the surface of the ground is at its maximum. When, however, the air is almost fully charged with moisture—that is to say when relative humidity is in excess of 90%—this process of water vapour molecules leaving water surfaces to move about in the air slows down, and at last the atmosphere becomes saturated. In these conditions the air ceases to take up more water vapour, and the exchange or evaporation almost ceases. It follows, then, that scent which is carried along with water vapour molecules also fails to diffuse. This explains why, in a mist or fog, when the air is super saturated with relatively stationary water vapour and evaporation has ceased, scent is bad. . . . '

The exudation of air, a comparatively warm earth, and more particularly the herbage that grows from it, clearly encourage a strong scent. However, warm air rises and goes on rising unless it comes up against a barrier of cold air. It follows therefore, that, if the air is warmer than the earth, scent will quickly disappear. That is why, towards the evening of a bad day's hunting, scenting conditions so often improve; for, while the sun declines and a frosty nip comes in the air, the earth temperature stays more or less constant, and scent is retained close to ground level. A frequently helpful factor here is that, when a night frost is expected, the wind often changes from warm westerly to cold easterly. If, after the frost, however, there is a sudden warm breeze bringing mild weather, scent conditions will be poor—unless and until the earth warms.

What else obscures scent? It is dried up by the ultraviolet rays of sunshine, which is a reason for early morning cubhunting in the relatively hot months of September and October and also why, on sunny days, there may be a screaming scent inside covert and none outside. Scent is washed away by heavy rainstorms, whose drops beat the scent oil into a water-and-earth emulsion, so preventing the diffusion of the molecules. The substance quickly evaporates, and its odours are dissipated in a very high wind. Scent is better at night, for the ground, having absorbed the sun's warmth, holds it after dark, radiating at the night's cold air. That is why wolves generally hunt by night.

So much for climate, how about ground and country? Poor soil carries a weak scent, whereas soil that is relatively rich in humus retains its scent-holding moisture. Plough does not hold scent well, primarily because soil itself is a deodorant and secondly because—compared with grass—it is cold. Also, if the plough's topsoil adheres to the fox's feet, the extrusion of scent from those glands must be to some extent inhibited. Dry plough carries a fainter scent than moist plough; snow preserves the flavour of scent; flowers, reeds, willows and leaves tend to mask it.

So, in general, scent will be good when the ground is warmer than the air and notably after the sudden decline of temperature that precedes a frost at night and in the evening. Moist ground is always good for scent and so—most authorities agree, in spite of Pollard's observation—is snow and fog. Except where the foliage is strong-smelling, the taller and thicker the herbage the better it lies; but a strong wind blows it away.

What of the man-made hindrances? Cattle and sheep, manure and other fertilizers, oil from agricultural machines and smoke, all tend to mask scent. So do people with their fumey vehicles. As I said in Chapter 2, the hunted fox takes deliberate advantage of these 'allies': he rolls in manure and canters through flocks of sheep; conscious of his give-away scent he will sometimes withdraw in his track, take a leap to one side, breaking the continuity of his trail and resuming his flight in a fresh track; or, finding another fox sleeping in a tree and pushing him out, he will lie there himself, shifting the burden of pursuit on to a fresh pilot. If scent is weak, on the other hand, the fox will know it, and, while hounds are casting and dividing and faltering on his line, he will saunter to and fro, will look back carelessly or even—albeit fully alert—will curl up in a secluded corner while they are quite near. The more weary a fox becomes, the fainter his scent.

Major Jock Mann, the senior joint-Master of the Vale of White Horse, having read this chapter, made some very interesting observations for me on the subject, as follows:

'If one is lucky enough, in these days of busy roads, to hack on with hounds, maybe they can tell you something of prevailing scenting conditions. If, as they go on, they are winding every smeuse, then scent is likely to be good. On the other hand, if hounds roll on the grass at the meet, then this is a bad sign. If, as you look into the light, you see the gossamer lying on the grass or even stretched across the bumps on arable ground, then you can be sure that scent will be bad. It is said that, when the hedges look black and clear, scent will be good, but I recall so many occasions when this has proved not to be the case that I consider it a very unreliable sign. Stormy weather is bad for scent, but when snow is likely then hounds will sometimes run very hard. Even in a snowstorm there may be a good scent.

I remember one such occasion when we could at times only follow hounds by their cry as the snow was so blinding we could not see. A fox will take to water; they are good swimmers. A wet fox, immediately he leaves water, leaves little scent. I have heard of a hunted fox lying in water to avoid being winded by hounds, but I have never seen it. In the springtime, I have seen hounds run extremely fast on dry ploughs with a cloud of dust enshrouding the pack as they drive on.

After an exceptionally wet day hounds put up a fox in a thick hedgerow at about 3.30 p.m. just as the rain had stopped. The way they settled indicated that there was a scent, and they ran on hard for an hour. By this time it was getting dark, and a mist was rising on the meadows close to the river. We had to keep as close as we could to hounds, as, with the light failing and the big overgrown hedges, it was difficult to see them. When eventually they were at fault, all we could see was their sterns waving above the blanket of mist as they feathered about. When they hit off the line, the sterns ran up together and dropped into the mist, as they went away with a cry that I can only describe as a roar, so strong was scent that evening.

When a fox is lying quietly in cover, he will give off very little scent, but let him move and become agitated then the emanation of scent will increase. Thus a fox that has lain a while will take a deal of finding unless he moves; but a fox that has recently lain down will probably be found by a hound hitting off his drag in covert.

Some hounds seem to have a special ability to find foxes. Their huntsman knows their voices and so will the other hounds who will quickly go to them. It is a lovely sound to hear that well-known voice proclaim, "There is a fox at home." How they do it better than all the other members of the pack, I do not know; whether it be by greater scenting powers or whether it is some uncanny intuition. Again some hounds are able to hunt a line down a road; but roads nowadays are so foiled by fumes of oil and petrol that the road hunter has an almost impossible task of puzzling out a line. It seems to run in families and is of such value that it should be preserved and perpetuated in the breeding plan.

There seems to be a condition of bad scent when hounds find it easier to hunt heel away. This is most aggravating, as precious time is lost when casting hounds, and away they go on the heel line, until it becomes apparent to the huntsman that this is so. Then they must be stopped and held forward once again.

It was during a day's hunting near Kemble, the home of the Red Arrows (aerial acrobatic team), that I noticed, whilst standing inside a covert, what I thought to be diesel tractor fumes. On looking outside, there was no sign of a tractor, nor had I heard one. I thought no more of it until I smelt the same smell at the next covert, and then I realized that this smell was everywhere. I asked Sidney Bailey, our huntsman, whether he had noticed it, and he agreed. That smell was everywhere we went, whether in covert or in the open. It can only have come from the aeroplanes which were doing a great deal of acrobatic flying that day, which included some very low level runs.'

As regards the confusion of hare scent, Mr M. F. Berry, sometime Master of the Fitzwilliam and the Woodland Pytchley, and for many years hunting correspondent to *The Times*, sent me this note:

'When hounds come out of cover and dwell on the line of the fox, it always appears to me that they are, so to speak, timing and making sure that the scent of this fox is really that of fox. If all foxes always smelt the same, why should they dwell? I am quite sure that, sometimes, particularly in March, on dry land and probably with an east wind, some jack hares smell exactly like fox. I have seen hares under those conditions hunted by staunch foxhounds who themselves would never dream of hunting a hare if they knew what they were doing.'

We read the signs, we watch the behaviour of foxes and yet it seems that, however much we may discover about scent, it remains something of a mystery. Let the late Frances Pitt, renowned field naturalist and for 23 years Master of the Wheatland Hunt, have the last word:

'If we really understood scent, if we could tell exactly when there would be good scent and when none at all, how dull our hunting would be. Scentometers are interesting things, but I pray earnestly they will never be brought to such perfection that they will tell us precisely what to expect. The fascination of hunting lies in its glorious uncertainty, and when we know what to expect I, for one, will give it up and stop at home. . . .'

Chapter 4
The Foxhound

BRITAIN

LIKE THE athlete's exacting career, that of the foxhound is a short one. For 2 or 3 days a week each 7-month season, he walks anything from 15 to 30 miles to the meet and between draws and may well gallop another 10 to 25 miles in pursuit of foxes. Even for a selectively bred canine that represents a huge expenditure of energy. Little wonder his working life rarely extends beyond five seasons.

Puppies are normally born between February and July. Litters of fourteen have been known, but six or seven is enough if robust puppies are to be expected: for this is about as many as the bitch can comfortably supply with her own milk. They are named at birth, the name of every brother and sister in the litter starting with the same first letter as the dam; or, if an outside sire has been used, that of the sire. A puppy's early life generally proceeds like this. The dew claws or rudimentary thumbs having been removed, toe-nails pared and worm-dosing administered, at about 8 to 10 weeks old he or she is sent out to walk, to live with that devoted farmer or other hunt supporter who has volunteered to bring him up. Sometimes the puppy-walker will take a second puppy, two being less trouble in a way since they amuse each other, rather than chew up carpets, slippers and cushions, not to mention the butcher's meat. Anyhow, thus farmed out, away from the hurly-burly of the kennels, the puppy matures and develops as an individual. It is an extremely important phase in a hound's maturation and acquaints him, among other things, with traffic, domestic animals and pets, which, in future life, must not be chased or interfered with.

How long should puppies stay out at walk? There are many different opinions. A. H. Higginson, lifelong Master in both England and America, took the following view:

'It is customary in many packs to let puppies stay out at walk until the regular hunting season is over, when the hunt staff have more time to devote to them; but I have always found that it pays many times over to bring puppies in a bit early in the season. . . . After all, it is a very important period in a hound's life, and, if they are allowed to "go back" at this stage of their existence, they never quite recover from it. More expensive it is, undoubtedly; but it is a false economy to stint your young hounds in any way, either in food or in care;

if your aim is, as it should be, to produce the best. Don't forget that on your young entry depends the future strength of the pack; and there is nothing more discouraging to a Master or huntsman than to see the youngster, over whose breeding he has spent so many hours of thought and care, ruined by underfeeding or neglect at this stage in his life. So get your puppies in from walk early—if you have a proper place to put them—and, once in, keep them warm and dry and give them plenty of exercise. In my opinion, except in the case of very late puppies, February or March is late enough to bring them in. . . .'

Soon after he returns to kennels, in mid-summer, perhaps when he is a year old, the young entry attends a puppy show at which prizes are awarded to the best-looking hounds. Then school begins. Once in kennels he is taught manners and obedience, to answer his name and not to chase after deer, rabbits and cats. He must be taught the meaning of certain terms, 'ware hare', 'ware wing', etc., and to keep away from a horse's feet. At the same time the foxhound begins to show that essential unwavering devotion to his huntsman.

About 6 to 8 weeks before the start of the cub-hunting season, that is in July, hound exercise begins in earnest. In the early summer hounds have simply been walked out by a dismounted staff; now the huntsman and his whippers-in (probably wearing hunt coats and bowler hats) are to be seen 'leading hounds out' on long early-morning hacks, 5 or 6 days a week. As part of their education, young hounds are coupled to old. This is the period when the young hound goes among deer and hares and is taught to ignore them; he learns to cross rivers and other obstacles without fear and generally gets to know his way around the country. This, too, is when the pack as a whole gets hard and fit. Perhaps the most important thing at this time is that they should not be rated too severely for 'riot'; for there is a danger that their hearts could be irrevocably broken by it.

The young hound is referred to as being 'unentered'. During his first season he goes through the process of being 'entered to fox'. After his first season, when he is probably about 18 months old, he is an 'entered' hound. He is never referred to by his age but by his season (a first-season hound is one that has recently been entered) or by his year ('Purley Shylock 74', for example, means that the 'Purley' hunt's hound, Shylock, was entered in 1974). When Shylock's name goes into the hunt's hound list we also find the name of his sire and dam: thus 1974—Shylock—Lenster Guardian 69 (under the heading, Sire)—Harmony 71 (under the heading, Dam) denotes that Shylock was by the 'Lenster' hunt's Guardian, a 1969 hound, out of the 'Purley's' own Harmony, who was entered in 1971. Every member of the pack—bracketed with their litter-brothers and litter-sisters—will appear in this list against their year of entry.

Packs are generally divided into two, the dog pack and the bitch pack, individuals in the former always being referred to as dog-hounds and those in the latter as bitches. A dog hound, that is frequently used as a sire, is referred to as a 'stallion hound'.

What are the factors involved in breeding foxhounds? To catch a fox, a hound must keep latched to his scent; and, not only must he interpret what he smells in terms of the fox's movements, but he must also distinguish between his quarry's 'heel-way' and true course. He must sense how the fox is running; his nose and brain must be properly co-ordinated. Nose will probably be the breeder's first concern; but like the wild dog, who was the foxhound's remote ancestor, he rarely hunts outside the close communion of the pack. Unless the hound can speak the moment he detects the scent, his fellow pack members will not be aware that the line has been hit; nor, when the pack as a whole has found that line, could they give the huntsman the message that this is genuine. Every hound must speak the instant he or she strikes the line, and speak to nothing but fox.

So the working of a hound's nose and the notes of his cry must harmonize. If he uses his tongue without a true message from his nose, he deceives both the pack and the huntsman and is condemned as a 'babbler'; or, if he uses his nose, yet moves silently and independently, he contributes little to the operations of the pack. The working of the hound's nose and the notes of his throat should balance. Sometimes a hound will become cunning and walk a ride or remain outside when hounds are drawing a thick covert, thereby getting a flying start when a fox is found. During a hunt that hound will probably also cut corners and run mute. Such a hound is known as a skirter. He is a menace and should be discarded.

From nose stems drive, which implies the hound's dash, enterprise and guts, his will to be up with his fox, to fly his fences, to persevere through thorn and bramble, to streak up the gradients and down the slippery slopes. The fox runs straight and fast—in the initial burst a good deal faster than the foxhound. His scent evaporates after 20 minutes—that is in *good* conditions—and, in these days of barbed wire, intensive agriculture, close networks of roads and other obstacles and a high population of foxes to confuse the line, a fast pack is needed, enabling the huntsman to hunt as close to his fox as possible. The other reason the foxhound is bred for speed is, of course, that he must keep in front of the galloping horses, whose riders are paying for the sport. He also needs courage to keep in front of that galloping field, courage to keep going at the end of a tiring day and courage to grapple with a fox that may turn and fight for its life. He must have a feeling for his quarry, too, what is known as 'fox sense'; and, like a team-games player, he must have pack sense.

A well-bred hound is an active hound: he turns sharply, he is quick off the mark and he responds instantly to relevant messages. He must possess mental alertness, coupled with physical rhythm. Since he may be required, during perhaps 5 or 6 hours of continuous activity in a day's hunting, in the very testing conditions of the modern countryside, to press three or four foxes, he must be a creature of great stamina and endurance.

D

What are the tangible hallmarks of activity and speed and stamina? The first two of these attributes are partly a matter of length of stride and fluency of leg movement. Long stride is the manifestation of a well-sloped shoulder or scapula—allowing him to reach well forward with his forelegs—and a good humerus, the bone which leads from the point of the shoulder to the elbow. Upon the length and position of this bone depends to a great extent the freedom of movement of the forelegs, which should be perfectly straight. The elbow ought to be set square and placed as low down as possible, so that the forelegs can move straight backwards and forwards. He should be fairly short from the knee to the ground.

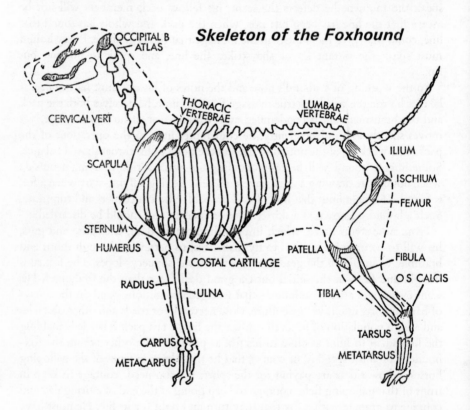

Skeleton of the Foxhound

The loins and pelvis must be wide and muscular. There should be no gap between hip and back rib, particularly in dog hounds. Nor ought the foxhound to run up from the ribs to the loins like a greyhound but should have a fairly straight underline. When you place your hand on top of the quarters and press gently down, there ought to be an impression of resilience and strength. He should have a rather short-coupled body, which implies that he should not be overlong in the back. As regards height, the dog hound, bred for an 'average' country, should stand about 23 to 24 inches at the shoulder, the bitch perhaps an inch shorter. His propelling power comes from his hindlegs, and therefore his femur, that is the bone connecting the hip and the stifle, should be noticeably long. His second thigh needs to be pronounced and muscly. He should be well let down to the hock.

Many views have been proposed on what is best for feet. Sir John Buchanan-Jardine, breeder and Master of the unique Dumfriesshire black-and-tans, in his classic, *Hounds of the World*, had this to say:

'The feet of the cat and the hare have both been used as patterns by various schools of thought. But a hound, after all, belongs to neither of those species but is, of course, a dog, so if one wishes to copy the feet of some wild animal, I consider it should be the wolf or perhaps the fox. . . . My own experience on the subject has been that most sorts of feet are capable of wearing well, provided they are not exaggerated. . . . A type that seems to suit many different sorts of country is a fairly compact lean hard-soled foot, with strong toe-nails, all of which are evenly worn down. . . . '

The foxhound's head ought to have a quality look about it, with a bright, enquiring and intelligent expression, and should be carried on a longish, slightly arched neck, which is clean and free from throatiness. It should be a swan-like neck, not only for beauty's sake but to help keep his nose on the ground. Every point of the hound should indeed reflect quality, including the stern which should be thick at the root and should be set rather high up between the quarters. His eye should show intelligence and grit, his deportment should be jaunty, his curved, slightly feathered stern should be the reflex of his moods—never tucked in to betoken fear but carried to reveal his cheerful temperament—and his jacket should be of 'best-quality texture' and sheen. Above all, as in the case of every thoroughbred animal, the foxhound should be well balanced and should show complete symmetry. No one point should be accentuated at the expense of another; and, unless every member of the pack is perfectly balanced, and, as near as possible, perfectly matched, they will not gallop all day—as they must do—together. Clearly the pack that hunts the line well huddled together is of far greater value than one that is spread out over half a mile. So their pace and rhythm must be even; they must be level. Most Masters will choose to draft hounds that run in front of, or behind, the main body of the pack.

'A chance-bred hound', said Lord Willoughby de Broke, Master of the Warwickshire Hunt, a great authority, 'is like a chance-bred racehorse: he may be very good at his work, but he is worthless for breeding. Not being carefully bred himself, the faults of his progenitors are certain to be reproduced in the offspring. . . . ' English foxhounds trace their ancestry back at least to the early nineteenth century. Hound breeders, like anyone else who is determined to produce an animal of excellent working qualities, follow the Mendelian law on heredity. The theory, worked out by the Austrian monk, Gregor Johann Mendel (1822–84), concerns the inheritance of definite different characteristics of the same breed. Mendel showed how any animal is the combination of a number of units, each of which has been inherited from an ancestor and that, by linking pure blood with pure blood, a self-reproducing strain is acquired.

The Master, or other person conducting the breeding policy at a foxhound kennels, will breed from homozygous parents, that is to say a sire and a dam of similar character, which are likely to produce offspring of the mutual stamp. In order that the spontaneous germinal mutations occurring in the breed are passed on by the most favoured mutants, clearly also they will breed from the best workers in the pack. In principle they will breed as closely as possible to the lines that are producing their good-working strain. 'The successful breeder of hounds', Cornelius Tongue ('Cecil') said in his preface to the first edition of the foxhound stud book, 'should follow the principles of the successful breeder of racehorses, as it is invariably found that those animals are most to be depended upon for the perpetuation of their species whose genealogy can be traced in the greatest number of direct lines to the great celebrities of olden times.'

Because pedigree is the only guarantee of excellence in work, to fashion a pack of really high-quality hounds, the breeder will make a careful study of that pedigree. Someone starting a pack, for example, may select an ancestral dog hound of great reputation, may then obtain a stock of brood-bitches owning as many lines back to that dog hound as possible and may put the bitches to a stallion hound descended from the chosen ancestor. This is how Ikey Bell, Master, first of the Galway Blazers, then of the Kilkenny and later of the South and West Wilts, advises the new Master to work out a female line:

'Make a list of your best bitches. Get a long narrow book, foolscap-ruled. Select a bitch from your list. On the left-hand page, at the top left-hand corner, write the name of this bitch. Below her name write that of her dam. Rule a vertical line after it, from top to bottom of the page. On the other side of that line, write the bitch's sire's name and year, alongside that of her dam's. You can continue with this procedure of writing out dam and sire of each bitch of the line immediately above as far as it interests you. This is termed working out the "F" line, or in other words the female ancestry or "tail female" of a hound. If a kennel has been home-bred for a number of years, it may surprise you how many of your hounds go back to the same female ancestress. . . . '

How close should this common ancestry be? Opinions differ. Here is the view of the late Earl Bathurst, Master of the Vale of White Horse (Earl Bathurst's) and one of the most respected authorities:

'I do not object to breeding rather closely occasionally if I am sure that the dog or bitch is absolutely right and a particularly good one. There are instances of this that have turned out extraordinarily well. As a rule the fourth generation is near enough, and, if one can arrange for what I call a double cross, that is when two separate hounds' names occur in the fourth generation of both sire and dam, it is most advantageous, again, that is, that they are both sterling good hounds in their work and go back in their pedigree to the old lines that are most fancied. . . . '

Ikey Bell's advice is similar:

'If your hounds are a well-bred lot, with a history sheet of constitution and stamina and no hereditary faults, such hounds can be bred closer to than those of a less excellent strain. It would be playing for safety if no name repeats itself prior to the fourth line, and then only *once*. On the other hand, if the hounds spring from different strains, it is necessary to breed closer, so as to form a uniform type. . . . '

To work continuously and exclusively on the line-breeding system induces inbreeding and degeneracy. 'Like should be mated to like,' runs a well-known maxim, 'with just enough outcross to guard against the danger of inbreeding.' That is to say, having established the good self-reproducing strain, to avoid the pitfalls of inbreeding, it is necessary to take infusions from other kennels. How will a hound breeder select his outcrosses? From dog hounds, not only of excellent breeding, conformation and working qualities but also, preferably, with lines of blood that 'nick in' with his own lines. A mutual ancestral name should, if possible, appear in the lines of the dam and the selected outcross.

If possible, the hand and eye and brain of one man should guide the breeding of a pack of hounds. Short Masterships and frequent changes of huntsmen must be detrimental to any kennels. As Lord Bathurst put it:

'Good hounds cannot be bred unless the qualities of their progenitors are known for several generations back otherwise there is no continuity or system of breeding. The short-term Master has probably had very little experience, while each new huntsman swears by the blood of some different kennel in which he was formerly at. The result is chaos. . . . '

Those words were written in the 1920s when comparatively long Masterships were still the vogue. Now, unfortunately, for financial and other reasons, not many Masters are able to hold the office more than a few seasons, and the desirable continuity is often lacking.

Major Robert Hoare, whose Mastership, first of the West Norfolk, then the Cottesmore and then the South Notts spanned 35 years, during the whole of which time he carried the horn himself, was one of England's most successful breeders of hounds. On reading over this chapter for me, he made the following comment:

'I have taken over packs of hounds which I did not like and which were anything but level, and I would like to pass on the advice given me by Sir Charles Wiggin as to what to do in these circumstances, advice which I found worked wonderfully well. He said the first thing to do is to breed a type, and, having got a type, you can then alter it to what you want. Initially only use one or two stallion hounds, and try to keep the whole of a few litters. That is, put a second bitch to as a foster, so that, if your chosen bitch has a dozen or more whelps, you can keep the lot. In a very short time you will have a level pack.'

How has the modern foxhound evolved? Hounds were probably first deliberately selected and bred for nose and other hunting qualities by the monks of the monastery of St Hubert at least 1,000 years ago, and there is proof that every hound alive today is descended from those hounds. But it was not until the mid-eighteenth century, in England, that the scientific breeding of the foxhound, for a combination of tongue, nose and conformation—to produce activity, speed and stamina—began, as well as the careful study and maintenance of pedigrees. In England we had the Talbot, otherwise known as the Southern hound, our descendant of the St Hubert's. In the middle of the seventeenth century, a fast-galloping hound, the result of the Southern crossed with greyhound, was bred in Yorkshire, and this came to be known as the Northern beagle; but, owing probably to the greyhound influence, the Northern was severely deficient in nose and tongue.

The Duke of Beaufort's began to keep hound-breeding books as early as 1728, the Cottesmore in 1732, the Brocklesby in 1746, the Belvoir in 1757 and the Fitzwilliam (Milton) in 1765. However, as I mentioned in Chapter 1, 1753, the year that Hugo Meynell took over the Quorn, really marks the beginning of selective hound breeding as we know it today. By intensive study and application of the principles of genetics, in so far as they were apparent in those days, Meynell bred the first model efficient pack of foxhounds. From that period, the dash and speed of the foxhound was increased, and the sport was vitalized. Meynell's Stormer 1791 as the ancestor of Squire Osbaldeston's influential Furrier and the Brocklesby Rallywood 1843, might be called the 'father' of the modern foxhound.

How did they look these early hounds? Rallywood, the nineteenth century's paramount hound, was comparatively light of bone, back at the knee, 'hare footed', rather harrier-like in appearance. 'This is the most beautiful little short-legged dog,' said the celebrated huntsman, Will Goodall, 'exceedingly light of bone, but with beautiful legs and feet.' This was the sort, too, found in the kennels of Lord Henry Bentinck (of the Old Burton), and of Lord Willoughby de Broke (of the Warwickshire), the two most highly esteemed breeders of the middle of that century. These Masters and most of their contemporaries laid far more emphasis on the merits of hounds in the field than 'on the flags'. Their comment was all about stamina, courage, nose and jumping power; but after the publication of the first volume of the Stud Book in 1866, and with the introduction of hound shows—Tom Parrington's national hound show began at Redcar in 1869 and moved to Peterborough a decade later—increasing attention was given to conformation.

Towards the end of the nineteenth century the foxhound got bigger. Because the most favoured mutants are taken to breed from, mating by selection often has a tendency to increase the size of the animal bred. The more it increased, apparently, the more the pundits insisted that plenty of bone and substance produced the right answer. From about 1890 up to the First World War, the heavy Belvoir hound—known as the Belvoir Tan, because it was mostly a coloured hound with white only at the feet and collar—set the fashion. Although the Belvoir did not show at Peterborough, their puppy show was regarded as a second Peterborough. Most of the prize-winners at the great show were Belvoir-bred, and the majority of kennels throughout England, Ireland and Scotland boasted Belvoir blood and the Belvoir look. 'Belvoir never goes far from itself', the pundits proudly boasted.

Ikey Bell, who was to play such a major part in swinging the pendulum back to the light hound, recalled this:

> 'At hound sales and in valuation even a moderate hound, if he was a "Belvoir type", commanded the big money. Absolute straightness, short knees and tan colour were of higher monetary value than shoulders and activity, while, to many at that time, a light-coloured hound was anathema and would be drafted for colour alone, however well made he might be in essentials. . . . '

The type showed increasing bone and lumber, the turn-in of his toes became exaggerated and he was so much over at the knees (knuckled over) that he almost held the ground with his toe-nails rather than with his pad.

Bell's comments were as follows:

> 'In kennels where bone had been bred to excessiveness it was noticed that shoulders "dis"-improved; and, in ratio to the excess of bone, forehands became heavier and chests broadened. These heavyish limbs, which hounds had continually to push forward at every stride, caused them to shorten the arc of their swing, to save them fatigue, and thereby cramped their liberty of movement. Turned-in toes had an equally bad effect, in many cases causing a hound to be "out" at the elbows and therefore "opening" the shoulder-blades. . . . '

Although the Belvoir and their allies continued to show fine sport on good scenting days, through too close breeding, they began to lose something of those two primary qualities, nose and voice; but many observers believed that there was another important reason for the diminution of these qualities, and that is that, in those days, they were regularly hunting 'bagmen'. It should also be added that, although the Belvoir still breed from the old Belvoir Tan lines, they are now a very quick pack, low-scenting and with fine ready music.

By 1914 the face of the countryside was fast changing, too. Not only was it becoming more difficult, owing to tarred roads, the spread of railways, the increased use of barbed wire and other aspects of modern agriculture, to get across the country; but also with increased use of artificial manures and with more vehicle fumes, bitumen and oil from farm machinery about, the ground and the air above it presented a considerably sterner challenge for the foxhound's nose than when the Belvoir Tan first came into prominence.

Searching for greater activity and lower scenting power, hound breeders began to look elsewhere for their outcrosses. They went to the Berkeley, whose country lies by the English bank of the Bristol Channel, the ancestral family hunt which had retained a lighter-built hound; to Sir Edward Curre, whose distinctive white-coated pack of Anglo-Welsh crosses from Monmouthsire became famous during the early years of the century, and to other famous Welsh packs. If somewhat lacking in staying power and having a reputation for 'babbling' and a bit too much independence of character, the Welsh hound had always been noted for his sharp nose, wonderful cry and constant perseverance. He was light-boned and full of activity. By crossing him with the qualities of stamina, pack sense and speed of the best English, a more effective fox-catcher was produced for modern conditions than the Belvoir Tan.

The Curre Fiddler 09 is said to be responsible for Ikey Bell's conversion to the Welsh cross, a conversion which marked the most important turning-point in the evolution of the modern foxhound. In the 1930s, 1940s and 1950s the Duke of Beaufort, Sir Peter Farquhar (Master of the Meynell, Tedworth, Whaddon Chase and Portman) and Major Maurice Barclay (of the Puckeridge) were probably the chief influences in the continuing process of blending the English and Welsh into the foxhound of today; and from the 1950s to the 1970s, when conditions of terrain became still more difficult and the ratio of plough to grass swung from 80% in favour of grass to 80% in favour of plough, their movement continued to evolve. The Duke of Beaufort and others, with Capt. R. E. Wallace, whose career began with the Eton beagles in the 1930s, and who went on to be Master of the Ludlow, the Cotswold, the Heythrop and the Exmoor, carried the 'activity and agility' movement one further, producing an even lighter quality hound. By the 1960s, Capt. Wallace's Heythrop type (together with the Duke of Beaufort's perhaps fractionally more solid and 'conservative-looking' hound) has become the prototype for winners on the flags at Peterborough; and most hound lists contain the names of more Heythrop and Beaufort sires than the names from any other kennels.

After reading through these notes for me, Capt. C. G. E. Barclay, Master and huntsman of the Puckeridge since 1947 and of the Puckeridge and Thurlow since 1970, added the following comment:

'The hounds that win at Peterborough hound show and other hound shows are from the packs that catch the most foxes, so there is no doubt that the best hound breeding is still on the right lines.'

Yet there can be no real prototype, not while individual whims remain, nor while the face of Britain includes such a wide variety of country. In Chapter 5 I shall highlight these matters of individual taste in hound character and of breeding hounds to suit topography, by briefly tracing the development of five uniquely bred packs of hounds: two from England, one from Ireland, one from Scotland and one from Wales. However, first let us consider the American foxhound.

THE UNITED STATES—BY ALEXANDER MACKAY SMITH

The evolution of the modern foxhound in the United States has been based on three factors: on the quarry pursued, on the country in which that quarry is hunted, and on the type of performance required by those who hunt hounds.

The quarry

Three species in the United States are hunted by foxhounds—red foxes, grey foxes and coyotes. The red fox, originally native only to the northern states, has now spread, through importations, from England and from northern native stocks, to all the states east of the Mississippi River, to the states between the Mississippi and the western desert and to states on the Pacific coast. In the desert area the native coyote, averaging 30 to 35 pounds in weight as compared with 10 to 15 pounds for foxes, continues to flourish and is slowly extending its territory eastwards. Furthermore the grey fox, the only species native to the south and originally found infrequently above the fortieth parallel, is now common in northern hunting countries as well. Fortunately all three species readily adapt themselves to encroaching 'civilization'.

Before the fencing of the western plains, coyotes were successfully coursed by greyhounds, but for the past hundred years, foxhounds, both English and American, have been used in those open and arid areas, both at night (when scent lies better) and in the early mornings, aided by the stronger scent of the coyote as compared with that of the fox. The coyote is a relatively free runner who gives good sport when scent allows.

Red and grey foxes are distinct and different species, mortal enemies who compete for the same territory. They never cross-breed, despite many statements to the contrary, mostly inspired by the reddish colouring on the flanks of many grey foxes, the 'red-sided grey' being considered by some to be a sub-species. Grey foxes have a different scent—an experienced huntsman can tell whether his hounds are hunting a red or a grey by the difference in the cry, as well as by the difference in the footprints. The grey fox finds his food and lives his life in a much more restricted territory than the red, usually where there is maximum cover, pine woods, close thickets and thick briar patches. In such an area he doubles and runs short, affording less sport to those primarily interested in galloping and jumping. Most Masters and huntsmen are nevertheless glad to have some grey foxes in their country. During the cubbing season, they provide invaluable education for the young entry and also help to keep the noses of the older hounds closer to the ground. As a matter of fact, if hunted regularly, a grey fox will lengthen his run and provide very respectable sport.

Native American red foxes are very similar in appearance to their British counterparts, particularly those from the more mountainous districts. They are, however, far less numerous per square mile for reasons variously attributed to less feed, less cover, less preservation and a drier climate. In consequence American red foxes range for their feed over a wider area. The great difference is that the American red fox will run far and fast, only going to ground if very hard pressed, so that there is no necessity for earth stopping in order to show good sport. The smaller fox population, the almost total curtailment, in recent years, of farm-raised poultry and the repeated demonstrations by Federal and State government game management officials that foxes have little or no effect on game bird numbers, all add up to the fact that the principal goal of American foxhunting is not to reduce the fox population but to maintain and preserve it—the chase not the kill being the reward. In consequence, American hounds seldom kill a fox, nor do they need to be 'blooded' in order to maintain their keenness—as a matter of fact they generally will not break up a fox when one is occasionally accounted for but pay little attention to it. A corollary is that American fox-hunting is not generally labelled as a 'blood sport' and so is not the target of the Humane Society or of the Prevention of Cruelty to Animals Society. Only a few packs use hunt terriers to bolt foxes, and none of them dig.

Eighteenth-century and Penn–Marydel strains

The early settlers of the northern colonies found little sport in hunting the straight-running native red foxes who, in that heavily wooded area, promptly distanced those who tried to follow hounds. The grey fox native to the south runs in circles and could easily be followed through the woods, however. Consequently Thomas, Sixth Lord Fairfax, and his contemporaries in Virginia, Maryland and the Carolinas, during the mid-eighteenth century imported from England packs of the strain known as the 'southern' hound, whose low-scenting powers and patience in persuing a line made them particularly effective in following the twistings and turnings of the grey fox. This strain was also well adapted for hunting sections where most of the land was under cultivation, requiring hounds with particularly good noses to carry the lines of both red and grey foxes across its cold ploughs. In such sections it was therefore perpetuated, notably in the flat lands between the Atlantic Ocean and the Chesapeake Bay, known as the Eastern Shore and including parts of Virginia, Maryland, Delaware and Pennsylvania. In 1932 under the leadership of Mr Roy Jackson, Master of the Radnor Hunt in Pennsylvania, and of John B. Hannum, who established a private pack in nearby Maryland, there was instituted a hound show for packs employing this same strain which was then christened Penn–Marydel, this being a combination of the names of the principal states in which it was developed. The Penn–Marydel Association has also maintained a stud book in which hounds of this strain have been registered, as well as in the kennel stud book of the Masters of Foxhounds' Association of America. Since the Second World War the Bryn Mawr hound show, held annually at the Radnor Hunt Club, White Horse, Pennsylvania, has offered a division for Penn–Marydel hounds.

The descendants of the English red foxes, imported in 1730 to the Eastern Shore ploughlands of Maryland, crossed the frozen Chesapeake Bay in 1774, spreading west and south into the grasslands of Virginia and Maryland. By 1850 they had reached Kentucky and Georgia. The eighteenth-century hounds used for hunting grey foxes were unable to cope with these red invaders. Hounds brought from Leicestershire in the early 1800s proving to be unsatisfactory, American foxhunters made a series of importations from Ireland, beginning with the famous Mountain and Muse imported into Maryland in 1814, two blue-mottled hounds of the native strain known as Kerry beagles, black-and-tan representatives of which are currently to be found in the Scarteen pack in Ireland. It was these strains crossed on the old 'grey fox dogs' which produced the modern American foxhound.

Field trial strains
From this foundation the performances required by different types of hunting have developed various sub-strains. Prior to the American Civil War (1861–5) packs of hounds were maintained by most of the large landowners in the south, including George Washington, who frequently joined their own hounds with those of nearby planters for a day's or a week's sport. The Civil War being an economic as well as a military disaster, these packs were either scattered or very much reduced in size, those still maintaining them having to work by day in much smaller holdings instead of entrusting the management of large plantations to overseers in charge of slaves. At night when scent lies better, it became the custom for neighbours to bring a few hounds apiece to a spot on a nearby ridge where hunted foxes were known to cross, to build a fire and to turn hounds loose to find a fox on their own. The cry of every hound being as familiar to the members of the group as the voices of their own children, there was great rivalry as to which hound would take the lead and maintain it, once a fox was afoot and running.

From these 'races' developed (in the 1890s) the modern foxhound field trial, at which hounds are assembled at a starting point at daylight, are turned loose to find a fox without further guidance from their owners and are scored by mounted judges, often as many as one to every seven hounds, who follow the various groups of hounds hunting various foxes, giving plus or minus work for speed, drive, nose, babbling, skirting, loafing and so forth. These hounds do not hunt co-operatively as a pack but as individuals, striving always to be in the lead when running a fox. Two principal strains of field trial foxhounds were developed in the second half of the nineteenth century. The larger in numbers, known as Walker hounds, were developed by the Walker family in Madison County, Kentucky, more particularly by the four brothers, W. Stephen, Edwin H., John Wade and Arch Kavanaugh Walker, born in 1841, 1843, 1846 and 1852 respectively, and by Sam Wooldridge (1879–1946) of Versailles County, Kentucky. On the black-and-tan strains used for hunting grey foxes and brought from Virginia, they crossed (1852) Tennessee Lead, a hound of unknown breeding stolen by a drover in Tennessee while running a deer. Crosses of English blood from the kennels of the Duke of Buccleuch (1857) and of the Earl of Eglinton (1892) plus rigid selection for performance by Ed Walker and Sam Wooldridge, both of whom were great riders to hounds, created the leading breed of modern American field trial hounds.

The second strain, known as July or Trigg hounds, originated in Maryland, descended in part from Mountain and Muse (imported in 1814), these strains being perpetuated in the packs developed successively by Dr Thomas Y. Henry of Virginia (1842–8), by George L. F. Birdsong of Georgia (1848–67) who added the blood of the Maryland-bred *July '59* and by Haiden C. Trigg of Glasgow, Kentucky (1867–1913) who added several Walker hounds to the pack. The temperament of the July-Trigg strain is sometimes criticized for not having the steadiness of the Walker strain, which perhaps in this respect is derived from its English ancestry. The registrations of field-trial hounds outnumber by perhaps 50 to 1 the registrations of pack hounds in the kennel stud book of the Masters of Foxhounds' Association of America.

Hunting countries

Night hounds can be hunted in almost any type of country where scent will lie, since night-hunters make no attempt to follow, but instead they rely on the fox circling back to the area where he was found. Field-trials hounds are followed closely only by mounted judges, their owners being restricted to such views as they can obtain by driving about on the roads in the territory hunted. This, of course, must be such that the judges have a reasonable chance of watching hounds for at least the major part of the time they are hunting. Neither variety (Walker and Trigg) is subject to any kind of encouragement, control or discipline. The American, Penn–Marydel, English and cross-bred hounds registered by the Masters of Foxhounds' Association of America, on the other hand, can only be hunted in countries where it is possible for staff and field to ride to hounds, so that they can be followed and can receive the help of their huntsmen when required. The tremendous amount of time, organization and labour required to secure landowner permission, to make it rideable and to preserve foxes within such a limited area, necessarily much reduces the number of 'organized' packs (145 in 1976), as compared with the hounds maintained by night-hunters and by field-trial hunters.

In the British Isles, where foxhunting originated, the average humidity during the hunting season is 65% to 75%, as compared with 35% to 45% in North America. Furthermore in Britain at night the clouds normally cover the islands, clearing away in the daytime, so that the ground warmed by the sun during the day tends to remain warm during the night, the air during the day being cooled by the winds which disperse the clouds. Higher humidity, plus the combination of warm ground and cool air, causes scent to rise. The northern latitudes of

England and Ireland, the warming influence of the Gulf Stream and the relatively even distribution of rainfall throughout the year make for a cool moist even climate and the best scenting conditions in the world. The consequent deep going, the long hours during which hounds hunt (from 11.00 a.m. until dark) and the many countries fenced with hedges (virtually unknown in North America) through which hounds must push, require a somewhat more powerful hound with more stamina than the American hound, who runs on the top of the ground, across larger fields with fewer fences, and seldom stays out more than 4 to 5 hours.

In the United States the nights tend to be clear so that the ground either freezes or is very cold. In mid-winter it may be twelve or one o'clock before the ground is sufficiently warm for scent to lie. Such conditions obviously require a hound with a particularly good nose and with the drive to keep constantly pressing a fox so that he never gets so far ahead as to cause scent to fail. Because of large woodlands and wire it is frequently not possible for staff and field to be in close touch with hounds. Consequently a good volume of cry is essential if hounds are to hear each other and if followers are to hear hounds. For the same reasons hounds must have fox-sense and the ability and initiative to recover the line on their own without help.

In the many countries where sheep and pigs are raised, the characteristic fencing is woven wire, with a tighter mesh close to the ground, and standard openings of 9 inches × 2 inches beginning 1½ feet above the ground and extending to the top of a 4-foot fence. This is usually surmounted by two strands of barbed wire to keep cattle from rubbing it. The smaller-chested American, Penn–Marydel and cross-bred hounds, when running a fox through such a country, turn sideways and slide through the 8 inch × 10 inch rectangles with surprising speed. Most English hounds and the larger cross-bred hounds, on the other hand, have too large a chest measurement to get through the wire. Trying to find a way round is often time consuming, and jumping it is extremely dangerous as hounds are then apt to be hung by a hindleg and cannot extricate themselves without help.

Pack hounds—how they are hunted

Although the height at the withers of the English hound is approximately the same, the body and total weight is considerably heavier (some 30%) than that of the American foxhound, which is closer to the body of the Fell hound or the English harrier. 50 years ago the conformation of the American hound was deservedly criticized for lack of uniformity, quality and soundness. His British counterpart was also deservedly criticized for straight pasterns that knuckled over, for exaggerated cat-feet with many a toe down, for excessive bone and weight and for lack of cry. Since that time hound-breeders on both sides of the Atlantic have been moving more and more towards a common goal, however, with most of the above faults erased, so that the top hounds at Britain's Peterborough foxhound show (particularly the bitches) are not too far removed in type from the top American and Penn–Marydel hounds at the Bryn Mawr and Virginia foxhound shows in the United States.

Wherever hound men and women gather there is apt to be much talk about different breeds and strains of hounds and far less talk about a matter of even greater importance—namely how they are hunted. Just as hounds that are followed on foot in the Fell districts of northern England are hunted very differently from the hounds followed on horseback in the Shires, so the night hounds that are not followed at all in the United States, and the field trial hounds that are left completely without the help of a huntsman, are hunted very differently from the packs followed on horseback by staff and field across countries recognized by the Masters of Foxhounds' Association of America. Necessarily the ways in which they are hunted are to a great degree responsible not only for their hunting qualities but also for their conformation and stamina.

Let us compare the methods of American huntsmen with those of their British counterparts. In Britain there is a long-standing tradition of hunt service, often passed on from father to son, which, unfortunately, is seldom the case in America. Furthermore, the methods employed by British huntsmen, the use of the voice, the horn, the handling of hounds in the field and so forth are comparatively uniform, so that a huntsman going from one hunt to another has little difficulty in adapting himself to his new pack. In the United States, on the other hand, methods vary widely. Perhaps a third of our huntsmen are either transplanted Britishers or have been brought up in the English tradition employing traditional methods. As for the remainder, some use the conventional copper horn, while others, particularly in the southern states, retain the medieval tradition of the cow horn which can be heard for very long distances but is more limited in the variety of notes used to communicate with hounds, staff and members of the field. Hound language differs widely—those who visit other hunts seldom get much information from listening to the voice of the local huntsman as to what hounds are doing. There are many ways in which the services of the whippers-in are employed and so forth. One quality characteristic of virtually all American huntsmen, however, is a high degree of woodcraft, the ability to read the signs of the countryside left by birds, animals, foliage, grass, wet ground, etc., the ability to foresee and to unravel the course and the stratagems of the fox. Most of them show excellent sport.

There are similarly wide differences between kennel management. Accommodations for hounds vary between a few elaborate structures of brick or stone with flagged lodging-rooms and yards and simple wooden buildings with earth yards, enclosed by woven wire. Some hunts feed prepared dog food, and others butcher and cook meat and Indian cornmeal or other grain; a few feed raw flesh, thanks to advances for controlling parasites which would otherwise be a serious problem, particularly in the southern countries. Few hunts are able to find satisfactory walks for puppies, which in consequence are mostly kennel-raised.

The extent to which hounds are walked out for exercise, to learn manners, and to become accustomed to cattle, pigs, sheep and poultry, also varies considerably.

Because of pressure exerted by shooting interests, most game commissions during recent years have stocked the forests of their respective states with white-tailed deer which have invaded the majority of the hunting countries. Various methods have been used to make hounds steady to deer—taking out only one or two couples at a time of the young entry, in order to learn from the older hounds that deer are forbidden; walking hounds out where deer are frequently found and chastising them if they make any attempt to follow; supplying the whippers-in not only with a hunting whip but also with a .22 calibre pistol loaded with bird shot; keeping an aggressive buck with horns in the kennel; the use of artificial deer-scent plus punishment to create a negative reaction; and so forth. A few packs will now pay no attention to deer under any circumstances, while the great majority can easily be stopped from running deer by the members of the staff.

Foxhounds of the future

The Walker strain and the Birdsong–July–Trigg strain of field-trial foxhounds were developed by men who were great riders to hounds, who observed closely the good and bad points of every hound and who were able to select and to eliminate accordingly. Since the advent of the automobile, however, most field-trial hound breeders have ceased to follow on horseback, being limited to what they can hear by night and what they can see by day, following as best they can in a car or truck, when hounds cross a road. Whether field-trial hounds are as good today as they were 50 years ago is a much mooted question. It does seem reasonably certain that they will not change much during the next half-century, however. Changes in hounds are brought about by changes in terrain and in the way they are hunted. Since the type of terrain used, because of the very nature of field-trials, is not subject to change and since they are simply turned loose and are not hunted by their owners, field-trial hounds in the future seem pretty certain to remain much as they are today.

As indicated above, changes in the conformation of American and of English pack hounds during the past 50 years have been extensive. Since breeders on both sides of the Atlantic have been working from different poles towards a type which is now relatively similar, we can expect in future a further refinement of that type rather than major changes. It is in the realms of hunting qualities and how hounds are hunted that we can look forward to considerably greater differences. This is because there will undoubtedly be major changes in the terrain of our hunting countries and in the obstacles encountered by foxes, by hounds and by their mounted followers. For example, before the advent of deer, most huntsmen in the United States, while casting, encouraged hounds to range widely: since we have almost no small coverts, planted and tightly-fenced, most foxes found are outliers. Today, however, huntsmen keep hounds much closer, in case a deer should jump up and one or two erring members of the young entry should need to be discouraged from pursuit. In consequence hounds hunt less independently and perhaps show less initiative in finding foxes than formerly, even though they are just as keen and just as effective once a fox is started.

We can be sure that, in the next 50 years, we shall see major changes in the conditions encountered in the hunting fields of the United States. We can also be sure that, during this period as in the past, the challenges presented by these changes will be met and overcome.

Chapter 5

Five Unique Packs

HAVING already touched upon the influence of the Curre, let us, in this survey of five unique packs of the British Isles, first take a closer look at the making of that Monmouthshire pack to see how they earned their fame. Then we shall turn from Wales to north-east England, thence to south-west England and from there to the south of Ireland, discovering how, through the development of the hunt concerned and the influence of its breeding enthusiasts, each hound-type emerged.

THE CURRE

Nose, cry and perseverance: those, as we know, are the three great qualities of the Welsh hound; and his shortcomings are lack of stamina and a tendency to independence and babbling. To counter these defects, several nineteenth-century Welsh Masters brought infusions of the best English blood to their kennels but none with such resounding and immortal success as Edward Curre, of Itton. In 1896 he went to the head of a heritage that was born in the eighteenth century, for he took over the Chepstow hunt, which began as harriers under his great-great-grandfather, John Curre. In 1869, the Chepstow, having a very small country, amalgamated with the Llangibby but separated again a decade before Edward Curre took over from Squire Lewis of St Pierre. He re-named the hunt 'Mr Curre's' and was Master for 34 seasons.

He explained this to a friend at the end of his career:

'I wanted a hound that had drive and voice and speed. I wanted them all of a type, without the woolly Welsh coat—which to me was unsightly—and I wanted them *white*, so that I could see them in the distance; for, even in my country, hounds often ran in places where a horse could not follow, and it would have been difficult to see the darker-coloured ones; but I did not want to lose "the hound of the country". . . . By using stallions from the long-established Welsh packs that possessed the most drive and speed and by cross-ing the produce with English stud book hounds which possessed low-scenting qualities and had plenty of tongue—and, wherever possible, the light colour which I wanted to get—I gradually acquired a type of my own; a type which, as you can see, reproduces itself generation after generation. . . .'

E

Establishing his kennels during the last years of the century with the best Welsh strains—some of John Lawrence's 'killing Llangibby', the Glog and the Neuad Fawr, during the pre-First World War era, Curre crossed these with such influential sires as the Milton Potent 01, Belvoir Weaver 06 and Watchman 07, the Duke of Beaufort's Leveller 10 and most extensively of all with his favourite, the 'hard-as-steel' Four Burrow Whipcord '05.

At the same time that the sacred Belvoir Tan had become a lumbering caricature of its former self, English Masters were hearing about the Curre and were sending their bitches along to the kennels which Curre (now Sir Edward) had built along the road from Itton Court in 1906. The die-hards were horrified. 'The Welsh cross is a blot on the escutcheon, a *mésalliance*,' complained Lord Bathurst, 'a marriage without quarterings.' However, the progressives held sway. 'Always on the look-out to improve my hounds,' wrote Ikey Bell, 'I soon paid Sir Edward Curre and his hounds a visit. I was astounded by their cry and their work in the field. . . . '

Then that colourful Anglo-American sportsman, A. H. Higginson, tells how, when out with a pack hunted by a 'brilliant amateur', he saw a hound make a hit across some plough when no other hound in the pack would own the line and was informed that it 'went back to some of Teddy Curre's blood'. 'It *made* my pack, I know that,' he said, 'and when I came back to England . . . I found that many of the best working packs in the land used some of the Itton Court stallions. . . . '

My day with the Curre, when hounds met at Itton Court, in April 1973, was a hot dry one; but scent was reasonable in covert, and, when at last they did get on terms with a fox, it was fascinating to watch this wonderfully level white pack, rather short-legged, close-coupled and of great agility, wriggle and persevere through the thorn and bramble brakes of the conifer plantations in which Monmouthshire abounds. They made that deep organ-like music so characteristic of the Welsh.

Several packs in Wales have gone exclusively for the native blood. From what I have seen of them, I cannot believe this achieves the best hunting qualities. I was out with the David Davies, whose country is in south Montgomeryshire, later that year. Here I saw the descendants of those broken-coated English–Welsh crosses bred at Llandinam by the First Lord Davies during the Edwardian era. This pack, probably now with 98% Welsh blood, have not been touched by an English outcross for over forty years.

How do they perform? They drew well, but their very independent character showed at the cast, when sometimes one or two couples would regain the line and say so, while the remainder were obstinately determined to find out for themselves; although they seemed to pick up the cold scent, as the Welsh breed should, they were too often unable to persevere with it.

At this time their joint-Masters, Lord Davies and his uncle, the Hon. Islwyn Davies, were in search of the right outcross to put these traits right. This surely proves that the Welsh strain, as Sir Edward Curre showed, needs 'foreign' blood to produce really efficient fox-catchers.

THE COLLEGE VALLEY

Sir Alfred Goodson, one of the great breeders of both cattle and hounds of our time, fashioned the College Valley hound to hunt those moorlands where North-umberland, Roxburghshire and Berwickshire meet around the Cheviot and Hethpool. His story is quite as absorbing as Sir Edward Curre's. It goes like this.

When, 67 years ago, the first Sir Alfred Goodson, Devonshire and Cheshire landowner and Master of the Haldon harriers, asked his son Alfred (or Bill as he was, and is, generally known) where he would like to do his farming apprentice-ship, the reply was 'where your ewes come from'; and the answer to that was the Cheviots. So, in 1909, Sir Alfred secured a place for the young man on the boun-daries of Roxburghshire and Northumberland. Soon finding the moorland and mountains closer to his heart than the rich enclosures he knew as a child, the farm student never looked back. He kept a horse with the Border hunt, and what excited him more than anything was the music and dauntless style of old Jacob Robson's hounds. A little before the Great War his father bought him the Border farm of Kilham, and soon a Yeomanry subaltern was whiling away his off-duty hours on the Somme imagining the cattle and the hounds he would breed for that faraway land, that rather poor-scenting country where the white grasses and mossy turf compete with the bracken and heather and scree on the naked mountainside of the Border.

So, when the Kaiser's holocaust was over, Bill Goodson set to and bred Aberdeen Angus cattle and Cheviot sheep; he bred harriers and beagles and hunted them with his friend and neighbouring estate owner, Capt. the Hon. Claud Lambton. Hare hunting was good fun; but the two young cattle farmers were sad about one thing—the way in which foxes were disposed of in their country. For this lay at the apex of three hunts, all of whom more or less neglected it: the Border, the Duke of Buccleuch's and the North Northumberland. Here the foxes were shot—and more often were wounded than killed—by shepherds, or were caught in the rabbit-catchers' snares and were cruelly maimed. So, when the Border agreed to surrender their unwanted north-eastern sector, Capt. Goodson and Capt. Lambton collected a pack of hounds and hunted the valleys of Bowmont Water and College Burn in the right and proper style. Soon afterwards the North Northumberland and the Duke of Buccleuch's lent them the steep-sided valleys of their own southern corners.

It was a close team. Capt. Lambton acted as field Master, saw to the foxes and organized the country, while Capt. Goodson was the huntsman and breeder of hounds. He was a born breeder. He bred bantams and racing pigeons 'from the age of six', and as 'Dalesman' (C. N. de Courcy Parry) was later to put it, 'This courteous and charming gentleman possesses that uncanny feeling or touch with all animals that enables him to breed the very best. . . . ' Originally hounds from

Jacob Robson's Border kennels and the Fell packs, with outcrosses from the Duke of Buccleuch's, were to form the basis of Capt. Goodson's pack. His best sires were put to his Goathland bitch, Rosebud 21 (by the celebrated Morpeth Random), who took his fancy, and another from that kennels called Friendly and also Bramham Chorus. The Friendly and Chorus lines did not prevail, but, even now, 95% of the pack go back to the foundation bitch, Goathland Rosebud. Later on, the outcrosses came from the Fell packs, particularly Blencathra Trueman, Coniston Chanter and Ullswater Marina.

Thus Goodson combined what he considered to be the best Fell blood, with the best foxhound kennel stud book stock that had been bred for hill countries. In the beginning the College Valley were catching 15 brace of foxes a season. Well before 1930 the tally for this small country averaged 60 brace.

Attracted by the legend, many of the great foxhunting names, who were to become firm friends of Bill Goodson, visited Kilham for a glimpse of the quality hounds he had fashioned: Lord Knutsford, Sir Peter Farquhar, Ikey Bell and Bill Scott. They saw and they were very impressed. When Ikey Bell watched the College Valley in action, he confided that he wished he had used Fell rather than Welsh blood when he bred his famous South and West Wilts pack, the hounds which were to mark the turning-point in the shape and size and weight of the modern foxhound. So, if Bell had seen the College Valley a little earlier, today's fashionable grass and plough country hound might have had a different shape and character; he might have carried his knees further back, stood more squarely on the hint of a hare-foot, he might have been longer in the humerus and snipier in the head, he might have shown a little more independence and perhaps a finer voice; but, over a flat country, would this have meant a more effective hound?

'The College Valley are mostly white in colour, full of quality and very level in appearance', wrote Sir John Buchanan-Jardine in 1936, 'and they are considered by many people who have seen them to be the fastest pack in Great Britain; certainly they account for a very high percentage of foxes and show great sport.' Dalesman went further, 'Goodson's white hounds are without any shadow of doubt the best pack to catch foxes in the hills of any in the world. . . . '

Sir Alfred Goodson (he inherited in 1940) insists on tongue first and next on nose and drive, coupled with stamina. For, as he says, cry, scenting power and drive are of little avail without great constitution and the ability to go all out on a long day.

Towards the end of 1972 I spent a week-end at Corbet Tower, Sir Alfred's present home, near Kelso, discussing the College Valley saga with him, enjoying a day's hunting and watching this celebrated pack show their special facility for casting themselves on over bad stretches, for knowing shale for its scentlessness, for realizing drenched bracken obliterates it and for automatically driving forward to seek beyond. The first of the four foxes they killed in College Valley that stormy, windy day was much too slow for them. After moving off from the meet at Hethpool, Martin Letts, the joint-Master and huntsman, cheered them onto the bracken slopes of Easter Tor. No more was required. Spreading quick as a fisherman's net they unkennelled their first in a few seconds and promptly killed him in full view of us.

Then, hunting southwards, they chased their second behind some rocks just short of Newton Tors. In went the terrier. Out came the quarry; but, within 200 yards, in his panic, he somersaulted over a rock and was swiftly dispatched. Fox number three was killed after a snappy run just out of view. They discovered their fourth by a place called Yeavering Bell. He gave them a 2-hour run with a 5-mile point and a fourth kill in the open. It was indeed a joy to listen to the College Valley and to watch this last hound hunt—a white ribbon, with a triumphant chorus, on the open hillside, now and then forming a speedy casting huddle and veering tight on their fox at every turn.

Whether the fact that several Fell pack Masters and huntsmen go to the College Valley for their outcrosses in itself proves the superiority of Sir Alfred's hounds is a moot point; but, having seen and heard both breeds in different conditions, my own opinion is that the College Valley have a finer voice and better pack sense and that they get away faster onto their fox than 'pure' Fell hounds. Perhaps a matter of greater interest to most hound-breeders is the use of College Valley sires by the most strongly admired of the old West Country harrier packs, a pack now entered to fox: the Cotley.

THE COTLEY

Of the few packs of hounds whose pedigrees can be traced through more than a century to their hunt's formation, the Cotley harriers, who hunt the green and tightly-enclosed hills, where Devon, Somerset and Dorset converge, probably provide the most revealing single lesson in the evolution of modern hunting.

For when Thomas Deane, of Cotley, formed his pack of hare-hunting 'lemon and badger pies' in 1797, the harrier was still the squirearchy's favourite hound. and in much of the West Country it remained so for up to 100 years and more; but, during the Victorian era, at the same time that enclosure programmes intensified, hares became scarcer and foxes more prolific. To adjust to these circumstances, Thomas Deane's descendants might have decided on one of two alternatives: to continue to hunt hares in increasingly difficult conditions or to draft their pack and kennel foxhounds. They went instead for a brave compromise, one that has proved an unqualified success: they bred up the weight and speed of their harriers to transform them into fox-catchers. So that today, although we see the Cotley listed in the foxhounds section of *Baily's Directory*, we also find them entered in the harrier stud book. In spite of the various introductions of foxhound strains in the kennels at Cotley, the blood of the old West Country harrier remains thickest in their veins. Nor has their character substantially altered since the eighteenth century.

This careful adaptation could never have been evolved without the unrelenting dedication of the family in whose hands the Cotley harriers remain today—the

Eameses. This ancient family of Devon yeomen provide a most fascinating side-line in the history of British hunting. The Eameses came in like this. Thomas Deane's heiress-presumptive married another devoted hunting man, Thomas Palmer Eames, who assumed control of the pack on the death of their founder, in 1855; and here a connection already existed, because the cousins of Eames Palmer, had hunted the Cotley country for at least a century before Deane's career began.

Thomas Palmer Eames was Master and huntsman for 31 seasons before he handed over the horn in 1886 to his much younger brother, Edward, who kept it until 1929. Then Edward's nephews, Richard and Deane, took over. In 1939 they were succeeded by Richard's son, the present Master, Lt-Col. R. F. P. Eames, who, in his turn, for more than 30 years, has continued to fashion the Cotley harrier to suit the ever-changing character of this corner of the West Country. And—in spite of a knee injury incurred on active service—to hunt them personally. So the Eames family have, during only four reigns, now held the Mastership and the horn for about 120 years.

The thread of these hounds' breeding is tenuous at one point only—in 1832, when an outbreak of rabies occurred at Cotley. (You can still see the railings of the original, now ruined, kennels, through which the hounds were shot.) However, Thomas Deane was not to be defeated by that. He bred extensively from the sole survivors of the tragedy, a bitch called Countess and her whelps, then at walk with the Eames who was to become his son-in-law. Here that splendid band of sporting clerics appear in the Cotley saga. For Deane was also lucky enough to secure the pick of the celebrated kennels of the Rev. E. C. Forward, who had died recently, besides presents from—among others—the Rev. Harry Farr Yeatman, whose kennels were full of the blood of Parson Froude's great pack. (Of these Jack Russell had said, 'They are light in their colour and sharp as needles—plenty of tongue but would drive like furies. I have never seen a better or more killing pack in all my life.' Later, after hunting with the Cotley, Parson Jack considered it a great triumph to secure a draft from them.) Anyhow, Deane soon kennelled a level pack of 20-inch harriers at Cotley again.

Under the Eameses, hunt records showed a steady increase in the ratio of foxes to hares: Thomas Palmer Eames accounted each season for about 130 hares and a few foxes, as chance occurred; but, under Edward, the average changed to the region of 60 foxes and 35 hares, until the hare interest dwindled to such an extent between the wars that, officially, the last was killed on 4 November 1938. Apart from the fact that the pattern of big Devon banks, topped with barriers of oak, ash and hazel was inexorably tightening, for all his nose and tenacity, the West Country harrier obviously lacked that element of speed and stamina necessary to press these tough hill foxes over a distance.

So far the only outcrosses to be used consistently came from the Taunton Vale harriers. New blood was needed—foxhound blood. Experiment was tentative: Tiverton strains were tried, and in 1918 they used the top award-winning Silverton Dalesman; then, with an eye to whiteness and Welsh tongue, they went once to the Curre. However, there was virtually no difference in the pack's appearance until a few years after the last war, when Col. Eames went to the College Valley, the stroke of genius which was to earn the Cotley the fame it now owns.

The Cotley being then practically pure West Country harrier and the College Valley a blend of Border, Fell and foxhound kennel stud book, no affinity existed between the two. So the 'nick' owed little to the study of genetics or line breeding. Col. Eames, who had for long been an admirer of the genius of Sir Alfred Goodson, decided in 1948 to use College Valley, after seeing Sir Alfred's Ruffian with Dr R. N. Craig, the baronet's brother-in-law, who was then Master of the East Devon.

Col. Eames's instinct said, 'Right build, an inch taller than mine, predominantly white, just what I want.' The first Cotley litter, sired by Ruffian, proved his judgment. The dog hounds grew to 22 to 23 inches, the bitches to 20 to 21 inches. To the retained light colour, superior nose, beautiful neck and shoulders and clean, hard-wearing feet of the Cotley was added the extra strength and pace of the Northumberland sire. (Fortunately, Col. Eames's initial anxiety—that their speed might prove too much for their noses—was quickly dispelled.) Soon another quality was added, from Sir Alfred's side: a loud bell-like tongue, typical of Lakeland and Border. This asset, Col. Eames told me, came from the College Valley Belford 58, who, at the time of writing, has sired three litters.

A single good day with this West Country pack was sufficient to convince me that only exceptionally gifted line-hunters, who turn tight on their quarry (a marked characteristic of harriers), are a match for this country, hounds, too, that will drive on across the pasture and yet can afford to be slowed up by the maze of tall thicket-topped banks of this part of the West Country. I attended such a day—the hunt's 1973 opening meet from Cotley, the Master's house. Then, after a rather scrappy morning, Col. Eames lifted hounds to a conifer wood on the south side of a combe, between Chardstock and the kennels.

From the north side of the combe I saw their very twisty fox make four or five great circles. I saw three roe deer cross their line and two fresh foxes roused, while the hunted fox made several sudden turns. Yet none of these obstacles deflected them. I saw each member of the pack momentarily checked as he or she struggled with the banks; but the white hounds of Cotley—with that priceless blood, nurtured by Thomas Deane, in their veins—followed the line in single file, giving the semblance of a string of white beads or drops of milk flying from a tap, until at last, after 50 minutes, they overhauled him in the open. It was a classic hound hunt: from the moment they found, Col. Eames demonstrated the habit of his ancestors, never speaking to the pack, never heeding to the holloas.

What a lovely pack of hounds this is! They remind one, if anything, of the Curre; and one wonders why Cotley blood is not sought after by other hunts, mainly, I suppose, because they are considered to be too small.

THE DUMFRIESSHIRE

To find the next unique hound of this study we must turn to an isolated hunting country on the western end of the Border: to Dumfriesshire. This is a country steeped in the tradition of the chase and the horse, a tradition stemming from the days of the Border feuds. For the ancestors of the Dumfriesshire foxhunters of today were largely cattle thieves—a quite respectable pursuit up to 400 years ago. That stretch of the Carlisle–Glasgow road that runs over the Solway Firth and through the Annan Valley had echoed to the sound of frantic hooves centuries before Robert Bruce was born. When the law began to catch up with rustling, the obvious diversion to fill the gap was the chase; then men appeared with reputations like the turbulent seventeenth-century John Irving, known as Jock o'Milk, who, when Lord Torthorwald ran him through with a lance over a cattle dispute, prompted this nice epitaph from the lips of James VI, '. . . yet he had virtues that Jock o'Milk, for he was a tight huntsman and could holloa to hounds till all the woods rang again'. The Annan coverts rarely ceased ringing to the horn and holloa of wild huntsmen like Jock o'Milk.

In the early nineteenth century, it was neighbouring foxhunting squires, lured by the challenge of the fast Dumfriesshire hill foxes and readily responding to the challenges of the local bloods, who hunted this country: men like Wullie Hay of Duns Castle in Berwickshire, who had been Master of the Warwickshire, Mr Murray, Major St Colomb and Col. Salkeld, who brought with him Joe Graham, one of the towering figures of Scottish hunting and virtually the founder of the Dumfriesshire. For in 1848 Salkeld gave Graham 16 couples of hounds 'to use for any purpose he pleased'. Graham could not afford to run an establishment on his own and might have sold the pack were it not for the happy intervention of the Seventh Marquess of Queensberry, who took over the Mastership, with Graham as huntsman. 'Old Joe' carried the horn through four more Masterships, dying, after 45 seasons, in 1893, when a monument was erected on Almagill, an obelisk still visible for many miles round, with the inscription, 'And now he has gone far, far away—we shall never hear his voice in the morning.'

With Dumfriesshire now firmly established as a foxhunting county by Joe Graham and his patrons, the way was prepared for the family who fashioned the county's famous Dumfriesshire black-and-tans: the Buchanan-Jardines, of Castle Milk. ('The Jardines are the soul of hunting', Old Joe told his great admirer, 'the Druid', 'and Castle Milk is our meet; most like an English meet of any; regular Badminton lawn business and everything for all!') The first of this family to become Master was Sir Robert Buchanan-Jardine, and the second his son, Sir John. A contemporary, a great friend and a fellow-breeder of many animals of Sir Alfred Goodson, of the College Valley, it was this Buchanan-Jardine who took over the hunt in 1921, at the age of 21, and bred the celebrated hound of the country.

As the Edwardian critic, 'Tantivy', put it, 'Dumfriesshire hunting men have been forced to the conclusion that, owing to their stoutness and wild nature, these foxes take a tremendous amount of catching. A *fast* hound is needed.' Col. Selkeld's hounds and their descendants, bred by Graham, are recorded as being 'a comparatively slow type—heavy, hard, persevering and accustomed to stick to their line, be it ever so cold'. In the 1880s, a bloodhound cross was tried, but Col. Charles Brook, who was Master during the First World War, saw little future for hunting after it was over and dispensed with most of the pack, and this gave Sir John Buchanan-Jardine in 1921 the opportunity to build up from the bottom.

He wanted a pack of pure black-and-tans, possessing a better cry and nose and greater speed than the average English foxhound. He achieved this, firstly by putting selected bitches to a field trial champion bloodhound called Ledburn Boswell. Sir John described a grandson of these experiments, Harlequin, a quarter bloodhound, as 'the best hound in the field I ever saw'. He also acquired a hound of Gascon breeding called Triomphe, and the foundation of his pack was the result of crossing Triomphe with Harlequin's sisters. He then brought in other black-and-tan influences, such as the Brecon Whipcord, which was by the famous Tiverton Whipcord, Silverton Woodman, an English foxhound–French stag-hound cross, and Croome Clansman. In 17 or 18 years of selective breeding the white was eliminated. What emerged were 26- to 28-inch dog hounds and 24- to 27-inch bitches, all with a tremendous shoulder and depth through the heart, great long-distance speed, a bloodhounds' nose and a golden voice, once heard never forgotten: a paragon to match this steep, varied country and its outsize foxes. The Dumfriesshire hound is very intelligent: he knows the tricks of the wiliest foxes.

I hunted two seasons with the Dumfriesshire when soldiering near Carlisle in the 1950s and have enjoyed several odd days since. These Dumfriesshire black-and-tans may not be the quickest of all when it comes to a sprint, but, in my opinion, they are the most difficult to keep up with over a long distance. Their pace never flags. The last day I rode with these magnificent hounds was in March 1971, the time of year when they are hunting the hill country.

I will describe that day. Major Sir Rupert Buchanan-Jardine, who already, by then, had carried the horn in his father's tradition for 25 years, drew Mosshead covert first. Finding immediately, we were led by Courstein and left-handed into Gimmendie Glen. With the Black-and-Tan's melody as loud as church bells, in spite of poor scenting conditions—and lovely to hear again—we now sped right, past Gibson Scale Hill and doubled back up the hill, killing him after 40 minutes' run, with Capt. John Bell-Irving (hunt chairman and a direct descendant of the legendary Jock o'Milk), Capt. Ronald Cunningham-Jardine (hunt secretary) and John Tulloch, at whose home, Tundergarth, we had met, riding one of his eventers, close behind David Culham, who was then in his first season as joint-Master, among the four or five who were up at the finish. The brush went to Johnnie Tulloch, our host's son.

They picked up the line of their second fox on the side of Burnswark, the site of an old Roman camp, and raced over the hill, through the young Burnswark covert and past Haregills, Douglas Hall Farm and Newfield, where he got into a drain; but they bolted him and overhauled him after a few hundred yards, a second Pony Club member—Miranda Bell-Macdonald this time—receiving the brush and holding it high above her head as she galloped back to her mother with smeared cheeks and an ecstatic cry of 'Tom's blooded me!' Meanwhile the Black-and-Tans trotted away to promising Burnswark old covert, to push up their third fox, to run him under the floorboards of Dansrig farm, to bolt him and to fly like the wind back to his covert, then right-handed past Mosshead and Tundergarth Mains to Castle hill covert, where he saved his brush in a cavernous earth.

Fly is the word. They take off, these Dumfriesshire black-and-tans, from 6 feet before a 4-foot wall or wire fence, to breast it at the gallop; you see them streak through tight spruce at the pace of jungle cats; and on a bad scenting day (like that occasion in March 1971) time and again I was entertained to their quick wide casts—Sir Rupert leaving it to them—the bell-like music a single instrument where the patchy line regained, then suddenly the full orchestra, and away with their inimitable lengthy stride. Of all the packs in the world it is Scotland's Black-and-Tans that I should be most sorry never to hear and see again.

THE SCARTEEN

Lastly, we have that other, even more famous, pack of black-and-tans—*The* Black-and-Tans, which hunt the banked grass country of Co. Limerick and Co. Tipperary.

'My boy, they were always there', young John Ryan was told in the 1890s on enquiring of his uncle, Clement, when these hounds came into the family. Made in an off-hand way, that was a fair answer. For it is believed that the Ryans kept hounds of the native strains as far back as the family history can be traced, and no one really knows when they first owned Kerry beagles.

What are these hounds? How, indeed, did they come to Scarteen? That they are of Gascon–Ariegeois stock, that much is certain. Still to be seen in south-west France, small and light-boned, with rather long ears, some black-and-tan, others black-and-white and blue-mottled, the Gascon–Ariegeois are small bloodhound types, prized by the old *veneurs* for their great hunting qualities and more especially for their deep resounding cry, which no less an authority than Sir John Buchanan-Jardine, founder, as we have seen, of the Dumfriesshire black-and-tans and author of the classic *Hounds of the World*, who put voice above all other virtues, described as 'absolutely the finest music of any hounds in the world'. Their advent to Ireland is popularly attributed to the 'Wild Geese', those perse-cuted Catholics who were rallied by King Louis to fight the English on Conti-nental soil. Some of these veterans, soldiers and sportsmen, too, are said to have heard, and been so delighted by, the Gascon and Ariegeois voice that they took some home and called them Kerry beagles.

Why Kerry? Mr Thady Ryan, the present owner, joint-Master and huntsman of the Black-and-Tans, proposes a different theory. He believes the Gascon–Ariegeois were also bred in neighbouring Aragon, Catalonia and Navarre; for hounds of that colour, size and type were remarked upon by Irish travellers in Spain and by Irishmen who fought up to the Pyrenees with Franco's army. Some years ago, Mr Ryan saw hound statues in the Canary Islands, at Las Palmas, showing identical conformation with his own. Ryan believes they came to Ireland long, long before the days of the 'Wild Geese', via the great Spanish–Irish trading island of Valentia, off Kerry. When crossed with the native Talbot type, the qualities of the dominant Gascon–Ariegeois blood, albeit in a somewhat taller hound, shone through. As for Kerry beagle, in those days the term simply referred to any light-boned hunting dog. The breed were kept and trencher fed, as they are today, by cliques of farmers over much of south-west Ireland. The Chutes and the O'Connells, the Butlers of Waterville fame and the Ryans of Co. Limerick, whose eldest sons have alternated through history between a John and a Thaddeus, kept packs of them; but only the Ryans' pack have survived.

John Ryan had them until 1781, then 'Tha' who moved house from Ballyvistea to Scarteen in 1798 and, by so doing, gave the hunt its additional name. Following a Ryan financial collapse, the failure of Sadleir's Bank, of Tipperary, John Franks, of Ballyscadane, took the family pack on trust for seven years. Then Clement Ryan, whose elder brother, Thaddeus, was constantly abroad soldiering, kennelled them at nearby Emly. He got the pick of the Chute and the O'Connell packs, when they broke up, and carried on until 1904, when his nephew, John, whose burning question opens my account, took over.

This John Ryan owned the Black-and-Tans for over 50 years. He hunted them up to the First World War, during which, in rest periods from the front line, he carried the horn for the 'Flanders' Hunt. Buried alive for three hours, when the Germans mined his regiment's trenches in 1915, John Ryan was officially reported killed, but he survived a prisoner-of-war camp to hunt the Scarteen again until 1929—the year in which they ceased to hunt carted deer—after which a succession of joint-Masters acted as huntsmen up to the Second World War.

In 1946, John's son, Thady, then aged 23, took the horn; he divided the Mastership with his father until the latter's death in 1955 and was on his own until 1971. Since then, while still owning the hounds, Thady Ryan has shared the command with Mrs Dermot McCalmont, widow of the Kilkenny's celebrated Master. Tommy O'Dwyer, who turns hounds to Mr Ryan, has served as kennel–huntsman since 1954, when he succeeded his father, Jack, who held that post for 30 years.

Thanks to such solid continuity at the helm and in the kennels, the character of the Scarteen Black-and-Tan has changed very little. His white markings were bred out long ago; he is jet across the back and flank, with head and legs of a rich deep tan. He remains a true Kerry beagle, possessing the very independent and engaging character of that breed, with a temperament that is easily upset by insensitive handling.

His conformation, too, is different from *Foxhound Kennel Stud Book* hounds: his shoulder is rather upright, yet permitting a great stride; he drops away a little on the quarter but is sufficiently strong at that point to carry it; he compensates for a long back by showing great muscle over the spine and loin; he carries his long-toed feet full on the ground under lengthy pasterns and well let-down hocks; his neckcloth bears evidence of his rich voice, while his French blood-hound ears reach across amber eyes to the tip of his nose. The dog hound stands 22 inches to 23 inches at the shoulder, the bitch nearly 2 inches shorter.

How have the Ryans kept the strain pure and at the same time avoided in-breeding? Mr Ryan did try a Dumfriesshire cross, but, perhaps because the lineage is so separated, the experiment failed. So he goes back for his outcrosses, as his ancestors went, to those Kerry trencher-fed packs that are congregated after Sunday Mass to hunt hare and drag, whose owners revel, as their fathers did before them, in the famous song and drive.

South-west Ireland was in flood the only time I could plan to hunt with the Black-and-Tans, and, as hunting was cancelled, I had to be content with follow-ing on hound exercise. So I never heard their wild music nor witnessed their unique manner of casting; but other visitors to Scarteen tell me that the description by Joseph Pickersgill, a veteran huntsman, who was joint-Master and who hunted them during the 1931-2 season, is as good as any:

> 'When the leaders are at fault, the tail hounds fan round them to left and right, driving on at the same time. If they are still at fault, they will make a big cast all the way round as a pack—not as individuals, as most fell hounds do—and most of this at the gallop. . . . I don't think I have ever seen another pack of foxhounds do a really big "all-round-your-hat" cast quite on their own. . . . '

The fame of the Scarteen goes farther beyond the native shore, perhaps, than any other pack in the British Isles. Every year, the Masters welcome American and continental visitors, and it must be quite a fillip for Thady Ryan to see Frenchmen, of whom there are often several strong contingents, flocking to Limerick and Tipperary to watch these Ryan hounds that stem from old Gascony.

True foxhunters always find it at once instructive, refreshing and exciting to witness a pack of foxhounds, bred outside the norm, at work, and it is worth a good deal of inconvenience and long travel to spend a day or two with any of these packs I have described.

Chapter 6
Kennels and Welfare

OW LET US SEE how foxhounds are kennelled, fed, exercised and generally cared for. Based on the accepted understanding that the hound
cannot hunt efficiently more than two days a week and that 12 couple
is the minimum the huntsman will lead out for a day's hunting, in the case of a
pack that hunts 3 or 4 days a week, somewhere between 35 and 45 couples,
divided into a dog-pack and a bitch-pack, are likely to be found in kennels. (I
will embroider on this later in the chapter.)

How will this formidable collection be housed? First, the situation must be a
healthy one. William Somervile set the right tone 250 years ago:

> 'First let the Kennel be the Huntsman's Care,
> Upon some little eminence erect
> And fronting to the ruddy Dawn; its Courts
> On either Hand wide opening to receive
> The Sun's all-cheering Beams, when mild he shines
> And gilds the Mountain Tops.'

Hounds sleep in a number of lodging rooms (probably three), each holding
15 to 20 couple and containing benches or beds about 18 inches high, which can
be folded up when the room is not in use or is being washed out. From each of
these lodging rooms a door leads into an open court, surrounded by some type
of grille, through which hounds can look and can be seen. Next door, perhaps
between the lodging rooms and the courts, will be the draw yard, into which
hounds are collected prior to exercise or feeding or any other purpose. The feeding yard is likely to be adjacent—on one side to the draw yard and on the other
to the boiler room, which houses the copper boilers, in which the meal and flesh
are cooked.

When I asked Major J. J. Mann of the Vale of White Horse hunt for his views
on cleaning lodges, he gave this advice:

'It can be time consuming when the traditional wooden benches are used,
because straw will always find its way through the gaps in the boards, and this
must be removed. The boards will also become soaked with grease and urine
and will require scrubbing. We have recently replaced the old benches with

solid concrete ones laid on rubble, which is topped with a layer of Aglite or other similar highly insulating aggregate. The result has proved excellent, and it is very easily cleaned. Also, it is very economical in straw.

A number of kennels have recently changed from the old coal-fired coppers to gas-heated boilers. These are easily controlled. They only need to be lit when actually required, thus obviating the continual stoking and banking up needed with coal or coke. At the same time other conveniences can be run off the same gas supply, such as a hot water heater, room heater or clothes drier. All this makes for easier and cleaner working conditions.'

Some salutary distance away from the central compound is the flesh hovel, where the carcases of horses and cows, which form the staple meat diet, are deposited for skinning and butchering. A cold room or freezer, in which to store good flesh, when there is a surplus, is a great help, so that, in lean times, there is a reserve to draw on. This should be situated somewhere between the flesh house and the boiler room.

Also beyond the main complex will be puppy houses, a granary, a straw loft and a hospital. In some other separate situation there will probably be another smaller lodging room, for bitches in season—also with court attached.

Somewhere handy for the kennels may be a grass yard, an expansive wire-netting enclosure, into which the entire pack can be turned for air and exercise. Besides giving hounds a chance of stretching their limbs and emptying themselves, it will afford the huntsman or kennelman the opportunity of spotting lame hounds or any that are off colour.

However, real hardening exercise is only to be had 'walking out'. The following advice, given by Col. M. Borwick, a former Master of the Middleton and the Pytchley, 40 years ago, holds good today:

'It is an axiom that hounds should be out of kennel as much as possible when the weather permits. When walking out, the vitiated air is cleared, and the kennel staff have the time and opportunity of effecting the sanitary measures which are necessary. Exercise is essential for the physical and moral well-being of foxhounds. All dogs like a walk, foxhounds none the less. The question arises, how long should a pack of hounds "have off", which means that they are merely walked out when hunting ceases. Several packs send hounds out for exercise for some two hours throughout the spring and summer with excellent results, the men riding either bicycles or cobs. When exercised like this, hounds get further afield and so take more interest in their work; they fight less, keep their condition better and put on muscle quicker when regular and long exercises start.

Regular hound exercise requires thought and imagination on the part of the man who conducts it. If made interesting and instructive, hounds will always be on their toes, putting heart into their work and muscle on their bodies. It is an important part of their training and, like all others, must be progressive

A Kennels Plan

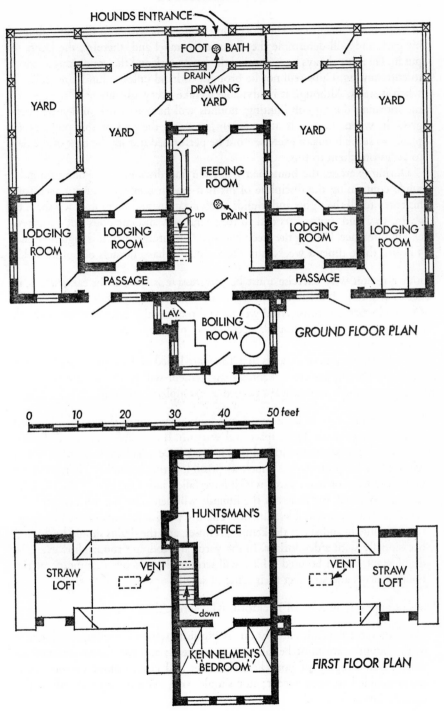

HOUNDS ENTRANCE

FOOT ⊙ BATH

DRAIN

DRAWING YARD

YARD

YARD

YARD

YARD

FEEDING ROOM

⊙ up DRAIN

LODGING ROOM

LODGING ROOM

LODGING ROOM

LODGING ROOM

PASSAGE

PASSAGE

LAV.

BOILING ROOM

GROUND FLOOR PLAN

0   10   20   30   40   50 feet

HUNTSMAN'S OFFICE

STRAW LOFT

VENT

VENT

STRAW LOFT

down

KENNELMEN'S BEDROOM

FIRST FLOOR PLAN

in both hours and pace. The discerning huntsman will note the condition of his pack and will determine the distance to travel and, thereby, the hours to put in. He must always have in mind the hard work and the conditions essential to cub hunting. Cubs will not be brought to hand unless hounds are really fit when it starts. Although it is advisable to take every advantage of the cool of the morning during cub hunting, hounds will have to work in dense undergrowth, when the sun is at its height, towards the end of this preparatory phase, so some hours of exercise must be performed during the heat of the day to accustom them to this.

During exercise, the huntsman will train and discipline his young hounds; while confirming the discipline of his first-season hunters, he must accustom his entry to all the sights and sounds of civilization, and he must teach them to swim, to avoid motor cars and to treat strangers and cur dogs with courtesy and indifference. During the week before cub hunting starts, it is suggested that 5 hours, three times a week, is not too much to have hounds out of kennel.'

Another reason why exercise must be progressive is that, in the early stages, in order to ensure pads are not worn thin, one must often lay off for long periods.

On road work one must avoid wet tar and roads which have just been gritted. No hazards are worse for hounds' feet. These jobs are nearly always carried out in early summer.

A time-honoured maxim holds that 'foxes are killed in the kennel'; and perhaps the most important feature of kennel management will be cleanliness. Borwick, whose own kennels were always quoted as exemplary, said this:

'Unless hounds live in healthy surroundings they cannot thrive; like humans they require fresh air, light, space and warmth. If they are overcrowded, they live in an atmosphere so vitiated that it must have a bad effect on their lungs. They must be protected as much as possible from breathing air tainted by faulty drainage or from yards which have fallen into disrepair. If the flags are not kept pointed, the faeces of the hounds will penetrate the soil beneath: the cause of many preventable ailments. The use of disinfectants is essential from time to time, in and about the kennel premises, and the drains should be flushed occasionally with a deodorizer. In the yards and lodging rooms, however, no disinfectant should be used which will irritate the mucous membrane of the hounds' noses and so affect their sense of smell.'

This last appeal is an echo of Beckford, who wrote this:

'As your sport depends entirely on an exquisite sense of smelling, so peculiar to the hound, care must be taken to preserve it; and cleanliness is the surest means. The keeping of your kennels sweet and clean cannot be too much recommended to your feeder; nor should you, on any account, admit the least deviation from it.'

Great names in the early history of the sport

1 Peter Beckford (1740–1809), Dorset Master of Foxhounds and author of *Thoughts on Hunting*

2 Hugo Meynell (1753–1800), Master of the Quorn and pioneer of scientific hound breeding

3 Thomas Assheton Smith (1776–1858), Master of the Quorn (1806–17), the Burton (1817–24) and the Tedworth (1826–58)

4 Charles James Apperley, 'Nimrod' (1778–1843), hunting correspondent

Scenes from the nineteenth century

5 *Taking a Toss with a Variety of Effects* by
Henry Alken (1785–1851)

6 *The Death Postponed* designed by Gill in
1822, engraved by James Pollard

An Edwardian meet

7   *The Cheshire Hounds* at Calveley Hall by
Goodwin Kilburne

The shires between the wars

8   The Pytchley Hunt Meet near Northampton
– 'Mr and Mrs Byng's novel way of carrying
horses to the meet by horse-box trailer'

9   Lady Zia Wernher, Joint-Master of Fernie's

A comparison of hound types

10 A Welsh hound – the David Davies Bristol

11 The Duke of Beaufort's pontiff in 1972

12 Foxhounds of Hugo Meynell's day

Hounds from uniquely bred packs

13 Dumfriesshire Dancer

14 Cotley Songstress

15 Curre

Hounds from uniquely bred packs

16 Scarteen Acrobat

17 Blencathra Trueman

18 College Valley Poacher

Hound puppies

Higginson has this to add:

'The benches should be folded up against the wall after the soiled bedding has been removed, and the lodging rooms and yards should then be swilled down with weak disinfectant. All droppings should, of course, be picked up and taken away, and this should be done *at once*, when it is seen. Hounds are naturally clean and will not foul their own bedding, but it is better to turn them out into the yards the last thing at night, as it inclines them to empty at that time. Some hounds have the filthy habit of eating their own excrement, and this is something that must be checked at once by punishing them when they are caught at it.'

C. R. Acton advises:

' . . . a foot-bath fixed in the doorway of each yard . . . these should be filled with a solution of alum, salt and water. This tends to harden the hounds' feet, and to clean them at the same time. If it be deemed too expensive to fit foot-baths, quite a good portable one can be rigged up by a feeding trough fitted with wooden rails, and hounds can be made to pass through it in single file when coming in from hunting or from exercise.'

Lice present a further sanitation problem. 'A dusting of some insecticide, which will eliminate them', as Borwick suggests, 'and which will not hurt their eyes, is most beneficial to their health.'

There is little disagreement as to the best policy for feeding hounds. In the old days foxhounds were fed exclusively on oatmeal pudding and boiled meat; but owing to more enlightened veterinary knowledge and advice a more varied diet is now given. Borwick, pointing out the importance of minerals, has this to say:

'Without vitamins the feeding value of any diet cannot be properly assimilated, and therefore waste occurs. In fact nourishment is paid for which is not assimilated. If food is properly assimilated, less will be required and the result is economy. . . . Adding minerals to their food is only a question of putting into the system that which they already lack or have lost through many hours of physical strain, which almost any day's hunting entails. It would therefore seem that, to stand their strain and to accomplish their arduous work with perfect ease, raw meat (whenever possible), a little raw vegetable finely chopped, cod liver oil and minerals should be added to their food, whch should be thick. Sloppy food only distends the hounds' stomachs and ruins their digestions.'

Happy is the hunt owning a kennelman who is proud of his cooking, as Charles Fox insisted:

'Scotch two-year-old coarse oatmeal, is undoubtedly the feed and well cooked. . . . You must know how, and you must work hard, otherwise the meal is half boiled or perhaps half baked (which is a dead waste). The water

F

must be at absolutely boiling point and kept so while the meal is spread out thin, persistently and steadily stirred, making sure the stirrer tool touches the bottom of the cauldron every time. The meal must be in just proportion to the water. . . . '

Higginson's recipe is this:

'The oatmeal is boiled until it forms a thick pudding, and then it is poured into the coolers . . . and allowed to harden, after which it is broken up in the feeding troughs, as wanted. To this, in summer, is added a small quantity of milk . . . soup from the flesh (boiled) and a quantity of chopped raw meat. I have always found that it is better to feed cold and thin in summer and thick and warm (not hot) in winter. Of course there will be a certain amount of cooked meat after the flesh is boiled and the soup is taken off, and this should be added to the other ingredients. . . . '

C. R. Acton's advice on food is as follows:

'The main thing to remember is that hounds must be fed thick. Solids are the natural food of hounds, not slush; oatmeal and flesh, mixed with a little broth, form the mainstay of a pack's food. The oatmeal should be coarse Scottish oatmeal, old going farther than new. Jorrocks used to say, "Always 'ave a year's meal in advance." Flesh can be obtained from a knackers, and it pays to have a weekly standing order for so much. Should any horses come in from farms or private sources, then the hounds can have some extra flesh that week. It will not hurt them . . . a good rule is a standing order of three horses a week for a pack of 45 couple. In the summer the amount of food should be reduced a little, but the kennelman must not water it down. Green food, such as boiled nettles, make an excellent summer addition. Epsom salts can be given in the feed during this time of year. Turnips and maize are given in some kennels, but I think that both are a mistake. Turnips are a laxative and too punishing, and maize is heating and bad for condition. . . . Biscuit should not be used as a staple diet but merely as an attraction at exercise. There must be clean water always in the kennel yards.'

How to feed gets as much priority from many Masters as the quality and preparation of the food itself. A. H. Higginson, in his general advice to the would-be Master, offers these time-honoured tips:

'The actual feeding of hounds should be done with the greatest of care, as it is of immense importance to their welfare. . . . Hounds, like human beings, vary in their appetites, one hound filling himself with a few gulps, while another will require coaxing to get him to do himself justice. The proper plan is for hounds to be called into the drawing yard, and then, when the feed is all ready in the trough, the huntsman or the feeder, as the case may be, should stand at the door of the feeding room and call them in, one at a time; first the dainty feeders, who pick and lap here and there, and lastly those gluttons, who would eat much more than is good for them, if they are allowed to do so. When they have partly sated their appetites, they should be called out; the kennelman should thicken up the feed for the light feeders, and those who need it should be given another chance. Here again, as in the case of exercising, it is not essential that you attend to the feeding, even if you hunt hounds yourself. It is a well-known fact that hounds will always go to the man who shows them sport in preference to anyone else. Still, it is a good plan to feed them now and again yourself, as it will often give you an insight into certain peculiarities of a hound which you may not know.

During the hunting season, feed your working pack when they come in—if the weather is not too hot. If it is, give them an hour to cool off before letting them into their food. Feed those hounds, which have not been out, between ten and eleven o'clock in the morning. During the hot summer months, when you are not hunting, hounds are better fed at three or four o'clock in the afternoon; and they are then walked out. As a rule, they should be fed once a day only, though the thin ones may have a lap at odd times. The feed in hot weather should be less thick than in winter, and it should also be given quite cold; while in the winter months the chill should always be taken off by mixing in some warm broth. In summer it is a good plan to boil up greens for hounds, as they are most excellent for their blood. . . . Hounds should never be fed on the day on which they hunt—until after they are through with their day's work.'

It is also absolutely necessary to hounds' general health that they should have constant access to water.

As with all animals so with hounds: a vigilant eye must be kept to ensure that excellent condition is maintained. As C. R. Acton expressed it:

'Hounds can tell one a lot about the man who handles them. If their coats are shiny and sleek and the hounds themselves are fat and listless, then they are overfed. If their coats are staring and dull, they do not get enough attention. If their ribs show up in summer, they do not get enough to eat. If their coats are shiny and sleek, and there is just the suspicion of rib showing, if their movements are active and their eyes bright, then the kennel man is a good feeder. . . . The chief anxiety should be to keep them from putting on flesh. Give a hound plenty of solid food and he can stand any amount of work; feed him on slush, and you will never build up the stamina that kills the evening fox. You can work fat off, but you can never work it on.'

Lord Willoughby de Broke went further:

'Condition is the key to success. If the question were asked, "What shows most sport and kills most foxes?" The magic word "condition" would be the safe answer. A moderate-looking lot of hounds will catch more foxes than all the Peterborough winners put together if they are in better condition. Authorities may not quite agree as to the exact methods by which the requisite fitness can best be gained and kept. Some will advertise more summer exercise than others, and everyone may not see eye to eye as to the amount of covering there should be on the hounds' ribs at the beginning of cub hunting. The feeding demands primary attention. There is good ground for supporting the rule that the quantity of food should be reduced in the summer rather than the quality.

In some kennels the thick oatmeal and flesh that is, or ought to be, served during the hunting season is watered down. This must surely be a mistake. Solids are the natural sustenance of dogs. They will no doubt swallow gallons of slush if they cannot get anything else, but, as it does not stay with them, it is doubtful if it does them any good, and it is really wasted. It is true that when they are not working under high pressure they will require less food; but it is good policy in the summer to let the consistency remain thick as in the winter and to give them less of it, with the addition of some boiled greens or nettles.

Hounds should also be halted at summer exercise where the young grass is long, and they will soon obey the dictates of nature and clean their digestive organs by eating it. By giving them thick food in a greater or a less amount all the year round, the sound quality of their tissues will be maintained. After a fortnight of slush a hound will become flabby; his coat, that true index of health, will lack lustre; he will lose his vitality, and his whole system will take weeks to recuperate at the very season of the year when he ought to be fit for long exercise. A hound's condition should never be let down below a certain level. It is so much easier to let down than to build up.'

Before leaving the subject of feeding I will quote once again from a letter which Major Mann wrote to me in 1974:

'We all know that some of the traditional ingredients of hounds' food are quite beyond the pocket of the average hunt; but, with the willing co-operation of farmers, a very efficient knackering service can be run, covering the whole country, provided the kennels have some means of collection, be it by lorry, van or Land Rover. I know this means someone to do the driving, but it forms a very useful "link with the countryside" and does a useful service to the farmers, who, when they have suffered the loss of a beast, do not then have to dig a hole in which to bury it.

According to circumstances, which really means the regularity of supply, the flesh may be fed raw. Hounds enjoy this and thrive on it during the hunting season, and financially it is a great saving. I believe hounds that are fed raw are in harder condition than those fed cooked food. The cost of Scotch oatmeal is prohibitive. For several seasons now, we have used a mixture of three parts oats and one part barley, ground on the farm in a hammer mill. The day before feeding, this meal is placed in the troughs, is scalded and is allowed to stand overnight. To this is added cooked flesh and broth just before feeding, the whole being well mixed together.'

To a great extent, of course, the foxhound is his own vet and his own keeper of condition. He looks after himself remarkably well. As Charles Fox put it:

'The hound, as a rule, is a robust hardy fellow, as he is much in the open, as he is not pampered or overfed and as his food is simple. He is also great at self-doctoring. Watch how he nips off a particular sort of grass that has a very rough blade, then note how soon after it is up again in the form of an egg, holding by its weft and warp a quantity of viscous matter commonly known as bile. In the land of the hop he loves the young leaves of the hop vine, their bitter taste is a cocktail to him. Watch again how he cleanses a wound if he can get at it by that wonderful member, his pinky ever-moist tongue and how he soothes the chafed webbing of toes with that same first-aid member. Then, being in a healthy state, there is nothing septic about his wounds, and if kept clean they soon heal.'

Since an effective preventive against distemper was discovered, disease is no longer the great problem it used to be. Mange is generally easier to cure, and as C. R. Acton says, 'In a well-cared-for pack the only possibility of the occurrence of mange should be through hounds happening upon a mangy fox.' As for hysteria or 'running fits', Higginson relates:

'My experience tells me that it is most apt to occur in animals whose powers of resistance are weakened by some affection or other, such as worms or improper feeding. . . . I know the best way to handle it: quiet, absolute quiet, and feeding with raw meat and milk only; meanwhile dosing with some form of bromide, best given under veterinary prescription.'

Another opinion is given by C. R. Acton:

'It is greatly a matter of feeding. Some kennels feed a lot of dog biscuit, and I should not be surprised if that had a considerable amount to do with it. Non-biscuit-feeding kennels of my acquaintance have never been cursed with this malady.'

The kennel–huntsman has many ailments to contend with, the least of which are lameness, cuts, thorns, blistered pads and torn nails. Clearly he must be a knowledgeable amateur vet. He must know about jaundice, worms and tumours and also how to cope with horse kicks and poison.

He must know, too, how to care for bitches in whelp. Borwick gave the correct treatment, as follows:

'When found to be in whelp, bitches must be allowed absolute liberty. Nature demands this if nothing else, and risk must be taken, even though the kennel may not be situated in an ideal position for that purpose. If fed sufficiently often, they will not be so apt to scavenge and pick up the offal which is so harmful. The surroundings of the kennel must be carefully overlooked so that they may not have access to any drain-infected water or filth from the slaughter house. . . . '

Higginson concurs, adding this:

'The normal period of gestation is 63 days; and, during the last 5 weeks of this time, a bitch is much better off without violent exercise. She should not be shut up, however, but directly she is seen to be in whelp she should be turned out to run about the kennels as much as she wants to, provided she does not get into the habit of visiting the back yards and garbage buckets of the neighbourhood, where she might well pick up food that would prove deleterious to her own health and that of her future offspring. She should be fed regularly, given plenty of meat—much of it raw—and all the milk she wants; and to this milk should be added either lime-water or precipitate phosphate of lime— preferably the latter. As her time approaches, special care should be taken that she does not get into the habit of sleeping in a place which necessitates special exertion in jumping on and off her bench.'

Regarding care of the whelps themselves, Borwick says:

'If, after a fortnight, the whelps begin to look out-of-sorts and become "pot-bellied" they are nearly sure to have worms. Many whelps are born with worms in them. It is safe to give some puppy worm medicine at 14 days old. At 4 weeks old, beginning once a day, a teaspoonful of finely minced fresh raw meat between three whelps should be given. . . . There is always the risk of acidity from the bitch's milk, in which case the puppies invariably do badly . . . if bismuth is given to the bitch, in many cases the acidity will help. . . . When weaned, the ideal diet for whelps would seem to be puppy meal, a very small quantity of minerals, cod liver oil, raw meat finely minced and orange juice, also a small quantity of kossolian salts mixed with the food three times a week.'

The breaking-in of young hounds is a very important part of kennel routine and requires much care and patience. It is hard work, too. As puppies come in from their walks, once they have become accustomed to kennel life and to the other hounds, they can be put on single couples and led when walking out. When they show willingness to follow, they will be coupled to old hounds, who will discipline them. Depending on individual development, some puppies may be coupled to old hounds at once, while others will need to be led for several days. Most Masters break in puppies as they come in from walk rather than wait for the end of the hunting season, when there would be a lot of puppies to cope with at the same time.

Lastly, discipline: the houndsman has come a long way since Beckford's day when unruly hounds were regularly flogged as a matter of course. Obviously what the huntsman requires is prompt and cheerful obedience from his hounds without subduing their dash and their independence of spirit. Higginson says this:

'Punishment is unfortunately necessary at times . . . but, when you think that it must be done, be sure your hound knows what he is being chastised for, and *don't ever do it yourself.* Hounds should always look on their huntsman as a friend and should feel that, in his presence, they are safe from chastisement. . . . Patience with young hounds will work wonders, and one must always remember that, just coming in from walk, they feel strange and lonely in their new surroundings, when they first get a taste of kennel life.'

As Borwick stresses:

'Hounds appreciate fairness and kindly treatment; they dislike nagging like human beings, and they learn to disregard it as quickly. To maintain order, punishment, when merited and if given, must be swift and sure.'

C. R. Acton expressed this from another angle:

'The huntsman must get to know his hounds, must make friends of them, must break down the shyness of some of the puppies. This can be done at summer afternoon exercise, and also it is then that the discipline can be gradually brought to bear that will mould the pack to his hand in the field. He must employ every endeavour and artifice to get them fond of him, he must make them play with him, he must reach each working pack to come quickly to his voice when he calls them, but, what is even more important, he must exercise a tremendous amount of patience in making them "stand" and await his signal to approach him. This will amply repay him during the hunting season. . . . '

It is to the hunting season that we shall now turn.

Chapter 7

Ethics, Organization
and Appointments

THE BOUNDARIES for Britain's 206 packs of foxhounds are laid down by the Masters of Foxhounds' Association, which was founded in 1881, and which consists of Masters of recognized countries and also some especially elected ex-Masters. It is this body also that regulates the foundation and growth of new hunts and the amalgamation of old ones. They lay down, too, certain rules, the principal of which are these:

'Foxhunting as a sport is the hunting of a fox in his wild and natural state with a pack of hounds, and . . . no pack of hounds of which the Master, or his representative, is a member of this association shall be allowed to hunt a fox that has been in captivity or in any way "handled". . . . '

Further regulations are as follows. Should a fox be run to ground one of these alternatives must be adopted: he should be left where he is; or he should be bolted and given a fair and sporting chance of escape; or, if it is considered essential that he be killed, then he must be destroyed before being given to the hounds.

Every effort must be made to prevent hounds hunting a fox in a built-up area. If a fox enters a house, etc., 'every effort must be made to stop hounds'. They should then be taken away and that fox not hunted again, the owner or occupier being at the same time consulted as to how he or she would like the fox dealt with.

A hunt may on no account draw for a fox in a neighbouring country. If they are led over their boundary they may continue hunting; but, if their fox goes to ground in that neighbouring country, no attempt should be made to get him out except under mutual arrangements previously made with the neighbouring Master, or Masters, concerned. In any event where there is more than one fox in the earth or drain, only one may be killed by the 'invaders'.

The hunt committee
The jurisdiction of the Masters of Foxhounds' Association is, of course, exercised only over hunts which they recognize; and here they deal only with the Master and hunt committee; they pretend no authority within the hunts. Although Masters invariably do join the association, they cannot be compelled to do so.

A hunt country is administered by a committee, which is elected or re-elected every year by the farmers and subscribers of the hunt. The committee members act, on behalf of the subscribers, as trustees for the hounds, the kennels and other hunt property. They make all the decisions regarding the raising of subscriptions and the size of 'caps'. They also elect, or re-elect, the Master or joint-Masters and appoint the honorary secretary and treasurer. Such appointments are generally made on 1 May, the opening of the hunting year. Thereafter the committee, under their chairman (who is often a former Master) continue to be responsible for the country and for the overall policy, while the Master's tasks are to show sport, to control the kennels and hunt stables and to plan the season's programme.

Jurisdiction over hounds
Packs of hounds are vested in the names of the trustees with a special trust deed. When the Master takes over, he and the trustees have an agreement drawn up, signed on behalf of each and stamped. The 'deed of agreement' states the number of hounds in the kennel, with the name, age and sex of each hound, that hounds brought into a pack by the incoming Master, in excess of the specified number he took over, shall remain his property and that they shall be available for selection to complete the specified number on change of Mastership, their progeny being merged in the pack, to become the property of the trustees.

If it is agreed that drafted hounds are the property of the Master, it should be stipulated that no hounds shall be drafted during the Master's last season, without the consent in writing of the committee and trustees. On giving up the Mastership the retiring Master is bound to leave in the kennel the same number of hounds that he took over.

He is also expected, by 1 May, to 'put to' a sufficient number of bitches to produce enough whelps from which to make the entry for the succeeding year. In co-operation, usually, with one of the trustees and the incoming Master, the retiring Master nominates the 'entered' and 'unentered' hounds to be left in kennel.

'Recognized' kennels
A 'recognized foxhound kennel' is one consisting of hounds kept for hunting the fox only and entered in, or eligible for entry in, the foxhound kennel stud book. To be eligible for the foxhound kennel stud book, hounds must have been entered and worked in a foxhound kennel for 5 years, and both their grand-sires and both their grand-dams must have been registered in the foxhound kennel stud book.

Control and costs
The Master, or joint-Masters, being appointed or re-appointed by the committee at the commencement of each hunting year, are granted complete control of hunting arrangements until the next 1 May. The committee at the same time undertake to pay the Master or joint-Masters a sum of money to go towards

their expenses: hunt servants, hounds, hunt horses, maintenance of the hunt premises and equipment, earth stopping, damage, repair of hunt jumps, etc. It is assumed that the balance of such costs is met by the Master or joint-Masters, privately.

Income is derived from members' annual subscriptions, from 'caps', which are collected from strangers out for odd days' hunting, from the hunt supporters' club, and from money raised from such functions as point-to-point races, bring-and-buy sales and hunt races.

The Master

The desirable qualifications of a Master of Foxhounds have been described in numerous ways. Most of the descriptions require a paragon. Lord Willoughby de Broke said this:

'No one is too good to be a Master of Foxhounds. If he be gifted with the average endowment of tact, administrative talent, power of penetrating character and all other attributes that form the essential equipment of a success-ful public man, so much the better; but he should at least be reared in the atmosphere and tradition of country life and should be fond of sport for its own sake, a good judge of horses and hounds and the possessor of a remarkably thick skin. For in addition to directing the sport in the field, the Master of Foxhounds is indeed a public man, who should have some faculty for the art of government, being ultimately responsible for the welfare of the country over which he presides. The character and ability of the hunt committee and secretary and the disposition of the owners and occupiers of land may make his task proportionately easy or difficult as the case may be; but there is no limit to the influence of the Master of Foxhounds if he has the power and the will to use it wisely and well, fortified by the resolve to leave his country, when he lays down his office, in at least as good state as he found it, and as much better as he can possibly make it. . . . '

In his book *Hunting*, Otho Paget wrote:

'A Master of Foxhounds, to be perfect, must embody all the virtues of a saint with the commanding genius of a Kitchener and the tact of a diplomatist. To find these qualities combined is well nigh impossible, so we must give up hope of ever finding the perfect Master and must content ourselves with ordinary men. It is a thankless task, and it has always been a wonder to me that anyone can be found willing to accept the responsibilities. . . . Everyone who comes out feels entitled to criticize and find fault with the Master. The man who is early at the meet asks in an aggrieved voice why hounds do not move off, and the man who is a little late is annoyed because they have gone before he arrives. The man who coffee-houses when hounds are drawing and gets left behind considers he has been very badly treated, and, of course, the Master is to blame.' . . .

Austin Wadsworth put the Master of Foxhounds on a very high pedestal:

'The Master is a great and mystic personage, to be lowly, meekly and reverently looked up to, helped, considered and given the right of way at all times. All that can be asked of him is that he furnish good sport; and, as long as he does that, he is amenable to no criticism, subject to no law and fettered by no conventionality while in the field. . . . '

To quote A. H. Higginson:

'When, in addition to the thrill which one gets from the exhilaration of the chase one possesses an almost personal interest in the achievements of the hounds which one has bred and watched develop from tiny whelps to mature foxhounds, one is amply repaid for all the trouble and expense and worry which fall to the lot of anyone who takes on a country; but the duties are arduous, and one must realize that it means the sacrifice of many other interests. . . . The Master is responsible for the sport, be it good or bad. He is in complete charge of everything pertaining to the Hunt . . . and he must be a master of organization as well as a master of detail. . . . A busy man might argue that the minor details of kennel and stable management, puppy rearing, earth stopping, damages, poultry claims, etc., could be attended to either by his huntsman, the stud groom or the hunt secretary. In a way this is quite true; but someone must instruct the huntsman and the stud groom; someone must dictate, to a great extent, the policy to be followed by the hunt secretary; and, after all, since it is the Master who is commander-in-chief and who is responsible for the quality of the sport shown, he is the man to do it. The existence of pleasant and personal relations with the farmers and the landowners of the country is of paramount importance, and no-one should become Master of a pack of hounds unless he is very keen and is prepared to devote practically his entire time to it. . . . '

That is an echo of Surtees:

'First and foremost they must be keen . . . it would be not a bit more absurd for a man to punish himself by keeping a yacht, who hates sailing and the sight of the sea, than it is for a man to keep a pack of foxhounds who has no ardent predilection for the chase. A qualified liking will not do for "a best fellow under the sun". He must be heart and soul in the sport—a real out-and-outer. Keenness covers a multitude of sins. . . . In addition to the *sine qua non* of keenness, he should possess a host of other qualities. He should have the boldness of a lion, the cunning of a fox, the shrewdness of an exciseman, the calculation of a general, the purse of Squire Plutus, the regularity of a railway, the punctuality of a timepiece, the liberality of a sailor, the patience of Job, the tact of an M.P., the wiliness of a diplomatist, the politeness of a lord, the strength of an Hercules. . . . '

A Master may be one who combines his office with that of hunting hounds, in which case a kennel–huntsman, who will probably act as first whipper-in out hunting, is employed. The Master, who hunts hounds himself—if not in name and although he is paid no salary—is virtually a professional. Otherwise the Master is one who confines himself to running the hunt and controlling the field, while leaving hounds, both in kennels and in the field, to a professional huntsman.

For those having the necessary talent, time and tendency, to become both Master and huntsman must clearly be the right ambition. A. H. Higginson said this:

'I cannot understand the point of view of any young man who fails to accept the chance which comes to him of hunting hounds when he assumes the Mastership of a pack. It may be that a man applying for the Mastership of a country might feel that it was not fair to his prospective field to take on the responsibilities of a job which he does not really know, because of the chances of giving them many indifferent days while he is gaining experience. . . . But, after all, a man must begin some time. . . . It will perhaps be understood that there are many countries . . . which cannot be called first—or even second class —from a point of view of sport, and I should advise a beginner who wants to hunt hounds to try to acquire the Mastership of one of these countries, where his mistakes will be more easily forgiven and his keenness more easily appreciated. . . . '

When a Master succeeds, besides taking over the hounds, the kennels, the stables and other buildings, he will get to know the hunt staff and their problems as soon as possible; he will study the breeding of his hounds; he will, at the earliest opportunity, visit the landowners and farmers, all those who are regular puppy walkers, and as many other folk, closely connected with the hunt, as he is able to; and—where they will allow it—he will get to know them personally; if he is not already familiar with the country, he will learn it by heart.

He must be a man who is not too sensitive to criticism, and like all good leaders he must be innately sure that his decisions (which may range from whether to enter a hound at Peterborough, whether to take on a particular hunt servant or whether to take hounds out on a frosty day) are arrived at by true reasoning, and then he must abide by them.

As for the Field Master, clearly he must be a bold and outstanding man to hounds with an excellent navigational sense, and must know the art of controlling the field with the minimum of fuss and effort, yet with unwavering firmness. In his book *The History of the Althorp and Pytchley Hunt*, Major Guy Paget exemplifies Lord Annaly, who had the Pytchley from 1902 to 1914, as the perfect man for this office:

'He had a naturally graceful seat on a horse, an iron nerve and—greatest gift of the gods—charm of manner.... He had, more than most men, the art of getting willing work out of others.... He was undoubtedly the best Field Master of his day; he was always in the right place; he never cursed or swore; but he was firm and pleasant. An old gentleman once said, "I've always liked hunting with the Pytchley hounds. You are always addressed as 'gentlemen', generally prefixed by 'please'. After all, if you hear 'hold hard, gentlemen, please', you are only too pleased to do so, if you can, and hope the Master is alluding to you, but, if you hear, 'Damn your soul, you blankety-blank fool, where the hell do you think you're going to?' you feel inclined to go on, as you hope you are not being referred to." ...

'Lord Annaly saw no unnecessary damage was done and was very down on anyone who rode over crops or jumped when hounds were not running, especially over gates. On one occasion he reproved a hard-riding member for the latter offence. "But I never touched the beastly gate," the offender retorted with injured innocence. "I know," replied the Master, "but all the other fools followed your example till one broke it and let all the cattle into the road." ... There was no better man to hounds in the whole of England than Lord Annaly.... He was amazingly popular among the farmers and always seemed to know every one of them personally.'

The hunt secretary
The Masters of Foxhounds' Association give the following guidelines as to the hunt secretaries' duties:

'He is responsible to the hunt committee, but, although he is in no way the servant of the Master, he should be able when necessary to act as liaison between the Master or Masters and the committee through the chairman. He should also be ready to help the Master with the puppy show and other entertainments, and with matters in which he can be of assistance without impinging on his responsibility to the committee, whose servant he is. His liaison will, of course, be still closer with a Master who is only acting Master in a count administered by a committee.'

The honorary secretary's task is to assist the Master with all administrative detail. Unless there is a separate treasurer, the secretary will be responsible for the accounts, for collecting subscriptions and for gathering funds raised by the hunt supporters' club and from such functions as gymkhanas, bazaars and dances.

Responsibility for the rideability of the country is usually also laid at his feet. In the words of the Masters of Foxhounds' Association:

'This includes the taking down of wire which entails much personal work and visiting farmers and certain districts; the putting up of rails, the insertion of gates, the provision of bridges in certain integral places, the maintenance of rides in hunt coverts. Some hunts find it necessary to employ one, or even two, men the whole year on this work, and it is important that, whatever help the secretary may obtain . . . he should have charge of these men, who will also be the labour for mending fences after the day's hunting. . . . '

The hunt secretary collects the 'caps' and deals as promptly as he can with all claims against the hunt by landowners and farmers. He has his ear close to the ground, keeping himself fully acquainted with the hunt's many different problems, personal, social, financial and political.

The hunt staff

The duties of the huntsman and his staff have already been dealt with and, as we have seen, a good deal more than three-quarters of the professional life of the hunt servants are fulfilled in kennels. The success or otherwise of a hunt is due in great measure to the spirit of a kennel. That spirit hinges on the character of the huntsman or kennel–huntsman. He must give his unswerving loyalty to the Master; he must carry out the Master's policy and instructions cheerfully and to the letter. He will contrive to impart to his whippers-in and feeders, from whom he will expect similar obedience and backing, every scrap of kennel knowledge that he owns.

The huntsman has also to be a very observant and alert man. Feeding hounds himself whenever possible, he must decide on the ingredients and density of the food and must take notice of any difference at the trough. He must be constantly on the look-out for signs of weakness and bad health; when walking hounds out, which he must do as frequently as possible, he should instil and confirm the discipline required out hunting; he has to supervise the kennels' sanitation, making daily inspections; he must have a good anatomical knowledge of hounds and basic veterinary know-how; and he should be able to treat wounds and to supervise bitches in whelp and to foster the whelps themselves.

It follows that the whippers-in, and sometimes the kennelman and feeder (whose special responsibility, besides preparing feeds and managing the flesh hovel, is often the immediate care of the whelps), should be competent to fulfil all those duties without supervision in his absence.

The Duke of Beaufort writes this:

'Probably every second whipper-in in the kingdom hopes to be a huntsman one day: half the first whippers-in succeed in becoming huntsmen; and the other half have come to the conclusion that to be a first-class whipper-in to a first-class pack is too satisfying a job to be changed for any other, even for the greater responsibility of huntsman. . . .

He is not richly rewarded in comparison with those whose eminence in other spheres is comparable with his. A huntsman may not walk with kings, but many a huntsman has ridden with princes. All huntsmen must be able to bear themselves easily among the leaders of their country, yet on a purely financial comparison they are badly off compared with, say, a First Division footballer, a radio comedian or, to put the matter on a more comprehensible basis, with the manager of a progressively run farm. A huntsman's wages in most countries are probably only a fraction higher than the agricultural wage rate; but, added to this, he receives his hunt uniform free and some help with other clothing. He has a free house and generally an allowance for fuel and light. In return for it he puts in a working day which, in the winter, begins very early indeed and ends late at an hour when, after long exertions in the open air, he is probably half drowsy with sleep. It is a hard life but a cheerful one.'

At the time of writing the Hunt Servants' Benefit Society, which has contributed so much to the welfare of the profession, has invested reserves of some £260,000 with an income of £26,000. The honorary membership is about 350. The Treasurer of the Hunt Servant's Benefit Society, Mr A. S. Clowes, of Ashlands, Billesdon, Leicestershire, is a former joint-Master of the Fernie.

Chapter 8
Hunting the Fox

Foxholding coverts

As explained in Chapter 2, the fox employs many refuges: a fork in a tree, a space behind a boulder, a willow thicket, a drainpipe, the ledge of a wall, a roof-top, etc.; but, most of all, he makes for the burrow in the ground, the earth that he and his kind have always fashioned or stolen from the badger or the rabbit. He is probably familiar with several of these, and the hunted fox may find earths as he travels.

The care of such coverts as hold the best of these earths will be of the greatest importance to the huntsman. Sir Charles Frederick, sometime Master of the Pytchley, gave this advice:

'No hunting country will yield its full measure of sport, however richly endowed it be by nature, unless the fox coverts be maintained in proper order. Directly a covert becomes hollow and fails to give a fox the warmth and security he expects, he will take to lying out, and it is the foxes lying out who are responsible for nearly all the poultry keeper's claims and grumbles. The outlier is a nuisance in other ways besides, for he is scarcely ever to be found when wanted and has a tiresome knack of jumping up in front of hounds and complicating matters in the critical stages of a hunt. The problem, therefore, is to confine Reynard to his rightful haunts. . . . A fox covert can never be too thick. . . . Foxes will not make their home in a covert permanently unless there is an earth in or near it where they can seek shelter from poaching dogs and other enemies. . . . '

Earth-stopping

Since the object of foxhunting is to kill foxes and to provide sport, clearly known earths must, if possible, be blocked. The Master, or his delegate, duly arranges that, if possible, in the country over which he proposes to draw, all earths within a comparatively small radius of the meet are stopped the night before hunting. Certain earths will be 'put to' in the early morning. The main considerations here will be the willingness and co-operation of landowners and tenants and the availability of the right men to do the job.

Some hunts are blessed with several willing and qualified earth-stoppers—keepers, farm workers, local tradesmen or anyone else who is capable and willing to undergo the discomfort and to sacrifice the time, others with perhaps only a boy—who may or may not be available. These will know in advance from the meet card that their services are required. Doubtless also the Master (or joint-Master), who is responsible for this precaution, will state his requirements a week or so in advance. The earth-stoppers will then set out in their appointed areas after dark, during the period when foxes are away hunting. It should be added that, on wet and windy nights, they could be unlucky; the foxes may then decide to remain down under.

Faggots, bundles or gorse, thorn or some such other fox-proof obstacle is generally used; earth only if there is nothing else to hand, because foxes can quickly dig through it.

How many hounds?

Most huntsmen have a favourite number of hounds to make up a pack for a day's hunting. Major J. J. Mann, senior joint-Master, and a former amateur huntsman, of the Vale of White Horse, put the case for his choice to me like this:

> 'I like 19½ or 20½ couple. (It's that odd hound that may catch the fox for you!) If one starts with about this number in mind, one can react effectively in the case of illness or lameness; but, if one starts with a small pack, then there is little margin for inevitable troubles. So how many hounds do we need in kennels? The number of hunting days per week govern the answer to that. Most hounds will do 2 days a week; I have known hounds that thrived on 3 days, but these cannot really be taken into account. Thus a 4-day-a-week country will make better use of its hounds than a 3-day-a-week. Taking account of injury, accident, ailment and, later in the season, bitches in whelp, I believe a 4-day-a-week country requires an absolute minimum of 55 couple. One could really only just get by with this number and that with good luck. With a pack of this size there are unlikely to be sufficient dog-hounds to make up a pack on their own. So a mixed pack would be made up with suitable bitches; and the other pack would be bitches only.'

In team with the huntsman

The fox, we know, is pursued by the medium of scent and sound. It is the hound's nose that finds the fox, that can track him and that can finally run him to his death or to ground; and it is by voice that the hound informs both the other hounds and the huntsman that he owns such contact. The hounds speak to their leader, the huntsman, and he responds by voice and horn. If we are familiar with the sounds and, as important, the tones of the hunt, if we are close enough to the scene, we shall know what is happening from minute to minute. We recognize the buoyant encouragement when hounds are sent to the draw, the optimistic coaxing when the huntsman tries his cast, the whipper-in's 'Gerr

G

along there!' when a hound drops back on the road, the crack of his whip that accompanies the deterring 'Bike!', when hounds riot, eat dung or hunt the heel-way, the triumph of the 'Gone away!', the long ecstatic call at the kill and the satisfied, or regretful, decision that says 'H-o-m-e'.

Since the music of the hunt, like any other language, harmonizes with the situation, so the huntsman's team, his hounds and his whippers-in, should harmonize with him, with his personality and his style. For his part he must love and trust his hounds and must do his utmost to secure their devotion and confidence. Because of this mutual love and respect, he owns perfect control of them; he has only to call once and they fly to him. They will try all day for him on the poorest scent. He has fostered in them the foxhound's greatest asset: courage. He has acquired infinite patience. He is never flustered; he never loses his temper. To become an effective huntsman, he had to banish all trace of self-consciousness. He is oblivious of his human audience; he projects all his genius and his heart into hunting his pack.

His whippers-in are there to assist him all they can, whatever the circumstances. They are the huntsman's advanced guard, they lay the pack on, they open gates for their huntsman, they take down wire, they stop hounds rioting or hunting a heel line and they look for hounds that are lost. As Beckford said, 'When there are two whippers-in, one ought always to go forward; when there is only one, he, to be perfect, should be a very Mungo, here, there and everywhere. . . .'

Drawing covert

Albeit there can be no hard-and-fast rules as to how a huntsman should handle his pack and should react to given situations, but only guidelines, let us imagine a day's hunting from the move off to the long call that tells us it is the end of the day.

The first draw from what we shall call this 'Blacksmith's Arms meet', used to be Chapman's, a triangle of gorse, which is unofficially used as a rubbish dump, a favourite scavenging place for foxes; but, since the dual carriageway was opened last summer, that is too dangerous. The foxes at Chapman's are no use. So this hunt cub-hunt that covert, as frequently and vigorously as they can, to disperse its foxes.

The next traditional covert, a safe distance from the road, is Roe Firs, a stand of conifers with a good fox-holding bottom to it; but, today, this must be ruled out because of shooting arrangements. (It is also too close to the dual carriageway.) So we are heading for a larch wood, called Dove Plantation. Owing to its very thick ground cover of thorn and bramble, it used to be necessary for the huntsman, in order to be close to his hounds, to dismount and to make part of it on foot; but now the foresters have quartered it with rides, which, although most unfortunate from the sportsman's point of view, as it lets poachers and dogs in, does at least make drawing a bit easier.

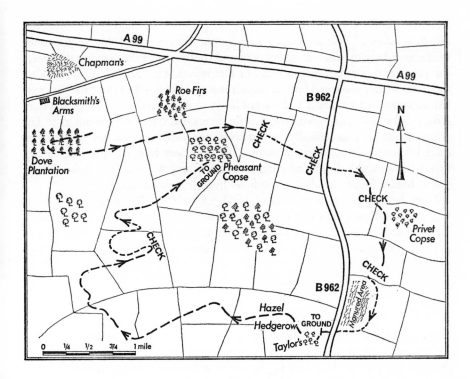

Today the wind is from the west. For a number of reasons our huntsman likes to draw upwind: this way the fox's scent is drawn towards the hounds; second, the fox prefers to run downwind; third, if he is flushed upwind, he will tend to break covert upwind, and, when he breaks covert and a holloa is given, hounds may hear it more readily. So we see our huntsman, faint December breeze on his face and hounds close at his heels, trot up to the east side of Dove Plantation while his whippers-in deploy on the flanks. To prevent the fox heading for Chapman's, the field have been taken to the north side.

Our hunt is blessed with a whipper-in with a particularly sharp pair of eyes which allow very little to escape him. He is a renowned 'scout'. Today he posts himself opposite the spot where foxes have frequently broken this covert on previous draws.

The ground shines with dampness; there is a sharp nip in the misty air; the sun is unlikely to break through: scenting conditions ought to remain fairly good. What will be the hounds' first clue of their fox? It may be at his 'kennel' or 'bed', the place where he curled up to rest after his night's hunting, or on his escape route from the covert. Or they may hit his 'drag', the scent that marks his entry into the covert earlier that morning, and the path up to his 'kennel'.

Hounds remain at the huntsman's heels until the whippers-in are in position and the scene is set. And then, with an 'Eleu in there!' and a wave of his hand, he dispatches them. These 20 couples rush for the covert—the third-, fourth- and fifth-season hounds with all the boldness and confidence of the veterans they are; the younger entries not quite so sure of themselves. They will continue to hear their huntsman's voice and horn at regular intervals during the draw: they always like to know that he is near and are not likely to draw well unless they can place him. It is by horn and voice, too, that the huntsman speaks his intentions to his whippers-in, and, incidentally to ourselves, the field; and he has no wish to catch his foxes asleep, to 'chop' them. That is no way to make sport. He hopes that, by horn and voice, he may unkennel his quarry in advance of hounds. Yet not so loudly that he awakes all the foxes in the neighbourhood.

Now hounds are well into covert, and we hear the lilt of the huntsman's voice up and down the rides, urging them to seek and find, 'Eleu in there!' . . . 'Leu, rouse him, my beauties' . . . 'Try over there then.' . . . 'Eu, push him up.' . . . 'Yit try-hy-hy-hy-h-y!' Exuberant encouragement of that sort for a few minutes. . . .

A find
. . . Silence from the pack. Until we hear the voice of one hound opening on a scent, an excited bell-like solo, echoing from the depths of the covert. Then, from the huntsman, who immediately recognizes the voice, a fresh cheer, 'Huic (hike) to Jupiter, huic huic huic to Jupiter, eu at him, eu at him, eu at him, then!' Now the whole pack open up behind this experienced single hound: there is a great crescendo of music, to many people the loveliest sound in the world. . . .

Gone away
. . . Now, from the huntsman's horn, we hear a series of quick stimulating notes, and, while hounds are still in covert, his resounding cheer echoes across to us, 'Huic, huic, eu at him, my beauties . . . for-or-or-or-orrard!' Next, from that first whipper-in, who was watching the east end of the covert so carefully, the piercing scream of a holloa; and our huntsman, putting his horse at a hunt jump let into the wire that surrounds the wood and cantering into the open, doubles his horn with; the exhilarating tones of a 'Gone away'.

He repeats that doubling of the horn, so that hounds know and the whippers-in know and the field know that this is his fox, and that he is determined to hunt it. Then, once he is reasonably sure that all his hounds are on the line, he ceases blowing. In fact, two couple of recently entered hounds are still in covert, and the second whipper-in, who had been keeping an eye on the far side, is busy calling them on, while the first whipper-in has galloped forward to a flank to see how hounds are running and to watch for the fox.

Scent proves reasonably good. Some hounds are running mute, some speaking, and, as the hounds that were mute catch the scent, they join in the chorus, and those that temporarily lose it go mute. They work as a close-knit unit. . . . The fox is heading towards Pheasant Copse now. Does he know a good earth there? No . . . he veers a little left-handed again, straight past that covert. . . .

Hounds cast themselves

. . . The Field Master has led us down this path and over that ditch and now, as we emerge between a tall hedge and a field of roots, we hear a second holloa—from a foot follower, who has seen the fox break into the pasture beyond. Hounds are firmly on the line. This is a steady pack: they do not cut corners; they turn tight with their fox.

However, in the middle of the field, their music peters out. The cattle herded into the corner tell the tale. Scent has been foiled. The huntsman remains quiet, pointing his horse's head on their line but keeping well back, lest he himself foil the scent. He lets them try for themselves: they should not expect help unless they are in real difficulties. They are still heading downwind. A hunted fox prefers to travel downwind; and now we are close enough to see 4 couple wheel to the right, and 3 half left, while the remainder surge across the ground where the cattle had stood. Then they are all together again, casting widely. We are reminded of the co-ordinated arcs of drill demonstration soldiers. Their noses are eager on the ground; they turn this way and that. Over there, suddenly breaking the hush by the gate that leads to the beans, Lucifer speaks. He is a three-season hound, a trusted one. Bountiful is next on the recovered line; then the whole chorus begins again; the race is resumed. . . .

Trying where the fox was last seen

. . . It spans the 300 yards that mark the bean field; but the far hedge fringes the B962 road, and here they check again, casting this way and that, up and down the hedgerow. Not a sign. The road smells of tarmac and vehicle fumes; they are reluctant to cross it. Then, from the opposite hedge, comes a car follower's message: he points down the road towards some sliprails: he says that the fox flashed through there, . . . somewhere there. It might have been the gateway; it might have been another gap; it was too quick to see properly. Oh yes, the *hunted* fox.

The huntsman calls hounds on and walks his horse down towards the sliprails. 'Yert, ye-ert, ye-rt!' He intones this soothingly. Hounds nose on past his heels but scent nothing yet. 'Ye-ert, ye-ert!' Quiet coaxing. . . . Two couple reach the sliprails . . . and suddenly, just beyond it, there is a new chorus. The leaders hit off the line together. Now the second whipper-in is here: he dismounts and pulls away the high top sliprail for the huntsmen to jump the lower one. The first whipper-in is already over the road and is watching beyond. We too have crossed the road farther up and have a closer view of them hunting over the plough, heading right-handed. . . .

Lifting hounds

... They are obviously some way behind their fox now, and no longer on good terms. In the middle of the next field they are brought to their noses. Our huntsman, who has hunted a fox on this axis on countless previous occasions, is pretty sure his fox is heading for Privet Copse, 500 yards beyond. They are getting too far behind him. So he 'lifts' them, calling them with him as he canters down the furrows. He is willing to bet his quarry went through that gap in the thorn hedge right ahead. Its an old favourite, that hole. Reaching it, he waves them on. 'Tr-y, Tr-y!' Bustling through the gap they pick up the scent right away. They are all on again now. The huntsman's eyes never leave them for a moment. ...

Systematic cast: I

... Although he proved right about the point, and about that gap in the hedge, he was wrong about Privet Copse, for now we see hounds lead straight on past that covert, then swing right-handed again, towards the road. They are running upwind now; and, once again, their careering column is transformed into walking groups. Nearly half a minute goes by before the huntsman is close enough to see what the trouble is. It is manure. There is a broad strip of ground adjacent to the road that is thick with it. He knows the two farmers standing by the gate. Did the fox cross the road? No—they have been watching like hawks but never saw a thing. The huntsman asks himself which earth this fox is making for. Was he headed? Could be he circling back to Privet? Did he follow the line of the hedge and cross higher up?

Hounds are not likely to make anything of this themselves. So the huntsman decides to try a cast that should strike the line whether the fox has doubled back, has changed direction on the manured area or has proceeded up the hedge. He makes his cast generally in a left-handed direction; he begins in front of the manured area, loops back a little way, then sweeps round in a wide arc that skirts the manure and ends on the roadside ditch and hedge, about 80 yards along the road. There they hit the line again and, after a short distance, re-cross the road. What happened, apparently, was that the fox was headed on the road and then ran alongside the hedge and ditch for a while to cross higher up.

Now we ourselves have crossed by the gate, where those two farm-workers were and can see hounds, hunting very well again, alongside a ditch leading away from the far side. ...

Gone to ground

... Hounds are not more than 150 yards down the side of this ditch when their chorus changes to intermittent and erratic soloes. Their fox is marked to ground.

There have been several complaints of poultry killing among the surrounding farms here. It is a natural earth. They dig up to the fox and shoot him with the humane killer, in accordance with the rules. He is given to the hounds, and in another moment the huntsman is there to join in their triumph with the tremelo notes of his horn, and with his voice, 'Who-oop! Who-oop! Who-oop, tear 'im up! Who-oop, tear 'im and eat 'im!' . . .

A blank

. . . Now we see a farmer talking to the huntsman. He is reminding him that a big dog fox has often been spotted 'in that old hazel hedge of mine'. The huntsman glances at his watch and exchanges a few words with the Master. . . . 'Yes, we'll have a go at that hedge for you,' he says, 'but first we must try Taylor's.'

Taylor's is a small oak wood a couple of hundred yards from the kill. . . .

'Eleu in there! Yit try! Eu push 'im up in there!' . . . Occasionally the voice of a single hound rings out from Taylor's Wood: a babbler. In spite of slow deliberate drawing, going patiently upwind through every inch of the wood, no fox can be found there. It is a blank covert. So we next hear a series of long horn-notes, the unmistakable, rather resigned and wailing notes of 'blowing out', followed by the voices of the whippers-in, laying hounds on to their huntsman. . . .

Find in a hedgerow

. . . Now we have reached that hedgerow where 'the big dog fox has often been spotted'.

'Eleu in there then! Yit try push him up! Yit try-hy rouse im then!' . . . Quite quietly: hounds are never far from their huntsman here. We watch them weaving and threading around the ditch and the hedgebottom, casting themselves briefly the few yards out to the headlands of the adjacent fields, and back again. A hare starts up on the headland; a young hound, Flyaway, romps after it, and a whipper-in's rating rings out, 'Flyaway! Ware hare! . . . Ahhh, Flyaway, leave it! Ware hare!' . . .

They are drawing this length of hedge well; but now they have gone too fast over a particularly thick patch of bramble. It is very prickly; they do not like it. Perhaps, too, the field have put them off. There is too much talking, A telling B how C fell off, C telling D how E funked that one with a ditch. The Field Master orders quiet. . . . The huntsman calls hounds back and urges them through it. . . . There he goes! Straight out of the bramble thicket. One hound is already hunting his line with a whimper. ' 'Ark, ark, 'ark, 'ark to Bellman, 'ark. Yoi at 'im there Bellman, old dog!' A few seconds later they are all away on his scent and again we hear the horn's sharp tied notes, 'Gone away!'

There go the whippers-in, one forward on the flank, one back to see all hounds are on. It is mid-afternoon; the frost on the air means better scent; the frenzied message from the pack confirms it. We give them a moment to get clear away, and then we canter on behind, hoping this will be a straight-necked fox, one that will give us a nice long point to round off the day. . . .

Systematic cast: 2

... But no—this is a crooked one, who travels up to a fence at one angle and emerges from it 40° in the other direction. In spite of the twisty course, they remain tight on his line for 10 minutes' hunting. Across the next two meadows we ride, with a big ditch and three nice hunt-jumps to cross. Then, very abruptly, they throw up, on the grass. It looks unfoiled. No stock, no humans. The huntsman has little idea what this tortuous fox's point is. He reckons he would do more harm than good simply to let hounds cast themselves straight ahead. So he begins another systematic cast.

We watch him circle them briefly upwind, about 100 yards, nearly back to the original line, the least likely course for the fox to have taken. No sign there. Having satisfied himself that his fox has not doubled back, the huntsman holds them round right-handed. He is approaching a ploughed field. In order to give them the opportunity of the best scenting ground, he avoids the plough. He circles around the grass beyond it, still veering right-handed until they are moving downwind again. With luck, if he continues this movement, he will strike the line again; he is leaving nothing to chance ... 'Ye-ert, ye-ert, ye-ert!' By those trees that mark the far corner of the plough, we notice a tremor in the pack, followed by one or two yelps, then the whole music. ... They are all on again now, hunting at right-angles to the left and south of their casting direction, downwind. We see them carrying a good head towards Pheasant Copse; and there, under the barbed wire on the near fringe of it, they mark him to ground. The huntsman dismounts, hands his horse to the whipper-in, walks up to the earth and cheers them, 'Who-oop, wind' im in there! Who-oop, wind 'im.' Three short blasts of the horn and another three and another three.

The Master arrives on the scene. There is a brief discussion. It is a big complex earth. Hounds have had blood today, and we, the followers, have enjoyed some sport. It is late, too, time for kennels. They decide to 'give him best'. The huntsman puts the horn to his lips for the last time and blows his single wavering note for home.

It is indeed the end of our day's hunting; but for the hunt staff, when they return to kennels, the serious work of the day begins. As for the Master, how many calls will he receive, complaining about the cattle that got through that gate, this farmer's seeds that were trodden in and that one's valuable fence that we crushed?

Cub hunting

> 'The happiest man in England rose an hour before the dawn;
> The stars were in the purple and the dew was on the lawn;
> He sang from bed to bathroom—he could only sing "John Peel";
> He donned his boots and breeches and he buckled on his steel.

He chose his brightest waistcoat and his stock with care he tied,
Though scarce a soul would see him in his early morning ride.
He hurried to the stable through the dim light of the stars,
And there his good horse waited, clicking rings and bridle-bars.

The happiest man in England took a grey lock in his hand
And settled in his saddle like a seagull on the sand.
Then from the shadowy kennel all the eager pack outpoured,
And the happiest man in England saw them scatter on the sward.

The happiest man in England turned down the stony lane
The heart of him was singing as he heard the hoofs again;
And where the blind ditch narrows and the deep-set gorse begins
He waved his pack to covert, and he cheered them through the whins.

He heard old Gladstone whimper, then Merryman give tongue;
He saw the green grass shaking as the whole pack checked and swung;
Then through the ditch came creeping a shy cub lithe and lean,
And nothing but a cocked grey ear betrayed that he was seen.

But once beyond the brambles and across the heath and clear
With half a league of open ground and not a whinbush near,
The happiest man in England blew the freedom of the pass,
And two-and-twenty couple backed the freedom of the grass . . .

He holds no brief for slaughter, but the cubs must take their chance
The weak must first go under that the strong may lead the dance;
And when the grey strides out and shakes the foam-flecks from his rings
The happiest man in England would not change his place with kings.'

Will H. Ogilvie

'I begin to hunt with my young hounds in August. The employment of my huntsman the preceding months is to keep his old hounds healthy and quiet, by giving them proper exercise; and to get his young hounds forward. Nothing will answer this purpose so well as taking them out often. Let your huntsman lounge about with them—nothing will make them so handy. Let him get off his horse frequently and encourage them to come to him—nothing will familiarize them so much. Too great restraint will oftentimes incline hounds to be riotous. They are called over often in kennels; it uses them to their names, to the huntsman and to the whippers-in. They are walked out often among sheep, hares and deer. . . . [The huntsman] draws small coverts and furze brakes with them, to use them to a halloo and to teach them obedience. If they find improper game and hunt it, they are stopped and brought back; and, as long as they stop at a rate, they are not chastized. Obedience is all that is required of them, till they have been sufficiently taught the game they are to pursue. . . .'

Peter Beckford, 1781

We have moved forward now to the following early autumn when the harvest is out of harm's way and the scene is set for the cub-hunting season, when the young entries learn to hunt the smell of fox and the litters of cubs are divided and dispersed from their birth-places.

In September it is still light before six, and, because, by mid-morning, scent begins to dry up in the comparative heat of early autumn, we set out in the dark, to be at covertside soon after first light. We are probably home by ten.

We? In fact the subscribers have no prerogative to be out at all during cub hunting, which is the Master's perquisite and his alone; but those who favour the still of an autumn daybreak, the early morning smells, the birdsong and the golden tints and who cannot do with too much of the atmosphere of foxhunting will doubtless telephone the Master for permission to attend. Of course, just as we know that the hunting field is not the place for schooling a young horse, so we must remember that the cub hunting season is not the time to ride a hot and tiresome horse or to look for gallops.

Why must the litters of fox cubs be dispersed? Because after the hunting season proper begins in early November, we do not want to find coverts blank, nor do we want just a few coverts holding foxes in strength. The hunt has a duty towards its subscribers: to show sport. Foxes are creatures of the woodlands whose first instinct is to find sanctuary beneath the trees and the undergrowth. By invading their strongholds we persuade the cubs that safety lies not in going to ground, but in fleeing cross-country.

But this hunting in the open is a graduation: it comes as the second phase of the cub hunting season. For there are two other factors dictating our policy. Firstly, there will be too many cubs. We have a duty to the farmers: to cull the fox population. Secondly, if the young hounds are to be encouraged, they must have blood. The cubs must be taught to run, and the young hounds must be taught to catch their foxes in the open; but cubs were born the previous spring, and, although they are neither as strong nor as cunning as their parents, they are already as tall and long, and in many cases just about as fast. The ground will be hard on feet at this time of year. All in all it will be difficult to kill the desirable tally of cubs and to provide blood unless—anyway in September—we 'hold up', that is to say, during the draw, we keep the covertsides under close observation, and, by voice and crack of the whip, we head any cub that breaks covert and turn it back in. 'Tally ho—ba-ack!' We hear and we say. For the whippers-in are assisted in this operation by the field.

Even later when runs in the open become the order of the day, there will be no holloaing. Young hounds learn little by being lifted to the holloa. They must work out the line for themselves.

When young hounds are hunting on the right line, the huntsman congratulates them with all his warmth; when they kill he cheers them to the echo, for he knows that, if they lust, above all else, after the blood of fox, half the trial of making a successful pack is won.

At the beginning of cub-hunting there will be a tendency to riot. Up to September, on hound exercise, the hunt staff will have used great patience to get them generally accustomed to strange sights and sounds and smells and to show them what *not* to hunt. 'Ware hare! Ware haunch! Ware wing!' This will have been all their message. It is not easy to prevent riot unless hounds are soon given an outlet for their hunting instincts. Out cub-hunting, the young entries will doubtless be accompanied by 10 or 12 couple of second-, third- and fourth-season hounds, their tutors, and it is, of course, essential that none of these speak to riot.

By the end of October the hunt will have put in some 25 to 30 days' cub-hunting and will have disturbed every covert in the country, once if not twice. With every cub hunting morning that passes, the less rioting there will be. By now the Master and the huntsman will have a very fair idea of the quality of their young entry and will draft those hounds which, owing to physical and mental handicaps, show themselves unfit to keep.

Terriers

When a fox goes to ground and the Master decides whether or not to dig him out, a number of factors are taken into consideration. Can the job be completed quick enough to make it worthwhile? (Understandably, the field object to being kept waiting.) Are there a surplus of foxes just here? Have there been a lot of complaints of fox damage? Has a long time elapsed since hounds tasted fox? Is the earth or drain reasonably accessible? What are the scenting conditions? If they are good, then would it be more advisable to leave this one and spend the time drawing for another in the open?

Most foxhunters hate digging. Not only is it unsporting; but it also wastes the day's sport. However, since foxes must be culled and hounds kept in blood, it is frequently necessary, by a combination of digging and terrier work, to bolt the fox. (Though, in view of the fox's breeding season, there is normally no digging after the end of January.)

The hunt terrier is not a recognized breed. It may be virtually any terrier capable of finding its way down an earth and facing a fox at bay. The little tan-and-white 'Jack Russell', smooth-coated or rough, is the standard. Charles McNeill, who was Master of the Grafton for 7 seasons and of the North Cotswold for 5 seasons and a great authority on hunt terriers, liked the following sort of terrier:

'A nice little short-legged terrier. . . . But he must not be wide in front. A tall terrier with good shoulders and narrow front, with a long lean head, is the ideal huntsman's terrier. The terrier should not be too "hard" but must have plenty of tongue, for in this way he is more likely to bolt the fox, and, if he does not, you may be sure, at least, that the fox is uninjured. Further, you have the advantage of knowing where he is if you have to start digging.'

The late Miss Frances Pitt, who was Master of the Wheatland and another expert on the terrier, held the following view:

'It should be somewhat small, for it has to creep down holes, and of slight frame, yet broad enough across the chest to have plenty of heart and lung room, combined with strength. Its head is rather broad and round, and its muzzle short, by show-yard standards. But that broad head contains brains, so that it is a shrewd and intelligent little animal. It is white in colour, save perhaps for a black or tan patch or two and has a broken coat of hard wiry texture. As for its pedigree, this is not entered in any stud book, but nevertheless is well known. The huntsman carries it in his head. . . .

I am definitely in favour of one point with regard to a hunt terrier and that is that it must be white. There are some grand types of dark-coated terriers, such as the Fell breed, black with tan or cream points, and the Border terriers of sandy hue, but they have a disadvantage, particularly the brown ones, and this is that hounds may mistake them for a fox. . . . '

Like the hound, the young hunt terrier is 'entered' to fox: to encourage him to go down the earth, foxes' masks and brushes are shaken at him and he is put at the earths of independent cubs.

Terriers used to be carried by a mounted hunt servant with a bag slung across his shoulder, but, nowadays, terrier men follow by van or Land Rover. More often than not they are soon up across the fields when they are wanted.

It saves a lot of trouble if the fox is encouraged to bolt; but foxes are shy creatures and like to conceal their movements. They are unlikely to bolt if they are crowded in. Therefore there should be no tramping over the ground above the earth. Hounds should be taken well to one side, and no one should be allowed near except the man in charge of the terrier.

Chapter 9

The Hunter

UP TO TWO centuries ago the horse provided the fastest and strongest land propelling power on earth: he drew the carriages that hauled the minerals from the heart of the earth; he opened the lock-gates and turned the millstones; he drew the ploughs, the mail and passenger coaches and the forest logs; he carried the overland caravans of the great merchants, he was transport for the nomadic herdsmen and of the armies of the world. *Cavalry en masse* was the most powerful man-made land force of all. No empire could have been fashioned without the flexibility and force of the mounted man-at-arms. The horse had much greater impact on the course of history than the combustion engine has had since his demise. Even now, although he is no longer a weapon that counts in terms of modern technology, he still gives pleasure for countless thousands of men, women and children—above all for those who ride to hounds.

Over a wide variety of going and obstacles, hunting demands stamina, sure-footedness, boldness and balance from the horse. It is the sport which still provides the best fundamental test for horse and rider; and it is from foxhunting that steeplechasing, eventing and showjumping are derived, and from which they still gain so much of their support. Hunting, indeed, still finds at least three-quarters of the best horsemen in most of the branches of equitation.

What sort of horse does the foxhunter need? To glance through *Baily's Directory* and to read, under the entry for this hunt and that, the type of horse recommended, makes an interesting study. For the rather flat Puckeridge and Thurlow, which was always composed largely of heavy plough, we are told that '. . . the horse required is a well-bred short-legged one, clever at banks and blind ditches, and also able to gallop through the deep. A big leggy horse is unsuited to this country. . . .' The Quorn, with their gently undulating Shire grassland and great variety of fences, tell you to ride '. . . a thoroughbred, the best that can be bred . . . he must be bold, fast, able to stay, and a big jumper . . .'. The Warwickshire, another good big country, propose much the same sort: '. . . the best hunter bred: he must be able to jump and gallop, timber especially, and stay; in fact be a thorough good hunter in the fullest sense. . . .'

Turn to the Morpeth, of Northumberland, where '. . . there are banks as well as fly fences . . . 70% pasture, 5% plough, 15% woodland and the remainder moorland . . .' and the simple advice is this, 'A blood 'un is the best horse.' Then look up the Exmoor, which 'consists mainly of moorland with some enclosed country and a few big woods. . . . The best horse possible, big or little; a fast, low-set mount is the most suitable. . . . ' For Cornwall's Lamerton ' . . . a clever horse is required, capable of jumping big banks, and good over rough going. . . . ' The Old Surrey and Burstow in the enclosed, built-up country due south of London suggest ' . . . a well-bred one on short legs, schooled over every type of obstacle, except walls. . . . '

How shall we define a hunter? A horse that has proved his capacity to carry a man or woman of a weight of 12 stone or more for a full day to hounds, 3 days a fortnight during 5 consecutive months of the year? For someone of 70, or for an adult beginner, this could imply a 'dead quiet' horse, one that may catch up at the draws and checks, then lopes along at the rear again, standing in a docile way when a gate has to be opened, going slow and steady as a rock down the banks but probably never leaving the ground higher than a couple of foot. Yet, for most of us, whether we ride to hunt, hunt to ride or indulge in a combination of those enjoyments, only a galloper and a fencer, one that will keep us with hounds on a roaring scent, will fit the bill. As prescribed by most of those *Baily's* entries, we need a horse of some quality. But what quality? What quantity? What virtues, what tests shall we demand?

Firstly, our choice must be 'sound in eye, wind and limb'. We shall make no decision without seeing a vet's certificate. How old is he? Proverbially a young horse is an improving horse; an old horse is one that goes back. What is his

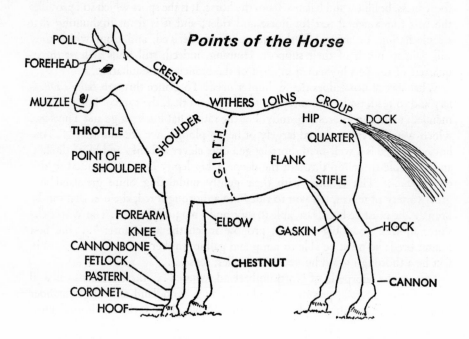

Points of the Horse

history? we want to know. Has he done any showjumping, for example? Is he up to our weight? Clearly if we are light we shall encounter much less trouble in finding something to match. Does his size more or less correspond to ours? If we are long in the trunk we are looking for one with comparatively long lines; and it is as well if our knees can lie flat against his, or her, sides, without projecting beyond the widest point of the chest oval. If we are small, we shall appear out of place on 17 hands; and tall horses, for the most part, tire easily and are not as surefooted as stocky ones.

The highest-bred horses are generally of little use for hunting. They lack the necessary stamina, their fine-drawn bones are more susceptible to injury, and, owing to generations of selective breeding, they do not grow a good coat and cannot therefore readily withstand the rigours of winter. The steeplechaser is required to move very fast over a short distance; whereas we need a horse that can keep up with foxhounds over a long distance. We speak of the 'three-quarter bred hunter type'. A half-bred horse—by a thoroughbred stallion out of a non-thoroughbred mare—makes the hardiest hunter. Or, in countries of trappy moorland and steep-sided valleys, one of the large native breeds—Connemara, Highland or Welsh—crossed with a thoroughbred, may produce the best result.

Many people nowadays scorn the importance laid upon conformation and looks by the purist judges of horseflesh. Clearly, just as the athlete and the greyhound, the boxer and the foxhound, are far more likely to give the prize performances and are less likely to suffer ailments and injuries, if they are well put together, properly developed in the right places and look bold and alert, than those lacking such qualities, so, too, with the hunter. All hunting men and women have their own ideas; I can only describe what is best from my own experience.

What, when his rug is removed, shall we seek first? Surely disposition and temperament. Do we get the *feeling* that he is a good character? Beware of evil eyes; favour big bold eyes that have width between them . . . and then let our own eye turn to his shoulder. A well-sloped shoulder affording a decent length of rein is what we are after, one that gives the impression he will carry the saddle well back behind his withers. These should be well developed: low short withers cannot give the essential base for the saddle. Searching for the bone structure, our eye should find the humerus joined to the scapula, or shoulder-bone, more or less at a right-angle, and the forearm, the bone of which is the radius, should be long compared with the cannon-bone. It should be well muscled, too. It is a combination of good shoulders and forearm that guarantees a long-striding step and marks the capacity to reach over the height and breadth of obstacles; but this is only possible if the necessary thrust and impulsion are coming from a properly developed hindquarters. If the quarters are weak, fine shoulders may be valueless.

The quarters ought to look round and muscular. They should be long, too, especially between the hips and the point of the buttocks, the hip joint and the stifle joint, and the stifle joint and the hock. They should slope away to strong

Skeleton of the Horse

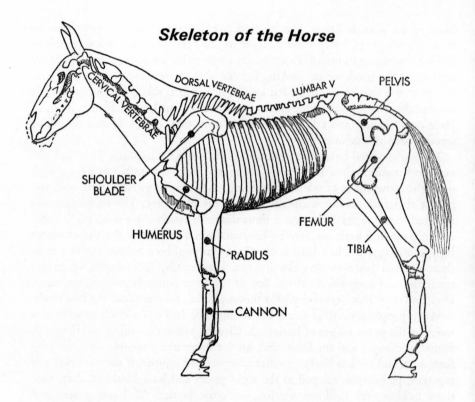

CERVICAL VERTEBRAE · DORSAL VERTEBRAE · LUMBAR V · PELVIS · SHOULDER BLADE · HUMERUS · RADIUS · CANNON · FEMUR · TIBIA

second thighs, symmetrical hocks, that turn neither inwards nor outwards, and back tendons that feel hard and clean. Turning our attention to the middle portion, the length of our prospective hunter's back ought to be the combined result of long withers, a long straight breast-bone and a loin of moderate length. If he is long in the back, this length must be supported by really muscular loins. However, short couplings are preferable: they produce a shape more likely to ensure collection, balance, spring and surefootedness.

Now to the front again: a very narrow-chested horse is unlikely to be a genuine weight-carrier and may tire easily, while one that is very wide between the forearms will be restricted as a galloper. On the other hand, our choice cannot be too deep through the chest, which is where we find the lung and heart room. The forelegs should be straight, with freedom at the elbows, the cannon-bone comparatively short, and the knee, which we should satisfy ourselves is nice and flat, ought to be in straight alignment with the forearm and cannon-bone. The fetlock joints should be hard and clean; for we do not want kinks or bulges that might harbinger unsoundness.

'No pastern,' they say, 'no horse.' It is upon this vital connection between the cannon and the hoof that much of our hunter's spring and suppleness of movement come from. Apart from the fact that a steep pastern makes for an inelastic tread, producing an awkward, uncomfortable and tiring ride, it is jarring for the horse. Upright pasterns are also the cause of much injury. Certainly, at the other extreme, very long horizontal pasterns are a sign of weakness; but we should definitely look for sloping pasterns.

Then let us take a close look at his head and neck, for they play an important part in his movement; and his balance, and ours with him, depend to some extent on how his head is set. We are not necessarily looking for a lean finely chiselled head, but there is no doubt that quality looks around the head are a good index of mobility, nerve and overall usefulness. In proportion to the rest of him, his neck should be long and free and wide in the gullet, thinning down as it approaches the head. It must be set neither too high nor too low and should carry the head at a balanced angle.

'Quality on short legs, with great depth through the heart is the right type for the hunting field', goes an old maxim, and a well-tested one, too.

The right type, yes; but has this horse, that is paraded for our inspection, been broken and schooled well? Has he always been ridden by confident and accomplished men or women? Or by people with poor seats and worse hands who have rendered him irretrievably nervous, hotted him up and jabbed him in the mouth? Is he a puller? Does he kick when he is in a crowd? Will he jump boldly and freely? Assuming it is during the winter that we are thinking of buying him, then let us insist on a day's hunting with him.

How smoothly does he box and unbox? Does he stand still to be mounted? . . . Now that we are up and away from the meet, let's get on good terms with him, find a sympathy through our leg and hand, get a dialogue going. Has he a cold back? Has he been properly and suitably mouthed? Does he walk out well? Does he show plenty of freedom and spring in his trot? Does he balance himself properly at the trot and canter? Is his head light, or does he drop it? Does he jump off his hocks and give a good feeling of power behind the saddle? Does he co-operate when we open and shut gates? Is he confident in traffic? How does he behave in the company of other horses? Are we sure we have not overhorsed ourselves? If we have done so, we are not likely to get much enjoyment for our money. Nor are we likely to see much of hounds.

So we make our decision; to buy or not to buy. If, in spite of some mild physical defect or two, he particularly appeals to us, if he goes well for us, if we find a harmony with him and he suits us in every other respect and if the price is right, then we shall probably be right to go ahead and buy him.

If we have time, patience, inclination and a way with horses, we may elect to make a young unbroken horse. Then we shall go through the long and painstaking procedure of winning his confidence, gradually introducing him to the bit, lungeing, putting on first the roller, then the rug, long-reining and driving, then riding every day and, at length, jumping. If all goes well, nothing is likely to suit us better than the mount we have made ourselves.

However, few foxhunters are so adequately placed as to be able to make their

H

own horses; and, apart from farmers, not very many more have either the time or the accommodation to keep the made horse which they have bought. Hunter management is something requiring deep study and an experienced tutor to teach the art, not just a book of words. Suffice it here to say that responsible hunting people, who keep their horses at livery, should have a sound knowledge of horsemastership. They should be able to satisfy themselves, from one day to the next, that their horse is being tenderly and efficiently cared for.

Firstly, the foxhunter who keeps his horse at livery should have a full understanding of the nature and characteristics of the equine animal, that is a herd animal with a herd instinct (which accounts for the reluctance of all but the best-disciplined to leave the herd out hunting). He has eyes towards the side of his head, indicating a beast which, in its primeval state, was no predator but was preyed upon. In his wild state he only gallops from playfulness or to escape, and then only for short distances. A herbivore, one that lives by grazing, he likes to feed little and often, which is why nature has given him a small stomach and why the hunter's ration must be divided into at least five meals a day, spread out evenly.

Nor did nature particularly intend that he should carry people, or anything else for that matter, on his back. Here man has made something natural out of what is unnatural. We require our hunter to work 7 consecutive months of the year, conveying a considerable weight across country for 4 or 5 hours at a stretch, 3 days a fortnight, or—in less exacting conditions—twice a week. So, to match the huge additional energy consumption, we devise a worker's diet of corn—bruised or crushed, probably, for better digestion—up to 15 pounds of it a day, and bran to supplement the hay and chaff which will be his bulk food in stables.

Doubtless we shall have him out in the fields during the idleness of summer, re-introducing him gradually before autumn to the hard food, which, combined with hard exercise, makes him a hard hunter; but, because he will find his stable diet somewhat binding and monotonous, we shall regularly vary it with linseed, green forage, carrots and swedes. We shall invariably feed him bran mashes twice a week or so to soften his corn diet and save him from constipation, though not the day before hunting; and, knowing that overfeeding is the cause of all sorts of ailments, his diet shall be related as precisely as possible to his exercise. We shall never feed him anything but the best forage.

Nature gives him a long coat to protect him from the bite of winter. Contrarily we clip him to keep him cool through the restless hunt and ridden exercise and to smarten him. We must therefore put a rug or two over his back during the colder months; and, when we return him to grass in the spring, it will be in a non-slip rug, until he grows a frost-resisting coat once again. We shall ensure that the field we allot is safe in every respect and is protected, if possible, from fierce winds.

Nature had him roam on soft pasture where metal-hard protection is not necessary; but we require him to carry us over long distances, on roads and rough places. We must therefore not only keep him shod but must change his worn shoes once a month. We should know the principles of cold and hot shoeing and can judge whether the job is well done.

His stable will always be hygienic. It will have light and air but will be draught-free. There will be a clean soft bed of straw (or, failing that, peat or wood shavings) for him to lie on if he chooses to get off his feet. We shall ensure that water is available for him at all times. A hunter should drink about 10 gallons a day. To keep his body toned, in the interests of hygiene and from pride and courtesy and a desire to honour our hunt, we shall groom him as well as may be and shall wash his eyes, nostrils and dock.

No matter whether we look after our own horse or keep him at livery, we shall know what atmosphere is expected in the stable: a cheerful one. We shall not look with favour on grooms that shout and clatter buckets. Horses, no less than any other animals, prefer quietly confident treatment. This also applies when boxing and unboxing.

Like all good horsemen and horsewomen, we know how bandages are tied, how to lift and inspect feet and how to detect lameness. We know the look of good saddlery and how it should be cared for, and we can tell in a trice whether the saddle and bridle and their accoutrements are fitting properly. We shall be constantly pre-occupied with our hunter's welfare, watching his condition from week to week, visiting him at regular intervals and seeing to his particular needs.

Everyone who rides to hounds ought to have a fundamental veterinary knowledge, at least a rudimentary understanding of splints and sprains, contusions and coughs, navicular and nettlerash, thrush and treads, spavins and sidebones, warbles and worms, colic and cracked heels, ringworm and ringbone; and all the other frailties that horseflesh is heir to. We shall realize, of course, that it is wrong to take our horse out at all if there is heat in a leg, or if he is off his feed, and that the vet must be called if such conditions continue. On a hunting morning our hunter will have a full drink and a feed of corn. On return from hunting there will always be a hot gruel prepared, and fresh bedding, too; and we shall understand what is wanted if there are outbreaks of sweating in the evening.

Our hunter will not develop muscle and stamina without an increasing amount of exercise from early in August, when we bring him up, until the season begins. This will be promoted, if possible, to plenty of uphill work, included in a programme of 2 or 3 hours' trotting and walking. During this time we shall revise his jumping performance. His exercise will, of course, be kept up during the season on non-hunting days—at the walk.

This is a truism that bears repeating: whether he keeps his horse at home or at livery, or with a farmer or a friend, or even if he hires, the foxhunter ought to be worthy of the name 'horsemaster'.

The high standard of horses seen in the hunting field today may be attributed in no small way to the Hunters' Improvement and National Light Horse Breeding Society whose premium stallion scheme, founded in 1885, enables breeders

to obtain stud services for a moderate fee. It works like this. With an annual out-
lay of some £30,000, which includes a substantial grant from the Horse Race
Betting Levy Board (taxes, in effect, from the betting industry), the society
awards 60 to 70 premiums. Owners of premium-winning stallions are paid a
£445 subsidy. Super premium award winners receive an extra £270 or more.
This additional is scaled down to £80 for thirteenth and fourteenth places. The
subsidies enable owners of non-thoroughbred mares to secure the services of
thoroughbred stallions for a tiny stud fee of £15 (or £25 for non-members). All
horses submitted for premiums undergo a meticulous veterinary examination, so
that breeders, who avail themselves of the service, are guaranteed totally sound
animals. Many of the stallions have good racing records behind them.

Among the host of famous horses which have been sired under the scheme are
Baccarat, Fidelio, Foxhunter, Goodwill, Halloween, Lauriston, Merely-a-
Monarch, Peer Gynt, Psalm, Specify, Sunsalve and Top Notch.

The society's offices are at 8 Market Square, Westerham, Kent.

Chapter 10
Riding to Hounds

BRITAIN

Oᴜʀ ᴄᴏᴜɴᴛʀʏsɪᴅᴇ is a heritage we treasure. Foxhunting is its greatest surviving tradition: a tradition of comradeship, courage, unselfishness, high standards and love of nature. Foxhunting provides the countryside's last surviving regular pageantry. This pageantry embodies the foxhunter's pride, his desire to make an elegant showing, one worthy of such a fine animal as the horse, of the illustrious hunt to which he subscribes and of the still beautiful land over which he rides.

He is aware that this land may cost, perhaps, £1,000 an acre in his particular hunt country and that, for better or worse, it largely belongs to, or is rented by, farmers. Therefore, without the support and goodwill of the farmers, the sport would be impossible. Indeed, if the ethics regarding riding over farmland were permitted to lapse, the owners—neither from spite nor fury but from sheer economic necessity—would simply shut out the hunts, and that would be that: no more hunting. So the foxhunter's first knowledge must be concerned with the precious countryside. He is aware of the rent per acre in his country; he understands agricultural cycles; he is familiar with crop sequence; he can distinguish between Jerseys and Friesians, Guernseys and Shorthorns; he has an inkling of the shepherd's problems.

He knows precisely *why* he may never ride across crops, *why* he must always shut gates, *why* he is out of favour if he gallops through fields in which stock is kept or over very sodden pasture and *why*, except when hounds are running, he should use gates or gaps rather than jumping. He knows that the good foxhunter never risks breaking valuable fences unnecessarily, and, if he does cause damage, then he reports the matter without delay. Since he is riding by courtesy of the farmers, he ought to return that courtesy, not only with common civility, by greeting them warmly by name in the hunting field, but by getting to know them and their problems and by learning how the harvest went, what was the milk yield, what was the lamb survival and what the price of hay. Unless he is sincere in all this interest, he cannot hope to be an integral member of his hunt.

Foxhunting is totally involved, too, with the wild life of the countryside. Consequently foxhunters, whether they come from Coventry or Clerkenwell or a Cotswold farmstead, must be countrymen or at least aspire to become countrymen. This implies, in true spirit, being conservationists, being lovers of wild life,

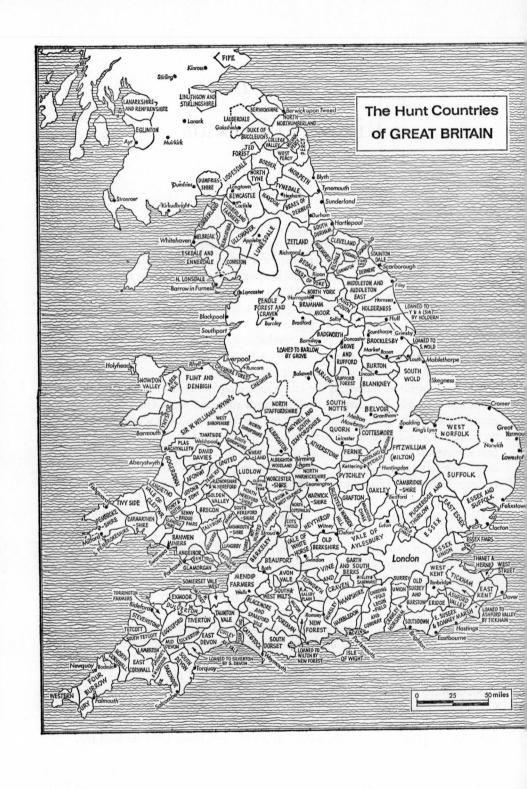

The Hunt Countries of GREAT BRITAIN

having a desire to see all indigenous species—animals, and plants, too—thriving at proportionate levels. Hunting is not just a sporting and social pursuit, it is a function of fox control: hunting prevents widespread damage to livestock and keeps nature in balance; and the foxhunter is well aware that, if the coverts are properly nursed by the hunt, with the support of the farmers and the foresters, all forms of wild life benefit. This is another reason why, apart from enriching his own life, the foxhunter should be a countryman, why he should learn the difference between a sycamore, a plane and a field maple, between a stoat and a weasel and between a crow and a rook and why he should develop a growing awareness of the ecological systems. If foxhunters are sensitive to the require- ments of farming and of wild life, no one can say they are superimposed on the land they use for their sport.

The hunting man's next responsibility—very nearly of equal importance to his responsibility towards landowners and farmers—is to the hunt itself. This means a good deal more than paying his subscription on time (and more than his sub- scription if he can afford it); it means arriving in time for the meet (and not going direct to the first draw, which is bad manners as well as being unhelpful) and generally bearing a reputation for integrity and decency within the hunting community. It implies loyalty to the Master. Knowing the holder of that appoint- ment to be one who sacrifices a great deal of his time, at all seasons of the year, to guide the destiny of the hunt, the staff, the hounds, the buildings and other property, the policies, the programme and the relationships with landowners and farmers, not to mention the fund-raising activities, and who pays through the nose for such honour; the foxhunter shows his outward appreciation by a willing- ness to help with the affairs of the hunt and with a heartfelt 'Good morning, Master' or 'Good night, Master' and a raising of the hat and a ready smile. The foxhunter shows his gratitude and respect by giving the Master all reasonable co-operation. Nor does he question the authority of the Master or Field Master out hunting.

The huntsman and his whippers-in should expect similar courtesy from the hunt follower. By the same token that they acknowledge the part played by the hunt subscriber in keeping the profession of hunt servant alive and healthy, the subscriber knows perfectly well that his sport depends to a great extent upon how well he co-operates, actively and passively, with the hunt servants. The fox- hunter greets the hunt staff by name, the huntsman as Mr —, the whippers-in by their first names. He remembers them at Christmas.

Between the moment that hounds are dispatched for the first draw and the end of the day, when the horn blows 'Home', the hunting man's help is mostly of a passive nature. That is to say, he takes immense pains not to interfere with hounds or with the tactics of the hunt. He keeps his horse away from hounds at all times. If unavoidably, he does find himself very close to them, to keep them out of harm's way by holding out his whip towards them with the thong dangling. He will always turn his horse's head towards them and in a close place will contrive to manoeuvre his quarters into a hedge or covertside. He is always at pains to remove himself from the middle of gateways and pathways whenever the huntsman, the whippers-in or hounds need access or egress. He endeavours to keep downwind of the pack, well back when they are casting and to one side—probably 100 to 200 yards and level with the tail-hounds—when they are running.

When he is sent to watch a ride or the corner of a covert, he must know when to holloa, when to shout 'Talley-ho over!' and when to shout 'Tally-ho back'. He reserves his holloas for those rare and very convincing occasions when he has seen the hunted fox, when hounds have lost that fox and when the huntsman agrees they have lost it. He takes no notice at all of anyone else's holloas.

He does not chatter at the covertside or does not make any noise at all at a check. He is always conscious as to whether the tail-hounds are all on after such occasions as a blank draw or a kill. From one moment to the next he is involved in the process of the hunt: he uses his eyes and ears and is ready at all times to give information to the hunt staff *when they require it*. He is also ready to hold their horses at the kill or at any other time that they need to be busy on their feet. He takes a continuous interest in the performance of hounds, keeping a close eye on prominent workers and knowing them by name. If he loses hounds, he has a habit of finding them by ear as much as by eye: he stands stock still every now and then for 4 or 5 minutes and strains to hear their music, the horn, horses' feet or several car engines in low gear: anything that may lead him up to them. For 'Be with them I will' is his motto.

Good countrymen have good manners, and foxhunting communities are, or ought to be, communities in which thoughtfulness, kindness and common chivalry abide. Even when hounds are running it is not quite a case of every man and woman for himself and herself. Even then the distress or potential danger of one's fellow-riders takes priority over the sport. Although the foxhunter always contrives to be at the front of the field, he moves into this advantage position inconspicuously and with the least possible inconvenience to his fellow-followers. He is ready to help and encourage children and beginners. He always feels responsibility for the welfare of others and is anxious that they, too, should see plenty of sport. If he is among the last through a gateway, as a more obvious example, and someone has had to dismount to open the gate for the hunt to go through, he waits until that person has safely remounted. Men open gates for women, stand aside for them at gaps, see they are safe with troublesome horses and ride outside when they accompany them on roadways.

The foxhunter is perfectly aware of the opposition to hunting, not simply the emotive anthropomorphic disapproval of the abolitionist crowd but opposition from people who believe (or who say they believe) the sport works against the national agricultural interests as a whole, from those who hold the view that anachromisms should, on principle, be eliminated and from motorists, whose only heartfelt opinion on hunts is that they clutter up the roads. There is, too, a psychological factor that should not be overlooked. Too often in history the man on a horse has been an oppressor—arrogant, unfairly privileged and tyrannical. There is a subconscious belief that he remains so. Horsemen have always elicited, and will always elicit, an inferiority complex in some pedestrians and motorists. It therefore behoves the foxhunter to make as little trouble as he can with road users or with those on their feet. He never blocks roadways, if he can possibly help it, he always shows consideration and courtesy, without any trace of condescension and he always remembers to say thank you. (It is not enough to raise the whip with a hard-faced nod when a motorist has the goodness to slow down. A loud 'Thank you very much' and a broad smile are the least that will do.)

It has been said that 'there are fools, damned fools and men who hunt in snaffles'. As a matter of hunting field principle, some pundits used to insist on standing martingales, others on running martingales, some on this saddle, others on that bridle; but a more flexible and enlightened attitude towards horse furniture prevails nowadays. Saddles and bridles ought to be of a type most suitable for the horse in question. The most important points are that they should be serviceable, clean and well kept and should fit impeccably. The irons should give plenty of room for the feet in case of a fall.

The horse is a splendid animal; the hunting cavalcade is the most beautiful sight in rural Britain. How the foxhunter dresses, therefore, has a collective aesthetic significance besides a purely utilitarian one; and the main factor about collective elegance is that it should harmonize. That is why we see uniform combinations of dress in the hunting field. The wearer of the pink, red or scarlet coat, as it is variously known, puts on white or cream-coloured breeches, mahogany or champagne-topped black boots with white garter straps and black spurs, a white hunting tie or stock with a gold or yellow-metal pin, a waistcoat (never a pullover), a black top hat and a pair of gloves. He carries a hunting whip with a thong and lash. The black coat variation of this may be with coloured breeches, instead of white, in which case butcher boots, not top-boots, are worn. The cut-away or swallowtail variation of the red or black coat is generally only seen in the Midlands. If a bowler hat is the choice, then it can only be butcher boots and coloured breeches. In the case of 'rat-catcher' a coat of some such material as tweed, Melton cloth or whipcord is worn with the bowler hat.

Fashions and form differ between hunts, but it is still generally accepted that, apart from the Masters and hunt staff, only farmers and children are entitled to wear the velvet hunt cap; and women riding astride. Unfortunately, the fashion of women riding sidesaddle, which is generally agreed to be extremely elegant, is all too rarely seen in the hunting field nowadays. For the most part women wear dark blue or black coats with velvet caps, cream breeches and butcher boots, or tweed jackets with coloured breeches.

Across agricultural Britain as a whole, the ratio of arable to pasture used to be 80% in favour of pasture. Now it is the other way round: we have 80% plough. At the same time farmers seem to use more, rather than less, wire as the years go by. These two factors, coupled with the value of land and the restrictions imposed by the proliferation of certain forms of specialized farming and smallholding, all combine to render hunting more of a follow-my-leader affair than it used to be; but, if there is less scope for taking one's own line, everywhere there are areas that offer escape and comparatively untrammelled cross-country riding; to take due advantage of the golden moments, all who follow hounds should aspire to become first-class horsemen and horsewomen. Apart from the sporting aspect, it is also much safer to take one's own line, much sounder to trust one's own judgment as to where to jump. Every time one waits in a queue, one is wasting time. By taking his own line, where it is practicable to do so, even on the slowest horse, the foxhunter is more likely to find himself in front—provided he knows the country really well.

The beginner must endeavour to learn every inch of it. He would be well advised to use a map for his first season and to follow the more enterprising veterans who know, of old, the ways through and round and over. His horse must be schooled for handiness, he himself must be agile, deft and quick, so that gates can be opened and closed in a trice and hazardous obstacles pulled aside and so that he can lead his horse through thickets, tortuous banks and bogs, if need be.

The wise foxhunter will, in any case, only ride a horse which he knows he can control, one that gives him an enjoyable day's sport without upsetting other horses and not a horse with a mouth like iron, that rears, shies, constantly throws its head or kicks. Kickers should never be taken out hunting, and, in fact, unless it be known that a horse has no tendency whatever to kick, it should have a red ribbon tied on its tail. If, through some dreadful chance, his horse does kick a hound, the rider fulfils two duties: he informs the huntsman immediately and, as soon as he gets home, writes a letter of apology to the Master.

The experienced foxhunter is aware that the frighteningly solid fences are the safe ones, not the thin, inviting-looking ones, and that iron railings are just as safe as timber. He searches instinctively for the safe take-off, and, if he is first up, he checks that it is wire-free and takes a look at the landing side. If he is in a queue, as I fear he often will be, he never cuts in front of another rider; he always waits until the rider in front of him has not only landed but is clear of the jump and away. In fast, grass countries there are occasions when he must gallop at his fences, but, if possible, he either comes into them at a canter or a well-collected trot—in trappy places at a walk—maintaining contact with the mouth and giving his horse that urging leg at the crucial moment. By projecting his own heart the other side of the jump, he puts his horse in no doubt as to his intention. Horses have an instinct for irresolution on their backs. If the horse pecks on landing, the knowing horseman gives him his head; he never tugs on the reins, for no horse wants to fall, and a horse that has made a mistake can only save itself. The rider ensures, each time he jumps, that he does not get left behind but brings his weight over the horse's withers as he jumps. At the same time he is ready to lean back if it is a drop fence. The foxhunter's horse will be prepared for the country concerned. He will not, for example, follow hounds in a bank country with a horse that has not been schooled to banks.

If the meet is within reasonable hacking distance and if there is nothing to prevent him doing so, the conscientious foxhunter will always ride on: a preliminary trot and walk are good for him and good for the horse, but never much over 5 miles an hour. During the day he will try to save his horse in various ways. Having hacked on a long distance, for instance, he should dismount and loosen off his girth for a few minutes at the meet; and he should repeat this procedure whenever the opportunity of a pause appears during the day, such as when hounds mark to ground. Before re-mounting he sees the girth is as tight as can be and checks it again when he is up. Since he is determined never to reach the bottom of his horse, he will never, if it is a good horse, allow it to gallop quite as fast as it wants to; he will always keep a little in reserve. He stands up in the stirrups and keeps as still as possible at the gallop. He never jumps unnecessarily. He tends to ride round the perimeter, not over the top, of hills. Otherwise he rides the shortest way—without, of course, interfering with hounds—that he can find. Whenever it is cold and draughty, during periods of waiting, he keeps his horse on the move.

Being a good man to hounds implies an eye for country, courage, resourcefulness and quick decision making, besides good horsemanship and horsemastership. It is the only universal sport left to the British countryside that requires and combines these qualifications. Little wonder that to be regarded as 'good to hounds' is such a prized accolade.

The organization with, perhaps, the greatest single influence for good in the hunting field is the Pony Club. Besides riding and horsemastership, the Pony Club teach their members the principles of foxhunting, the duties of the hunt staff, the meaning of hunting terms, what goes on in the kennels, recognition and care of crops, woodland, and pasture, how to read a map and, of course, how to behave and how to help in the hunting field; and they prepare them for a number of stringent tests on those subjects.

Since the longer-term future of foxhunting depends, to a great extent, on the knowledge and attitudes of those who are now growing up, this education is clearly of the greatest importance. And what more refreshing aspect of foxhunting is there than the eager child?

> 'They're sure of sport to-day, Papa
> 'Tis such a hunting morn!
> They'll very soon be here, Papa
> Hark, there's the huntsman's horn!
> Look, look, beyond the chestnuts there,
> Oh what a lovely show!
> They'll find at Barkby Holt, Papa
> Oh won't you let me go?'
>
> Anon., *Sporting Magazine*, January 1835

THE UNITED STATES. BY ALEXANDER MACKAY SMITH

When our British ancestors first landed on the Atlantic coast, riding to hounds would have been impossible, even if they had been inclined to do so, simply because virtually all the land along the seaboard was heavily wooded. Only on a few of the offshore islands, notably Long Island, and in the Shenandoah Valley was there any natural grassland. Gradually, the wooded areas were cleared, and riding to hounds became possible. The roads were so bad that virtually everyone, male and female, were accomplished in the saddle. Furthermore, there was no wire. The fencing was either stone walls or various types of rail fencing, including morticed post-and-rail, stake-and-rail, where the rails are held together by a pair of stakes driven in the ground at each end, and the old-fashioned snake-, or worm-, fence, in which no posts are involved, but the rails are supported by being laid in a zigzag pattern. Hedges, ditches and banks were virtually unknown in the eighteenth century, although some attempt was made to establish hedges of Osage orange during the first part of the nineteenth century, a not very successful experiment.

When the quarry was the grey fox, not much hard riding was required, since this particular species preferred to run in circles in dense cover, only occasionally crossing an open field. Riding to hounds on the line of a red fox required a much faster horse and a much bolder rider. As a matter of fact the eighteenth-century gentlemen, of the old school, deplored the advent of the red fox in the Southern States during the first part of the nineteenth century.

After the Civil War, when night hunting became popular, partly through necessity, hound breeders and owners continued to ride to hounds, cutting across from one point to another so as to keep in closer touch with the pack but not attempting to jump fences. The development of foxhound field-trials during this century produced a set of rules which forbade owners to follow on horse-back, that privilege being extended only to the judges (preferably one judge to every seven hounds) and to followers having no direct interest in the competing hound. Owners, however, are allowed to follow in the roads in automobiles or in small lorries known as 'pick-up trucks'.

Riding to organized packs of hounds presents a very different picture. The aim is to enable everyone in the countryside to see, to hear and to enjoy the work and the cry of the pack, whether they follow on horseback, on foot, on a bicycle or in an automobile. The hunt supporters' clubs, which have become so popular in Britain, have not been copied in the United States, but nevertheless non-mounted followers are encouraged, as long as they do not get in the way.

As in all hunting countries, there are those who ride in order to hunt, and those who hunt in order to ride. In other words there are the dedicated followers whose pleasure is in watching and listening to hounds at work, and there are those who are interested chiefly in galloping and jumping, taking very little interest in the hounds. In the former group there are many who never jump a fence but are classified as 'hill toppers', following along the roads and through gates, but still managing to see and hear a great deal. Because most of our farms are mechanized, there are not nearly as many people riding to hounds who make their living chiefly from the land as there were in the days when horses provided farm-power and the mares produced, to the cover of thoroughbred stallions, the young hunters that needed schooling.

It is obvious that foxhunting can be carried on only through the courtesy of those who own and rent land over which hounds run. The first consideration, therefore, in riding to hounds is the permission and co-operation of the land-owners and a corresponding co-operation on the part of those who ride over their land. This includes keeping hounds in kennel when the going is really soft and avoiding wheat and other young crops, as well as the few farms found in every hunting country which are off limits. There are American hunting countries where all the fencing is stone walls as, for example, in some parts of Ireland. Virtually all of the original rail fences have rotted away and have been replaced by wire. A few of the more opulent hunting countries have been re-fenced in rails, but, generally speaking, riding to hounds in America means riding over hunt jumps or panels, as they are called. The larger the number of riders in the field, the more extensive the panelling should be. Since our stone walls are often jagged, it is customary to replace some of the top stones in jumpable places with a tele-phone pole or other piece of timber which will not cut a horse's knee should he make a mistake jumping the wall.

The common timber for rails was the American chestnut, a wood which splits easily and which is very durable. Unfortunately a blight killed every chest-nut tree in this country during the early part of the century. Nevertheless the dead trees were cut down and split up into rails, which were largely used as panels up to the end of the Second World War. At the present time, however, rails are most difficult to get, even using live chestnut oak, which makes a very acceptable substitute. The most common type of panel has thus become the 'chicken coop', which is rather like the 'tiger traps' found in some British hunting countries. These are in effect two sides of a triangle made of oak boards, the apex usually from 3 feet to 3 feet 6 inches in height. It is very effective in turning all types of grazing livestock, who do not like the width at the base of the triangle and will avoid jumping the obstacle. The same width requires a horse that is jumping should stand back a suitable distance; he cannot get his knees hooked underneath the obstacle as he can in the case of a rail fence. 'Chicken coops' also have the advantage that nobody can leave them open nor can lower them in height as in the case of gates or rail panels. Oak boards are expen-sive, but they are obtainable. A well-built 'chicken coop' will last for 20 to 25 years.

This jumping of panels means that the horse always has a reasonably safe take-off and landing, so that falls are far less frequent in America than in Britain. Furthermore, in the United States, the going is much less deep than in the British

Isles; horses are virtually galloping on top of the ground, which makes it possible for a heavy man to ride a somewhat lighter type of horse, and thus favours the thoroughbred. Because there is so much less water in the ground, it is also possible to hunt when the temperature is below freezing, if one is careful. There is much more snow, even in states as far south as Virginia, than in Britain, and some of the best hunting occurs when there are a few inches of snow on the ground, especially when that snow is melting and the sky is overcast. Being able to distinguish the footprints of the foxes and other forms of wildlife in the snow adds very much to the pleasure of hunting at such times.

Some of our hunting countries are fenced with barbed wire, but an even more common type of fencing is woven or 'Page' wire with a mesh of 8 inches by 12 inches in the upper staves and a smaller mesh below, the latter being designed to hold small pigs, lambs, etc. Page wire is 4 feet high and is usually surmounted by one or more strands of barbed wire. The American strains of hounds, with relatively smaller chest measurements, are able to slide sideways through the upper staves, which they do with remarkable speed. On the other hand, the larger-chested English hounds have to find a way around or under the wire or jump it. The latter is always dangerous, since a hound is very apt to get caught by a hindleg in jumping the wire, a position from which he cannot possibly extricate himself without help. Hounds have to be very carefully watched by the hunt staff if they are known fence jumpers.

Because most American hunting countries are panelled countries, an intimate knowledge of the location of these panels is essential if one is to ride to hounds successfully. Usually the responsibility for staying with hounds rests on the shoulders of the Master or of a Field Master, but, if one has the bad luck to become separated from the main body of the field, knowledge of the country is essential if one is to stay in the hunt. The longer most people hunt, the more they become interested in hounds and their work, riding across country gradually assuming a secondary importance. You can readily select the dedicated hound-men and women, because they do very little talking and are constantly using their eyes and ears, not only in watching and listening to hounds but also in watching all the other factors which are favourable or unfavourable to hounds and to their quarry. This close concentration almost invariably enables them to get a good start when hounds find and maintain a forward position, throughout the course of a hunt.

About 10% of the organized hunts in the United States are drag hunts, simply because their countries are too built up to allow foxhunting. Most of these drag hunts take great pains in laying a line, which closely simulates the line which would be taken by a fox, however.

One of the great advantages of foxhunting is that it is one of the few equestrian sports which is not competitive. 50 or 75 years ago, most of the organized hunts were clubs with restricted membership. Today, however, virtually any well-behaved individual on a well-behaved horse is made welcome. For those interested in pursuing the subject further, the book, *Riding To Hounds In America*, by William P. Wadsworth, Master of the Genesee Valley and, like his father before him, former President of the Masters of Foxhounds' Association of America, can be highly recommended. It is published by *The Chronicle of the Horse*, at Berryville, Virginia.

Chapter 11

Accidents and First Aid
in the Hunting Field

BY MICHAEL W. GIBSON, BVMS, MRCVS.

ACCIDENTS in the hunting field are no different from any other accidents, in that many could be prevented. Attempts by the rider to jump unsuitable obstacles with a tired or green horse, especially in deep going, will frequently end in disaster. Young horses, and those that are unfit or have been laid up for some time, should only be lightly hunted.

Condition of horse and saddlery before hunting

The horse should always be carefully observed before hunting. Any signs of lack of droppings, not eating up, abnormal discharge or generalized discomfort should be fully investigated. Check the horse's temperature. Many horses will not eat up in the morning if they are plaited first thing, so it should be left until the last job. In some cases, overnight plaiting can cause signs of generalized discomfort similar to mild colic. Horses that are leaving early in the morning should be fed last thing at night, as they may not have time to eat and digest their morning feed; consequently they may go without food for at least 24 hours.

Before leaving for the meet, the tack should be checked for correct fitting. Sores can be caused very quickly by badly fitting tack, and a rider cannot expect to be in full control and his horse to jump well, if there is a large sore in the mouth or on the withers.

Precautions out hunting

Despite the many advances made in veterinary science in the last few decades, first aid to horses in the hunting field has altered very little. It is still largely dependent on a combination of common sense and ingenuity. The most useful pieces of equipment are a clean handkerchief and a bandage, which take up very little room in the pocket and serve for a variety of uses, from mending tack to tying up a roadside gap. Paper tissues can be used for a dressing but should not be used to plug wounds, as some may get left in. It is quite pointless to pour powder, antibiotics, etc., on a mud-covered wound, when you are going to wash it off half an hour later. It is liable to do less good to the horse than to the rider, who then considers the animal as 'treated' and continues on his way! Iodine in particular can cause more tissue damage than it does good.

Treatment of wounds

Where possible, bandage (using a stock if not carrying a bandage) to bring the edges of the wound together. If there is very little gap, it may be better to leave it until the wound can be properly cleaned and dressed, otherwise dirt may be bandaged in. If bleeding is excessive, make a hard pad, such as a tightly rolled handkerchief, and bandage it on firmly. If the bleeding is very difficult to control, it may be necessary to apply a tourniquet—a bandage, and a piece of stick to twist it, will often suffice. Undue movement is liable to start the bleeding again; therefore do not expect it to stop completely until the horse is back in his stable.

Little can be done in the field for minor over-reaches into the bulbs of the heel. They should always be poulticed that night, as they are generally very dirty and prone to infection. If the over-reach is large and gaping, then it should be bandaged, if possible. The higher up the leg the wound is, the more serious it is apt to be, especially if it involves the tendon or joint/tendon sheath. Damage to the tendon or joint, particularly with the presence of oil, should be treated with great care and expert advice quickly obtained.

Although the exterior wound-holes may be small they are often serious, as they can be very deep and can penetrate vital structures or can be left with foreign bodies inside them. Where possible, remove any foreign body, and plug the wound. If there is a chance of any debris being left in, get professional advice, as septicaemia or, possibly, death can result. Stake wounds in the abdomen area should always be carefully examined because of the possibility of penetration of the abdominal wall and herniation of the guts, with consequent peritonitis. If there is any chance of this, pack the wound well and do not move the horse *at all* without veterinary assistance. To do so, greatly increases the risk of herniation. If there is marked internal haemorrhage the horse's membranes will be noticeably paler.

Loss of a shoe, and consequent treading on the nails, is a frequent cause of trouble. Often the horse shows only slight lameness at the time, but continued work will aggravate the situation by wearing the sole and working dirt into any holes. It is advisable to poultice the foot after pulling a shoe, even if the horse is not sore. Penetrating wounds are always the most liable to cause tetanus and infection. All horses should be permanently immunized against tetanus, and, if not, they should be given tetanus anti-toxin after any wounds.

Limb fractures

Any form of sudden acute lameness, with very marked pain, must always be considered as a possible fracture. If possible, use a low-loading vehicle to transport the horse and to obtain professional advice with a view to radiological examination. If the limb is swinging, and particularly if the skin is broken, euthanasia may be the only answer. Damage to the point of the hock at the insertion of the tendon may cause panic when the horse puts weight on the injured limb. Then

I

the animal can become very difficult to control. The use of temporary splints in horses is usually futile because of the physical problems.

Vertebrae fractures

A completely broken neck usually means immediate death, but an animal with a partially broken vertebra may show some signs of movement but may be unable to get up. Often, a horse lying on the ground is only blown and, if the saddle is removed, will soon get up of its own accord. If the horse remains lying on his side, sit him up in the 'sitting dog' position and allow him to rest there for a few minutes. Lack of feeling in the limbs or tail often indicates a damaged vertebra. The degree of sensation can be ascertained by the use of an ordinary pin. If a horse gets up and is then unable to stand or move properly, it may be caused by partial damage to a vertebra or merely by concussion which will wear off. If a hind limb is broken, a horse will often be capable of getting up if rolled on to his other side.

Horse stuck in a ditch

Very often the horse is only blown, and, if his saddle is removed and if he is allowed to regain his breath, he will often get out on his own. If this is not successful, try to get the horse in the 'sitting dog' position, and then lift him with his tail, giving suitable encouragement—vocal or otherwise. If still recumbent, the next step is to dig away the side of the bank and to fill in the ditch partly (for example, with straw bales). The use of ropes is always potentially dangerous and should be left as a last resort and should preferably be used with the aid of experienced assistance. The chances of injury to the neck can be lessened by using a rolled-up sack round the neck with its ends tied by the rope with a non-slip loop. When pulling with the aid of a tractor do not tie the rope to the draw bar, but take a couple of turns round the pin and hold the rope end. In this way the pull can be varied or can be quickly released. The direction of the pull should, as near as possible, follow a line drawn from the tail to the head and should be an even pressure, without jerks. It is not recommended to attach ropes to the limbs, and only limited pressure should be applied to the tail. Always make sure that the horse is well clear of the ditch after pulling him out; a horse will often half get up, will stagger and will fall back in. Having got the animal out of the ditch, roll him so that the side that was underneath in the ditch is now uppermost and massage briskly. It is no use sticking pins into the horse to see if he has broken his back when his hindquarters are numb from lack of circulation and cramp.

Lameness

At the first signs of lameness, dismount and examine the foot and limb thoroughly for any signs of foreign bodies, wounds, sprains, etc. Remove any obvious cause, and, if the lameness persists, walk quietly home. A thorn in the coronary band can cause acute lameness until it is removed. Always note how and when a horse goes lame as it may be of great help to the veterinary surgeon in diagnosis and consequent treatment. Swelling or tenderness in the area of the joints or tendons should always be regarded seriously, even if the horse is not unduly lame. To continue hunting may cause irreparable damage.

Injuries from kicks will often not cause lameness until the horse stands and gets cold. The severity of the injury depends on the position and force of the kick. Kicks on the bone are usually more serious.

Azoturia (tied up)

Typically this occurs when a horse has had little or no exercise for a few days or is on an unusually high ration, especially high protein or added glucose; the horse shows signs of stiffening up soon after exercise commences. Azoturia can appear in varying degrees from slight stiffness and/or blowing, to widely spread cramp of the loins and hindquarters, with marked sweating and pain. Lead the horse slowly to the nearest road and get transport back to the stable, making sure to keep the loins warm. Heat, for example infra-red lamp, electric blanket, hot towels, should be applied to the affected area, and the horse should be given mash and salts. Once an animal has suffered from an attack of azoturia, the condition is very liable to re-occur.

Mild azoturia should be differentiated from mild colic or hindleg lameness.

Colic

Out hunting, the first indications of colic are often a general sluggishness, followed by obvious abdominal discomfort, sweating and a tendency to lie down. Loosen the girths, and keep quiet, walking if necessary to stop the horse going down and rolling. If it does not pass off in a short time, call your veterinary surgeon. Early signs of colic can easily be confused with azoturia.

Nose bleeds

These should always be regarded as potentially serious, particularly if the blood is frothing, indicating that it has come from the lungs. Allow the bleeding to stop, if profuse, and then walk quickly home. Cold water may be applied to the head if necessary. When there is bleeding after a fall, there may be damage to the frontal sinuses and concussion.

Heart and lungs

In these cases there is marked respiratory distress on exercise, often accompanied by excess sweating with slow recovery to normal. Dismount, loosen girths and allow to stand quietly until recovered. Do not move until the respiratory rate has reverted to normal for some time. With heart conditions there may be pain causing 'nappiness' or unnatural 'hotness' because of the fear of pain on exercise.

Girth and saddle galls

As soon as the gall is noticed, it should be ascertained whether it is possible to pad the tack in order to remove the pressure; if so, a piece of sacking, cloth or even gloves may be used. If this is not possible, the horse should be taken home. Be sure to check the fitting of the tack before it is used again.

Nettle stings

A horse can often be badly stung after falling in a ditch or going through high nettles. The response can vary from the appearance of a few weals to a thin-skinned horse going nearly mad and throwing itself over backwards. If the reaction is violent, the rider should get off immediately and should try to calm the horse by walking him quietly about, well away from any nettles as the animal may go down and roll. In bad cases the horse should be given sedatives and anti-histamine, or cortisone drugs.

Poor performance

There is usually a reason for bad performance or a sudden change in behaviour of a horse out hunting, and it should always be investigated before the next day's hunting. Some examples of this are: fading, although apparently fit and well, can be caused by such things as anaemia or heart murmurs; not jumping well (especially if jumping short) can be caused by a back problem or sub-clinical azoturia; sudden pulling can be caused by damage to bars of mouth or inside of cheeks; unusual shying or refusing can be caused by eyes.

On return to the stable

A horse should not be allowed to drink a large volume of cold water immediately on return to the stable but should be offered half a bucket of tepid water. He should be thoroughly checked for the presence of small wounds or thorns, which should be treated and poulticed, if necessary, to remove dirt and to lessen bruising. Any parts of the horse that are washed off should be dried carefully, particularly the heels. Washing-off water gets dirty very quickly, so always finish with a bucket of clean water. A hose-pipe is often the simplest method. Many horses will break out in a cold sweat after hunting. The use of string rugs and heat lamps can be very beneficial. Horses should always be looked at last thing at night to make sure they are warm and dry. Animals that are not checked may easily break out and get cold, resulting in a chill. It may be irritating to have to keep rubbing ears dry and changing rugs, but it is preferable to missing the next day's hunting.

If you do not feel fully satisfied with your own diagnosis and treatment of your horse's injuries or ailments, call in your veterinary surgeon promptly, stressing the degree of urgency as appropriate to the seriousness of the case.

Chapter 12

Following on Foot

I N SOME countries there are more enthusiasts to be seen following hounds by car, by bicycle and on foot—members of hunt supporters' clubs and visitors —than there are with the mounted field. Of these, the genuine dismounted follower, he who leaves his conveyance out of harm's way and walks with the hunt, may be just as welcome with the Master as the man who rides to hounds. To know which of the two would be the most popular in any given case, one would need to enquire which was the most knowledgeable and considerate countryman, which the most helpful to the hunt staff and which the best sportsman and foxhunter.

If such rivalry were to be considered, subscriptions and caps apart, the sensible foot-follower is clearly at a huge advantage. For being unencumbered with a horse, there is a no reason why he should damage farmland. Uninvolved with equitation, he has only himself and the progress of the hunt to think about. Being more or less unrestricted in his cross-country performance, he does not depend upon 'jumpable' places and gaps; rather he crawls through wire, climbs stiles and locked gates and worms his way through thickets. He is never subject to the herd pressures imposed on the mounted field, and, albeit his pace may be slower, he can really 'take his own line'. The fact that hunting has been slowed down by present-day conditions gives him a further advantage: he can keep up nearly as well as, often more easily than, the horseman.

He is able to be more detached, more objective in his view of the hunt and more aware of the sport as a natural and integrated function of the countryside. The really observant dismounted foxhunter soon learns, in a way that is denied to the horseman, who is preoccupied with riding and with getting himself across country, that there is a great deal more to the sport than controlling foxes by hunting and all the organization that goes into that process, more to it than the science of houndwork, more even than the tradition of several hundred years. It also forms part of an ecosystem, with men and women playing a part, if an indirect part, in prey–predator relationships. For, at a stretch of the imagination, the foxhound could be placed at the head of various food chains which go from the fox to rodents and birds and beetles and thence to other insects, plants and fruit. And from there to the soil—is it acid or lime?—and from there to the rock beneath—is it limestone or granite or sandstone?—which influences the whole ecosystem concerned.

This sense of ecology is borne in easily on the foxhunter, more particularly the foot follower; nature is simply recognizable to him, because he is doing what his remote ancestors did, he is fulfilling a natural activity. Being a devoted countryman, he is fascinated by the changing seasons. During the cub-hunting the acorns are fattening and the blackberries are ripe, the swallows are still with him and there are butterflies in the hedgerows. A few weeks later, with the season well under way, all is dormant; only an interrupted patchwork of grass covers the nakedness of the landscape, only ivy clothes the trees. By the time the whole season is drawing to a close, there are catkins on the hazels and yellow on the gorse, the trees and hedges are growing green and the birds are nesting again; and the foxes, whose lives are interwoven with this growth, are heading for parenthood. All such country lore is integral to the tradition and spirit of foxhunting.

Whether or not he is directly interested in farming, the foot-follower cannot truly earn the title foxhunter and countryman unless he has some grasp of agriculture and stock farming and is responsible enough out hunting to try to make amends where damage has been done. After all, there is very little of our countryside that has not been given over to farming. It has transformed the landscape, it dominates the natural ecology and it renders most lowland fox-hunting a slow and tortuous business. Anyway, if it were not for the landowners' and farmers' general devotion to the sport, hunting would have been committed to history long ago. It is up to those 'walking to hounds', no less than the horse-men, therefore, to keep off crops and to shut gates—at least. If he is in a country containing significant quantities of commercial woodland, then he should also interest himself in the forester's work.

Hunting on foot offers a wonderful opportunity for developing an eye for country—a sense of navigation, an instinct for the lie of the land and a built-in rural *sens du practicable*. This is best learned with the aid of map and compass. The most suitable map to carry out hunting is the 1-inch-to-a-mile Ordnance Survey map, which packs a host of information into this comparatively small scale. Some hunts have these maps made up expressly to contain their country, and folded into 4-inch squares, neat, sturdy, weather-resisting and handy for the pocket. If such specially designed hunt maps are not available, then it is a simple matter to make up one's own, with Fablon stuck over the surface to keep it firm and dry.

The 2½-inch-to-a-mile map gives considerably more detail. It shows practically every wood, pond, stream, track and farm building and states all their names, where they are known. Squares of 2½-inch map could be made up to cater for areas of country that might be hunted from any particular meet and folded into handy segments; but most foot enthusiasts regard that measure to be more trouble than it is worth. Perhaps the best compromise is to carry a '1-inch' map of your country (possibly two maps for better handiness), which you have composed with scissors and gum from a number of Ordnance Survey sheets, covered with Fablon and kept in a polythene case; and, on a wall at home, to hang a complete 2½-inch map, with the hunt boundary outlined and the principal meets circled off for quick reference. By discovering the names of landmarks from local followers on hunting days, by jotting them down lightly on his 1-inch map and by cross-checking them at home on his 2½-inch map, the foxhunter will soon build up a useful pattern of reference points.

From the beginning, he should study the language of the contours and other indications of relief and should get to know the conventional signs, so that he can 'set' his map with the help of a compass and can always read it at a glance without laborious reference to the marginal key; and his orientation will soon be so efficient that he will have little recourse to his compass and less to his map.

While he gains this happy familiarity with his country, he also learns a little about the hunt: the names of the Masters and the hunt staff and what their hunting careers have been; how, in principle, the hounds are bred and which are the prominent workers; how many couples are kept in kennels and how strong the young entry is; which days the dog-hounds are hunted and which days the bitches; and how many foxes have been accounted for in recent seasons. The comparatively static conditions of the cub-hunting season, when he will play his part in holding up cubs, will give him more chance to absorb information. He will develop his awareness of wind direction; he will learn to sum up the shape, size, density and character of each covert and to know the reputation of each as a foxholding covert. As the season progresses he will get to know the principal earths, both natural and artificial, and the areas of his country, which are good and which are poor for scent holding.

As he subconsciously fits the jigsaw of horn, hound music, voice and hoofbeat, the music of the chase will become more familiar to him each time he goes hunting, until eventually he can always read the progress of the hunt by sound, if he is close enough: the huntsman's cheery encouragement during the draw; a whimpering cry—a babbler or a single hound on the line; if it was a confident cry it will be followed by the huntsman's urging to ' 'Ark, 'ark, 'ark!' A long series of slow tied notes when the huntsman summons his hounds from a blank covert; or tumultuous hound music, followed by the doubling of the horn when the fox has broken covert, and the main body of them are away with him. 'For-or-or-or-orrard!' Then the holloa of a whipper-in or a follower. A sudden hush and the huntsman's patient 'Yert, y-ert'—a check. The crack of a whip, ' 'Ware riot!' A whipper-in rating a hound who's hunting the line in the wrong direction, ' 'Ware heel!' The long triumphant horn note with a flip at the end of it, which means gone to ground or a kill, and the single, rather plaintive, note that means home.

When the follower reaches covertside, he keeps as quiet and inconspicuous as a mouse, for he knows nothing starts a fox so quick as human voice and movement, and instinctively he tunes in for the whimper there, the duet there, the cracking whip, the receding hoofbeats, the high abandoned call of a young hound, the sonorous confidence of a fourth-season hound, the subtle intonations of horn and voice. All the time he watches for the fox, and, when hounds break covert on the line, he identifies the prominent workers, making a mental note, 'That's Ursula, there's Whimsical . . . and Dulcimer.' As he watches them feathering, he understands a little more how they work out their line; and, through the mosaic of knowledge he acquires, the chances are he will guess which way this fox will go, where his scent might be foiled and where all the other hazards are which hounds are likely to encounter. At a respectful distance he follows on and he sees. . . .

Here are some more golden rules for foot followers: never holloa till a fox has passed you, and then count twenty; always help the mounted followers by opening gates for them and by closing them when they have all passed through; take special responsibility for roadside gates; if you are in your car, always switch off your engine if hounds are near—petrol fumes make a hound sneeze, and he cannot hunt and sneeze at the same time!

If it is done conscientiously and wisely and with a sportsman's sense of fun, it is doubtful whether any pursuit can give, at once, such exhilaration, exercise and intimacy with the countryside as following hounds on foot.

Chapter 13

Hunting on the
Fells of Lakeland

FOXHUNTING on the fells of Lakeland is quite a different matter from fox-hunting across the pasture and plough of lowland England. Horses are not used—for those fells rise, at angles inclining from 40 to 80°, up to heights well over 3,000 feet above the sea. They are formed of volcanic rock, sloping down and away under the broad smooth lakes of Windermere, Crummock, Loweswater, Ennerdale, Derwentwater, Buttermere, Wastwater, Bassenthwaite and Ullswater, and into ghylls, steep-sided and rock-strewn, with bubbling waterfalls marking their ascent and punctuated by lone trees, oak, ash and thorn, contriving a life from the recesses of the precipitous stone.

Considering the lure of Cumbria's beauty and the Lakeland Tourist Board's concerted efforts to attract visitors, the area is remarkably unspoilt. If you are following one of the six packs of fell hounds, you may, soon after your initial climb, become divided from the remainder of the field, and you may find yourself alone, with no human habitation in sight and only nature's sounds to break the hush; you may well decide, in company with many others, that this is the loveliest of England's unspoilt areas. For it is, to a great extent, the backcloth to hunting in the Lakeland fells that renders it uniquely thrilling—the grand sensation of gazing from open heights to deep waters, embowered with ancient trees, and across to the distant slopes opposite, which are one day a patchwork of purple and gold, broken by a rainbow, and the next day one great cloak of snow.

Then there is the ever-changing scene all around you. Here there may be bracken frost-bitten to a deep coppery hue, with unseen becks tinkling beneath it; there, past a larch spinney, to a patch of heather, interspersed with blaeberry, from which grouse explode and as quickly vanish (their nesting hens and young are a sporting prey for quick foxes); here a slope thick with shale fragments (fell hounds are bred and 'entered' to climb their treacherous slip); there a boggy tract, with sphagnum moss, a rosy-verdant squelch, and bent-grass and cotton-grass leaning against the wind; here a sprawling outcrop of boulders concealing one of those cavernous 'borrans', which are among the foxes' favourite refuges; and, suddenly, now to an expanse of vivid pasture, where Herdwick, Rough fell, Kendal-type and Sweldale sheep are grazing—and carrion crows and buzzards are circling overhead (hoping, perhaps, that a sheep will die).

Sheep farming is the dalesman's first occupation, and in the spring and early summer the lambs are a ready prey for vixens with cubs to feed. Chinks in the defences of hen-runs, too, are soon discovered by those extra-wily hill foxes. So, three days a week, from late September till May, the fell packs are out culling the fox population. A fell huntsman who can regularly kill foxes is indeed a hero to the farmers.

Nor would any of them disagree with that big sheep farmer, who was also chairman of the Westmorland Agricultural Executive Committee, when he declared recently that 'hunting is literally the only effective form of fox control we have in the fells'. When, as a wild life journalist, I asked Mr Jack Chard, who was, until 1973, Conservator to the Forestry Commission for north-west England, whether foxes were having an adverse effect on the attempts being made to cultivate and diversify the wild life of Grizedale Forest, he replied, 'No! Almost entirely due to the efforts of the local fell hounds—they are not.' (Grizedale's nearest hunt is the Coniston.) The role of huntsman was a reserved occupation during the Second World War; the hunts are now regarded by the Ministry of Agriculture as 'fox destruction societies' and are duly rewarded for handing in the brushes.

However, hunting in Lakeland is important, not only for the livelihood of the shepherd and the chicken farmer, and to preserve the balance of nature, it also remains the sporting dalesman's firmest tradition. Many of their families have followed the hounds and have joined in the post-hunting jollities—the 'tatie pot', the beer and the hunting-song choruses—for ten generations and more. It is not known when foxhunting began in the Lake Listrict, but when Hutchinson wrote this note on the inhabitants of Loweswater in his *History of Cumberland*, published in 1794, the roots were clearly already deep:

'The people live in harmony, and they express contentment. The peasantry have one enjoyment here, which is prohibited to most men of their class. Through the liberality of their lords, a hound is kept in nearly every house. Two or three inhabitants take licence to kill game and to command the pack. As soon as harvest is in, an honest cobbler shifts his garb and becomes huntsman and, every second or third morning, collects the dogs and calls the sportsmen to the field; the cottagers climb the mountainside, where they can view the chase and, without much exertion, enjoy the pleasure of the hunt; after which they retire with cheerful minds and invigorated constitutions to their peaceful homes. . . .'

Except for the huntsman himself, who wears a scarlet coat and black velvet cap with his collar and tie, brown breeches and woollen stockings, and his 'whip', wearing something even more subdued, the fell-hunters do not dress up. They wear stout ankle-boots and tweed caps, breeches, knickerbockers or thick trousers, and anoraks, oilskins or gabardines; and they carry their thumb in a hazel crook. Their subscriptions and 'caps' are diminutive, and for the most part voluntary, and bear no comparison with the hefty levies imposed by the 'southern' or 'low-country' hunts, or 'fancy packs', as some fell-hunters are wont to call them. For there are no hunt horses to maintain, no 'wire fund' to be sweetened, no crops to be ridden over, no loose stock to be compensated for and virtually no damage to be repaired. To raise money to maintain the pack and pay the huntsman, they stage dances, beauty queen contests, tombola evenings and sponsored walks.

Except perhaps when they unwind at an inn after their day's hunting, they are men of scant words. Whether farmers or quarrymen, shepherds or cobblers, publicans or roadmen, they are true sons of the fells. A few of their elders have never travelled farther in their lives than Penrith or Carlisle. Out hunting they are joined by other local inhabitants, such as solicitors, vets, accountants and doctors, who speak their language; and, in the milder seasons by a sprinkling of tourists, who, it is hoped, *try* to speak their language. As for foxes, they are at once the dalesman's enemies and guides, villains and heroes. He loves nothing better than stout challengers.

The fell fox was once almost a distinct breed. He weighed up to 25 pounds, and so grey was his coat, wiry his frame and long his stride, that the local people called him a 'greyhound fox'. They still do but with pursed lips and headshakes; for there are fewer of his kind now—the average weight being more like 15 or 16 pounds. During the nineteenth century, when the neighbouring lowland hunts imported foxes to increase their stocks, the populations spread towards the fells and crossed the smaller reds with the 'greyhounds', so that the 'typical' fell fox become a somewhat more diminutive and less adventurous creature.

As befits his rugged open habitat, he still shows greater stamina and strength and a more flowing stride as he scales the gradients or threads his way along the steep watercourses and scree-beds. The fell fox can climb like a cat and can squeeze through the narrowest of entrances.

Apart from their superior agility, cross-country performance and capacity for survival, their characteristics are much the same as those of their lowland cousins. They mate in late December to early January, and in March the vixen gives birth to the cubs, which are ready for a diet of lamb or chicken by May. The hill fox lives mainly on beetles, frogs and voles, and also, whenever they can find them, rabbits, leverets, game birds, poultry and rats.

The populations have increased enormously. 100 years ago a fell pack might kill 10 brace a season; by 1920 25 brace, and now perhaps 35 to 50 brace.

Fell foxes spend most of the day at their kennel, sleeping off the meal they hunted at night and ate at dawn. This kennel is usually on the fell side, a cliff ledge ('bink' or 'benk'), a pile of boulders or a patch of bracken or heather. The less wary will lie up in the valley. Hounds, setting forth in the middle of the morning, pick up the 'drag', the trail which the fox leaves between his hunting grounds and his kennel, where it is hoped to 'put him off' the fell, as hunters call it. Trusting their great strength and stamina, most Lakeland foxes seek safety in flight on the open hill; some will find refuge in a river, a few will make for a lowland earth or badger's set, others for the underground cave fastness or a 'borran' and some for a 'benk' or 'bink', the ledge of a cliff-face.

This can be dangerous for hounds. On the same day that I enjoyed a day with the Ullswater, a delicate rescue operation was carried out on the nearby Helvellyn range. Three days before, the Ullswater's fox had piloted hounds along a cliff-top and had then taken a diagonal route along a benk. Only Rascal, a three-season bitch and award winner at Rydal, the largest of the Lake District hound shows, followed him down the benk. Although the ledge narrowed, the fox moved on, but Rascal could neither advance nor turn, and the huntsman and his friends were unable to reach her. A storm set in, and it was not for three days that Rascal, starving and shivering, was brought to safety by a team from the local Outward Bound school.

The average rainfall in the Lake District is very high (which helps scent); but, rather than the steady drizzle so familiar to Highlanders, here fine spells are interspersed with torrents. Snowstorms are frequent in mid-winter, and, over the years, hounds, huntsmen and followers have suffered terrible disasters when heavy falls have occurred. Mist is probably the most usual hazard: when the vapours converge in earnest, fell hunters lose not only the hunt but every land-mark they know and the cry of hounds becomes their only guide.

'Breed a hound to suit your country', insist the pundits, and there is no doubt that a hound of somewhat special character is required for the steep shaly gra-dients, boulder-strewn crags, stone walls and precipitous water-courses of the Cumbrian fells. The conventional lowland foxhound, whose model is seen at Peterborough each July, is not by any means fully suited to Lakeland. For those daunting slopes, a hound needs to be as rangy and wiry as can be. The fell hound experts say his bone should be light with little flesh on it, for he has to be really fit and fast to get up to those hill foxes before they find a borran. Not all Lakeland venerers concur on the degree. (At times that I have visited them, it was clear that the Blencathra, the Coniston and the Melbreak showed a good deal more rib than the Ullswater.)

Fell hounds are not urged to their work as conventional hounds are urged by their huntsman. They must work on their own all day. So one of their main characteristics is reliable independence. They hunt in twos and threes.

The fell hound's character and his conformation have evolved as a result of much trial and error over the past century and a half, blood from other hounds, besides the mounted packs and the Welsh having been grafted onto the old strains. His big well-placed shoulder gives mountain strength and combines with a lengthy humerus and long flexy pastern, to minimize concussion when careering down the gradients and jumping walls. He shows a sound hare foot to grip the rocks and a very well let-down hock and usefully developed second thigh for uphill impulsion and speed.

Fell huntsmen set a particularly high premium on cry—'giving mouth'—for, much more often than in lowland countries, their music is the only sign to indicate their whereabouts. In most fell-hunting countries there is no limestone, and, except across expanses of thick bracken, scenting conditions are generally good; but, since a long cold 'drag' must frequently be puzzled out, hounds must be low scenting.

In the old days fell hounds were kept by individual farmers, shepherds and others all year round and were brought to agreed meeting places on hunting days; and, although they are now concentrated at kennels for the hunting season, they still return to their walkers between May and September. Those walkers retain hounds from puppyhood to retirement (in their seventh or eighth season) when they have the option of keeping them in old age rather than see them put down. At a meet you will often see individual hounds break away from the pack to greet their 'summer masters' and, when hounds are drawing, you hear walkers addressing their hounds with 'Good lad, Cracker, good lass, Melody, Goo-arn, then!'

So impressed have some foreigners been by their performance that visitors from as far afield as Canada, Finland, France, Holland, South Africa and the United States have bought hounds from the Lake District packs. The College Valley bred partly from fell strains, and the Lochaber and Sunart Farmers', a footpack, formed in the western Highlands in 1970, to help offset the banning of the gin trap, went automatically to Lakeland for their drafts.

Foxes are bolted more effectively from the 'borrans' of the fell than from the earths of the lowlands; and the little Bedlington–Border crosses that are bred for the job, some brindled, some honey-coloured, some silky-coated, some wiry, are very quick and quite fearless. The basic breed of Lakeland working terrier was man's servant, so they say, before the Romans came. A single terrier will keep a fox at bay all day and all night if he cannot bolt him. These terriers are an integral part of each hunt, and there is always a good turn-out of terrier men available to help. Fell hunters love the 'bolt': it is the moment for terrier owners to show off their charges, where hound speed may be seen close to, and an occasion to catch up and recuperate. Sometimes you see 40 or more people round a 'borran' (or 'hole', if earthy) and, when the terriers go down, the sporting cry is given, 'Stand back, stand back! Give fox a chance!'

Steeped in tradition and colourful personalities, the fell hunts are very proud of their history and of their heroes. In terms of present identity, the Melbreak, whose country lies in West Cumberland, is the oldest. The Melbreak was founded by William Pearson of Bannockrout, in 1807. His huntsman, William Collingwood—'Old Collin'—carried the horn for over 50 years. Of the hunt's steep record of marathon runs, the longest was in the 1880s when a fox took them through 13 parishes, in Cumberland, Westmorland and Lancashire. Their longest Masterships were those of John Benson (1865–1917) and Major Ernest Iredale (1917–65).

The Blencathra's country is immediately to the east of the Melbreak's, with

Bassenthwaite Lake as the two hunts' northern dividing mark. The Blencathra boast John Peel who hunted their country, besides what is now the Cumberland, from 1798 until his death in 1854. John Crozier, a protégé of Peel's, who founded the Blencathra in 1840 and was in charge of them for no less than 63 years, bred from the famous old huntsman's pack. Here is a description of Peel by a friend:

'He used to wear a grey coat with buttons at the back, what we call a lap coat. Tall and straight, a bit of a rough diamond, and as cute and keen a man as ever dealt in horse flesh, he had a good heart under his grey coat and was a friend of every farmer in a country that was overrun with foxes. He rode the shortest stirrup ever I saw a huntsman have; his knees were very nearly up with the saddle of Dunny, the brown cross-breed he usually rode when I saw him: clean leg, plenty of bone, a fast Cumberland nag. But more often Peel was to be seen on his feet, striding. . . . '

70 or 80 years ago, Jim Dalton became another legendary Blencathra huntsman, and Johnny Richardson, who escaped from the Germans after being captured at Tobruk, has built himself a similar reputation. His service was mostly under Mr Alan Peck (Master from 1948 to 1971). Richardson also has a close understanding with Sir Alfred Goodson, and there is much College Valley blood at his kennels at Threlkeld. The Blencathra catch upwards of 70 foxes a season, and how the old chant rises in the pub after this hunt have enjoyed a good run with a kill at the end:

'. . . *D'ye ken that bitch whose tongue was death?*
D'ye ken her sons of peerless faith?
D'ye ken that a fox, with his last breath,
Cursed them all as he died in the morning?

Yes, I ken John Peel and Ruby, too,
Ranter and Royal and Bellman as true,
From the drag to the chase, from the chase to the view,
From the view to the death in the morning.'

The Coniston, who kennel at Greenbank, Ambleside, above Lake Windermere, have a strong family tradition—with the Logans as Masters and the Chapmans as huntsmen. The present Master, Bruce Logan, has held office since 1954. His great-great-great-uncle, Anthony Gaskarth of Coniston Hall, a farmer and a butcher, too, who—after angrily seizing two hounds from a Duddon client in payment of a meat debt in 1825—bred up the forebears of this famous pack. In 1908, John and Bruce Logan, Gaskarth's great-nephews, arranged to amalgamate their pack with another private pack called the Coniston, of which the Rev. E. M. Reynolds had been Master since 1881, and to form a new subscription pack under the same name.

The Chapman family boast as strong a Coniston tradition as the Logans.

Anthony Chapman (whose stride and energy in the autumn of his life are quite astounding) gave up as huntsman in 1976. His great-great-uncle, Tom Chapman, came from the Patterdale (one of the hunts that merged into the Ullswater just over a century ago) to be huntsman in the 1850s, founding a reputation not easy to follow. A visiting reporter wrote this towards the end of Tom's term:

> 'He's the best huntsman in England; if you'd seen him chanting hounds as they were questing, it would have fair lifted the cap off your head; it went to your very soul, there was such grand music in his tones. When he was huntsman at Patterdale he was courting a girl at Kendal, whom he afterwards married. He often left the Patterdale kennels at ten o'clock at night after a day's hunting, walked the 20 miles to Kendal to see his sweetheart and then walked back the next day. That's the stuff that Chapmans are made of . . . '

Though the Eskdale and Ennerdale, whose country lies against the coast, south of the Melbreak's, were not established until the 1850s, they can trace their history back to 1785, when Mr Lamplugh Irton, of Irton Hall, kept the first regular pack in the Eskdale district. His hunt was amalgamated, in 1900, with the Ennerdale to compose a subscription pack under the Mastership of Tommy Dobson (known popularly and famously as 'La'al Tommy') who had by then completed no less than 53 years as huntsman, beginning at his own expense with a single couple of hounds, when he was a young miller. From miller and huntsman to Master in the Edwardian era—it has been said, and with truth, that 'English democracy began in the Lake District'. Dobson was served by another great fell huntsman, Willie Porter, who went on to be Master from 1910 to 1952; and now his son, Jack Porter, is Master and his grandson, Edmund, is huntsman.

Next after John Peel's, the name Joe Bowman—of the Ullswater—towers above all others in the collective biographies of the fell huntsmen. Taking over the horn from the Ullswater's first huntsman, Abe Pattinson, in 1879, Joe Bowman—'Old Hunty', as he was called—remained in office until 1911, when he was obliged to retire on medical grounds. After a rest cure, he was huntsman again from 1914 to 1923—completing a full 40 seasons altogether. Bowman's 20- and 30-mile runs —some of them undertaken when he was in his 70s—were renowned throughout Cumbria, and he would turn out at any time of night—often after a long day's hunting by fixture—for farmers that were woken in the night by the sounds of raiders on their chickens. Taking his hounds, without any hesitation, to the scene, he would hunt the fox past first light and, if necessary, right through the day.

It was not simply that Bowman ranked with Chapman, Porter and Dalton as a huntsman and houndsman, but he was also a grand mixer and humorist and the leader of the fun when the fox was killed and the singing began. Considering the hunt is the hub of social life in a fell country, such qualities are precious. In the pubs around Ullswater, the veterans still talk of Bowman, over 'tatie and beer', as though he were still alive, and sing of him too:

'We're away to the meet and a hunting we'll go
For nothing's so sweet as the glad tally-ho,
With the Ullswater's hounds we'll travel along,
Awaking the country with laughter and song.
The fire's on the hearth
And good cheer abounds,
We'll drink to Joe Bowman
And his Ullswater hounds.'

Joe Weir, who followed Bowman for 43 seasons, is still cherished as one of the very great old fell hunters; and now the Ullswater's huntsman is Dennis Barrow, who served a 9-year apprenticeship as whipper-in to the Coniston. The Hasell and Lowther families have always been the principal backers of the pack. The joint-Masters are Capt. the Hon. Anthony Lowther, whose ancestor, 'The Yellow Earl', Lord Lonsdale, headed the hunt's first subscription list in 1873, and Mr John Bulman, who was previously Master and huntsman of the Windermere harriers for 15 seasons. The Ullswater have two countries, one around the lake, between the Helvellyn range (west) and the M6 (east) and the other in the Pennines, around, and to the east of Appleby. They kennel at Glenridding, by Helvellyn.

The most recently established of the Lakeland fell packs—founded by Mr Thomas Robinson, of Bainsbank in 1919—is the Lunesdale, who hunt an expansive tract in the Pennine foothills between, and south of, the two Ullswater areas. It includes the old Sedbergh country which, up to 1905 (the Sedbergh's year of birth), had been the Ullswater's. Unfortunately a western portion of the Lunesdale country is spoilt by the M6. Although young, this hunt has gathered all the great spirit of the older packs. A committee runs it, the chairman being Mr Harold Watson, with Mr Oliver Berry as his joint-secretary and John Nicholson as huntsman.

But for the motorway, all these hunt countries remain marvellously unspoilt. They can indeed be little changed since foxhunting first began here. Even the walls—or most of them—have been up for a century and a half.

The hunts are helped and advised by their own central committee of fell hunts, who have a link with the Masters of Foxhounds' Association. The committee's secretary is Mr Oliver Berry, of Ellergreen, Kendal, also a joint-secretary of the Lunesdale.

Visitors to the hunts are welcome, provided they are quiet and observe the 'countryside code'. They are encouraged to pay a generous 'cap' each time they hunt. Hounds are as expensive to feed here as anywhere else. Huntsmen are only paid about £35 a week, a tiny wage considering the hours they keep and the responsibilities they shoulder (and, with no employment at the kennels during the summer, they must then find other work, such as helping on a farm or wall repairing).

Car followers are rarely welcome. Especially in autumn and spring, they are

Hounds at exercise

20 Michael Farrin, Huntsman of the Quorn,
with hounds at exercise near the kennels

21 Judging the two couples class at the annual
Show in July

The kennels

22 A pall of steam over the South
Pembrokeshire hounds at post-hunt feeding time

23 Bitches of the Galway Blazers on their beds

Sussex meet in springtime

24 The Crawley and Horsham at Shipley

Devotion

25 Captain R. E. Wallace, Master and
Huntsman of the Heythrop, with his hounds

The hunt

26 Huntsman Harry Goddard putting hounds in to draw after a foggy meet at Lilley during the Enfield Chase Hunt

27 Hounds crossing Ford Brook and screaming away into the distance during the afternoon Vale of Aylesbury Hunt from Haddenham

Duties in the hunting field

28   The North Shropshire Hunt Secretary
collecting caps

Duties in the hunting field

29 A Cottesmore gate-shutter checks the catch
after 'the field' have passed through

Australia

30   The Melbourne Hunt coming through a
eucalyptus grove

usually to be seen, bumper to bumper, immediately below the point where hounds are working. Apart from the fact that they frequently head any foxes pointing off the fell and are inclined to fill the hounds' noses with their exhaust fumes, they are a curse to other road users. Anyhow, who, boxed up on a lakeside road, albeit armed with a pair of fieldglasses, can hope to earn the magic of fell hunting?

For this can surely only be sensed, on the heights, with the smell of bracken and boggy moss in the nostrils, within earshot of the hounds and their huntsman? Every time I hear the sounds of a fell hunt, I sense they belong—with as strong a claim as the buzzards' cries—to the hill; and I am sure that they mark the spirit that binds the dalesman to the fell as no other force has ever done.

Chapter 14
The Irish Scene

GROUSE SHOOTING in Scotland, sailing in the Carribean, safaris in east Africa, skiing in Switzerland...and foxhunting in Ireland: that synonymity has rung truer than ever since the agriculture of the Midlands swung so heavily in favour of the plough.

Having also enjoyed the sport on the Continent, in America and the whole of Great Britain, I believe that Ireland remains the finest foxhunting land in the world. It is the first place that springs to mind for a hunting holiday: firstly, by virtue of the spirit of the country people, whose love of horses, hounds and the thrill of the chase seem to lie a little deeper in the blood than with most other peoples of the world; then the quality and general performances of their horses, bred foremost as hunters, have always been the envy of every foreign judge of horseflesh; on account, too, of the Emerald Isle's lovely rich pasture—so beneficial to horses and cattle—and the limestone base and the gravelly brooks that help it grow. Except in the non-hunting north-west, there is so little plough that the heart of the hunting man or woman, flying into Cork or Shannon, delights at such an unbroken sea of grass.

The landscape is a foxhunter's paradise. Gently rising and falling, whichever way you look, the vivid pasture is intersected by a fine variety of enclosure: hedges, banks, limestone walls, thorny doubles—banks, with a ditch fore and aft and a hedge on top—bullfinches, timber or water. The visitor never knows quite what he will face next. There is wire, of course, far too much wire, but Irish foxhunters know how to circumnavigate it. Huge areas of conifer plantations have grown up during the past quarter of a century. Although there is comparatively little natural woodland, the English visitor is at once impressed at seeing large expanses of gorse wherever he looks. Those Irish nineteenth-century foxhunters knew the key to fox populations. Whyte Melville recorded that Sam Reynell, a famous Master of the Meath, found that country without a single gorse covert, and 'left it with 30 or 40 sure finds'.

Hunting apart, the Irish landscape is lovely to ride over. In one direction or another, mountains form a backcloth to the rolling pattern of grass enclosures. For those familiar with Britain's neatly clipped enclosure, there is a delightful wildness and unkemptness about the Irish farmland, where gorse wastes and thorn thickets thrive unchecked, where bewhiskered hedges ramble and lean.

The Hunt Countries of IRELAND

There are no motorways, little traffic, few railways and scant sign of urbanization. As can be seen from the accompanying map, the Irish hunts are concentrated largely in the south and the east and not in the north-west, where the bulk of the arable land is.

The history of Irish hunting follows much the same general pattern as in Britain: the deer was once the king of venery. Then, following the seventeenth and early part of the eighteenth centuries—in which the ascendancy squires dominated the scene with their private harrier packs—the foxhunting cult caught the imagination and remained supreme from the second half of the eighteenth century onwards. In the beginning foxhunting did much to bring landlord and peasant together and to help soften political bitternesses.

However, right up to the time of independence, it also served to accentuate the deep feelings of resentment over landownership, and to promote Land League agitation; and, in the nineteenth century, demonstrations were so bitter and the warnings sent to Masters so convincing that, in many parts of Ireland, hunting was frequently cancelled or was suspended for long periods.

Feelings about landownership and tenantry still bedevil Irish hunting. While private landowners are restricted to comparatively small acreages, the Land Commission have allotted numerous small plots in the east and south to aspiring farmers from the non-hunting west. Not having been brought up in a foxhunting country, many of these *émigrés* show little sympathy for charging foxhunters and quite frequently deny them access; and, of course, the division into small plots not only means that Masters must negotiate with a great many different owners, but it also means more wire.

There is another feature distinguishing the character of Irish hunting from British, and that is money. Irish hunts are less lavishly backed, which is why you often find the Anglo-Irish and Englishmen and Americans at the head of affairs.

In summarizing the hunts as they were in 1977, I shall begin at the heart of Ireland—at Westmeath—and I shall work southwards.

During the seventeenth century, a large area of Co. Westmeath was hunted by the first Lord Longford from Pakenham Hall. Sam Reynell, who afterwards hunted the Meath for 20 seasons, kept hounds at Condilever, up to the time of the potato famine. The county pack was founded by Sir Richard Levinge in 1854. In 1976 Major Hesse and Mr J. C. Beveridge joined Major Patrick Tandy in the Mastership. John Smith has been huntsman since 1966. In terms of variety and unspoilt beauty I believe the Westmeath possess as sporting a country as any in Ireland.

Adjacent, in north Meath, is a small country, the Ballymacad, whose tradition began in 1792. For the first half of the nineteenth century their huntsman was a Jorrocks-like character and famous fox catcher called Charley Bowles. The present hunt was started in 1885 by a Mr Kilroy. In 1947-8, they had Major Chatty Hilton-Green, of Cottesmore fame, as Master. This was between the 3 Masterships of Capt. Speid-Soote. Mrs C. Cameron took over in 1961 and Peter Donaghue has served at the kennels since 1940.

60 miles by 30 miles, the Meath country lies adjacent, in the west, to the Ballymacad and Westmeath, reaching eastwards almost to Dublin. John Watson, ex-Hussar, leading light in the polo world, son of the equally famous Robert Watson of the Carlow, and described as 'the greatest Master that the Emerald Isle ever produced', had the Meath from 1891 to 1908. When John Watson took over from the Earl of Fingall, the pack had just been decimated by rabies, so he built up a new lot, based on the Milton blood at his father's kennels. The kennels

at Nugentstown, Kells, were built in Watson's time. Mr G. H. Kruger took command in 1971 and was joined by his wife in 1976. Mrs de Stacpoole is secretary.

Between the Meath and the sea lies the Louth, whose strongest influence since the seventeenth century, when Cromwell gave Lisrenny to that family, has been the Filgates. Mr Billy Filgate, who took over in 1947, carried the horn until 1973. Then M. McKeever took over as huntsman and Mr R. W. McKeever joined in the Mastership. Miss Mary Shirley has been secretary since 1959. This is another delightful, rambling bank-and-ditch country with less than 25% plough. The kennels are at Lisrenny.

The Louth country measures about 45 by 15 miles, while the Kildare, to Dublin's south-west, with 36 miles north to south and 22 east to west, is the largest in Ireland. The kennels are at Jigginstown, near Naas. Founded by Thomas Conolly late in the eighteenth century, this hunt boasts an impressive roll of Masters, including Sir John Kennedy, John La Touche, Lord Clonmell, Major Talbot-Ponsonby and Major Michael Beaumont, and as many famous professional huntsmen, too. The drive, tenacity and fox-catching record of this pack in the nineteenth century earned them the nickname of the 'killing Kildares'. An American, Thomas Fields Long, became Master and huntsman in the late 1960s and was joined in 1973 by Mr Bertram Firestone. 3 years later Mr J. P. N. Parker took Mr Long's place. Capt. the Hon. Patrick Conolly-Carew is Field Master, and a most popular and dedicated Co. Kildare man, Jack Hartigan, was huntsman from 1946 till 1976, since when Mr Parker has carried the horn. T. H. M. Reeves is the secretary.

The Shillelagh and District, situated between the Kildare and the sea, was originally hunted privately by the Fitzwilliam family, then, under its present name, by the farmers on a committee basis. Messrs James Kerr and Richard Woods support Mr Patrick Kilbride (who also carries the horn) in the acting Mastership. It is a rugged mountainous country, running down to the Carlow plain in the south, where they march with the Wicklow, Ireland's smallest country. Founded in 1901 by hare hunters, the Wicklow were entered to fox in 1932. Their kennels are at Raheenagunan, home of the present Master, Mr J. F. Webb. Miss Mary Webb took on the duties of Hon. Secretary to the Wicklow in 1973.

South-west of the Shillelagh and District lies the Carlow country. John Watson, of Ballydarton, whose father had kept a pack to hunt wolves, became first Master of the Carlow in 1808, continuing in office until 1868, when he handed over to his son, Robert, who had already proved an outstanding huntsman. (It was Robert's son, John, who had the Meath for 17 years around the turn of this century.) In 1900, Robert sold his hounds to the Carlow Hunt Club. Mr W. E. Grogan was at the helm for 20 years before Mrs Hall began her famous innings, with Grogan still carrying the horn and breeding the hounds. In 1950 she was succeeded by her son-in-law, Hardy Eustace Duckett, who hunted hounds. The Carlow country is reputed to have the biggest double banks in Ireland. The hounds were disbanded a few years ago, but the Carlow Hunt Club still flourishes under the guidance of Mrs Alexander, of Milford.

Going west again we come to the Leix, Laios or Queen's County, a country mainly of bank enclosure and very little plough but fairly heavy going in parts. It is excellent scenting. Lord Portarlington had the first going concern in the country around 1815, and the Hamilton-Stubbers' long association with the hunt began 50 years later. Mr Desmond Lalor has been Master and huntsman since 1964, and Miss Robinson secretary since 1952.

West of the Leix, in north Tipperary and east Galway, is the Ormond, whose kennels are at Modreeney house in Co. Tipperary. The hunt was named by Lord Lismore, who started hunting the country in the 1770s. Having a great many Anglo-Irish landowners in the country, the Ormond suffered especially badly from Land League agitation, and hunting was stopped for long periods in the late nineteenth century and early twentieth century; but this trouble subsided when a Catholic, Sir William Austin, became Master in 1912. One of the finest amateur huntsmen, Major Bobby Peel, came in from the Blazers to carry the Ormond horn in 1950, and he established a beautiful pack of hounds there before moving on to the South Dorset in 1952, when he was relieved by Major Preston. Capt. D. Swan, who is also huntsman, was appointed Master in 1973. Mr J. F. Calahan, Jr, is the secretary.

William Barton, of Grove, began hunting the Suir Valley—to the south of the Leix and the Ormond—around 1808; and thus began the Tipperary. Between 1840 and 1843 the Jack Mytton-like Third Marquess of Waterford was Master of the 'Gallant Tipps', but he left for his own county after having his kennels maliciously burned down. Other famous Masters were Richard Burke (1912–17), Sir Thomas Ainsworth (1928–32), and Capt. Evan Williams (1953–72). Mrs Sylvia Masters, who was joint-Master and huntsman from 1935 to 1953, was the first woman ever to ride 100 point-to-point winners. The kennels are at Tullmaine. Mr M. R. C. Higgens acts as Master for the committee; he is also huntsman. Mr J. Carrigan has been secretary since 1969.

Another excellent, if small, country lying north-west of the Tipperary, is the North Tipperary, a hunt which was formed after the Second World War. Their kennels are at Kilteelagh, near Nenagh, the home of Lt-Col. J. A. Dene, whose wife has been Master and huntsman since 1974. The secretary is Mrs Powell. Opposite, on the Tipperary's eastern side, the North Kilkenny country was fashioned from a tract known as the Freshford, which was lent to Major John Alexander by the Kilkenny Hunt Club in 1931. It is a wild sparsely populated and particularly good scenting country, with little wire. In 1971, Mr Loughlin Bowe —and in 1975 Mr Michael Dillon—joined Mr John Murphy in the Mastership. They also hunt hounds. Mr Michael O'Reilly is the secretary.

The Kilkenny, who are astride the River Nore, date back to the eighteenth century, being founded by John and Richard Power. It was the first established county pack in the south of Ireland. The Powers went in for high-class English blood and probably had the best pack in the Isle, a tradition which has persisted. Famous Kilkenny Masters were Col. Hartropp (1880–2), the Earl of Dysart (1882–4), Col. Frank Chaplain (1876–80), who hunted hounds himself with Ben Capell—afterwards a famous Belvoir huntsman—whipping in; Sir Hercules Langrishe (1890–1908), Ikey Bell (1908–21), whose celebrated career began with the Galway Blazers in 1903, Major Dermot McCalmont (1921–68) and his son, Major Victor McCalmont, who joined him in 1949 and who remains Master and huntsman. The kennels, at his home Mount Juliet, Thomastown, are still the envy of the foxhunting world. Over the years the Kilkenny have taken a great share of the prizes at Clonmel, the national Irish hound show. Mr G. A. Salmon has been secretary since 1950.

South of the Carlow, with a long coastal border and a country of about 30 square miles, are the Wexford, a hunt started by Col. Spigot, of Slevoy Castle, in 1780 as a private pack. James Harvey took over in 1841, and his family have always been closely connected with the hunt. The following year, David Beatty, of Borodale (grandfather of the First World War admiral, whose brother was Master of the Island in the Victorian era) took over. Fell huntsman and writer, C. N. de Courcy Parry (Dalesman), carried the horn during the 1927–8 season and became quite a legend in Wexford for his daredevil behaviour. That role is now fulfilled by Mr Newton Popplewell, the Master. The secretary is Mr A. J. B. Boyd. Also in Co. Wexford is the Bree, founded in 1888, whose Master, since 1965, has been Mr J. A. Spring. Miss Judy Spring turns hounds to her father, Messrs Jim and John Mernagh are the secretaries and the kennels are at the Master's house.

North of them, also against the seaboard, the Island cover 31 by 32 miles of Co. Wexford, a nice light country, even at its wettest, with stone-faced banks. It was hunted by the Esmonde family from early in the seventeenth century, but Mr William Bolton really started the Island, as we know it today, early in the nineteenth century. On Bolton's death the hounds and country were lent to Lord Milton, afterwards Earl Fitzwilliam. The famous Robert Watson hunted the country for him as the 'Carlow and Island' until 1904, when Lord Fitzwilliam, who obtained drafts from the Milton and Fitzwilliam, transferred hounds to Coollatin. They are now at Ballynadara, Enniscorthy. Mr G. Chapman, who also hunts hounds, joined Mr Kevin Byrne in the Mastership in 1973 and is now in sole charge. Mrs C. J. Skrine is the secretary.

Under the Wexford, Kilkenny and Tipperary countries, east of the Comeragh Mountains, and against some 20 miles of the south coast, is the Waterford hunt, an area measuring about 15 by 20 miles. Edward Fitzgerald was founder of this hunt in 1840. Then the Third Lord Waterford, who, as I said, was Master of the Tipperary from 1840 to 1843, purchased Fitzgerald's hounds together with Henry Briscoe's to form a new pack in his own county, and this was known for many years as Lord Waterford's or the Curraghmore (his home). Ever since the hunt was founded, his family, the Beresfords, have played a big part in running it. The present Secretary of the Irish Masters of Foxhounds' Association, Mr Richard Russell, whose father was Master (1914–23 and 1926–7) was himself in command here from 1927 to 1957. The Masters now are Messrs J. S. Rohan, who also carries the horn, and Major Hugh Dawnay. The kennels are at Mr Rohan's house, Woodhouse, Stradbally. Dr P. J. Shanahan has been secretary since 1959.

Going west again, beyond the Tipperary, are the Scarteen, which I have described in Chapter 5, so I shall now turn to the West Waterford, a well-foxed sporting country, with small enclosures, about 20 miles square. Founded by the Holroyd Smith family in the middle of the eighteenth century, this hunt has had several lady Masters: Miss Musgrave, afterwards Mrs Glen Browne (1927–31); Miss Anne Hickman, afterwards Mrs P. G. Grey (1937–9), who had Miss Robin Walters (Mrs Hall Watt) turning hounds to her; and Miss Anne Gregory, with Miss Hickman (1939–40). The famous amateur huntsman, Major W. W. B. Scott, was Master here from 1947 to 1949, immediately before he went to the Portman. In 1953, Mrs Morgan, of Bishopstown, became huntsman, her husband joining her in the Mastership in 1954, and hounds are kennelled at their house, Bishopstown, Lismore.

Adjacent to the West Waterford, in Co. Cork, is the United Hunt Club, which was formed in 1871, when the Fifth Earl of Shannon bought and amalgamated two packs of hounds then kennelled in that county. Mrs J. A. Russell was joint-Master with Mr John Murphy from 1888 to 1889. Having bought the hounds from the committee, he was sole Master from 1889 to 1895. Mr Russell's son (father of the present Secretary of the Irish Masters of Foxhounds' Association) was Master from 1923 to 1925. 17 miles north to south and 26 east to west, the United, describing their country, tell us that 'in some cases the banks are very narrow and some stone faced; not much wire'. Mr Van der Vater, whose huntsman is T. Meade, was appointed Master in 1968, and the kennels are at his home, Midleton. The secretary is Mr D. J. Daly.

The Avondhu, a smallish country, sandwiched between the Tipperary, the Duhallow, the United and the Scarteen, were formerly harriers, not being registered as foxhounds until 1932, under Mr Tommy O'Brien. In 1973 the committee appointed Capt. J. D. Moore as acting Master. The secretary is Miss Mary O'Brien, and the huntsman is Mr John Noonan.

By the sea, south-west of the United, the South Union hunt a steep glen country. The hunt was founded by Mr T. W. Knowles of Oakland, Kinsale, in 1830. Mr W. P. Worth-Newenham, who hunts hounds, became Master in 1971. The secretary is Mr D. Sullivan. Adjacent, to the north, in the Barony of Muskerry and Co. Cork, are the Muskerry, whose joint-Masters are Mrs R. P. Murphy and Mr T. N. Tanner, with the Rev. Leslie Bryan as amateur huntsman and kennels at Cloghroe house, Blarney. This hunt thrived largely under the Tonson-Rye and Hawkes families from the middle of the eighteenth century and, subsequently, under a succession of cavalry officers serving with the Ballincollig garrison. They now meet on Wednesdays and Saturdays, Cork and Macroom being the best centres of this good bank and wall country. Mr M. O'Driscoll is the secretary.

North, astride the Blackwater valley, in Co. Cork, the Duhallow is another good bank country, well wooded and composed almost entirely of rich grazing. It has one of the longest continuous histories of any hunt in Ireland, stemming from the pack established by Henry Wrixon of Ballygiblin in 1745. In 1822, his descendant, Sir William Wrixon Becher, gave the family hounds to the country. Mrs R. I. Nelson became Master in 1969 with Harry Clayton as huntsman. Mr Kevin Thompson has been the secretary since 1971, and the kennels are at Black Rock, Mallow.

The Carbery, Ireland's most south-westerly hunt, situated in west Cork, began their history with the Cashelmore hounds being established as the Carbery by the Beamish family in 1787. The hunt remained more or less in their hands until 1914 when Patrick O'Driscoll became Master for 38 years. Since 1952 his sons, Messrs Edward and Patrick O'Driscoll, have held the joint-Mastership, while Barry O'Driscoll carries the horn. The Carbery have rather more than their share of plough but very little wire. The West Carbery, of which Edith Somerville (see Chapter 17) was Master from 1903 to 1909, has Barry Ryan Finbarr as Master, Bertie Hourihane as huntsman and Wing-Commander Thallon as secretary.

The adjoining Macroom was got going again in 1949 after a lapse of about 20 years. Mr Justin White has been joint-Master and also secretary since 1958, with his joint-Master, Mr P. St. A. Horgan, whipping in. The kennels are at Mr White's home, Ballyverane, Macroom.

North of the Duhallow lies the Limerick's fine grass country with an inviting pattern of banks and ditches and walls, 30 miles by 40 miles, all in Co. Limerick. They trace their history back to 1734, when twelve gentlemen of Limerick formed a hunt club; but the county pack stems from Mr George Fosbery's pack, which he and his friends assembled in 1825. The joint-Masters are Lord Daresbury (since 1947), a former Master of the Belvoir, and the Earl of Harrington (since 1972). H. Robards is huntsman, and Mr J. R. Sheehy has carried out the duties of secretary since 1973.

North of the Limerick, a brand-new hunt, the Co. Clare, were first recognized by the Irish Masters of Foxhounds' Association in the 1976-7 season. Their Master is Mr C. Sparling, who also carries the horn.

The largest hunt country in Ireland's middle west, about 30 miles square, is the Co. Galway (The Blazers), again nearly all grass—over limestone, so that the going is good and light—and with walls of loose stone to jump. The Galway Blazers derive from Robert Persse's Castleboy hunt, the county hunt being established in 1840. During the first half of this century several well-known hunting names stand out in their succession of Masters: Ikey Bell (1903-8), Joe Pickersgill (1911-22), Major Bowes Daly (on and off between 1928 and 1948) and Major

Philip Profumo (1948–52). Lord Hemphill, the present senior joint-Master, first came in for the 1957–8 season. Mr F. J. Mannheim joined him in 1963, Mr J. B. McGowan in 1974 and Mr E. Crotty in 1976. Lt-Cdr R. D. V. Stoney is secretary to the Blazers, and the kennels are at Craughwell.

In the similar East Galway country, part of which is in Roscommon, the fox appears to have been hunted first by Lord Eyre in the latter part of the eighteenth century, he being succeeded by his nephew, Giles, from 1791 to 1829. This hunt was disbanded from 1848 to 1883, and again in 1956, being re-formed in 1970. Messrs Dempsey, Gwyn-Jones and Bishop and Mrs Ordway are Masters, Mr Dempsey also carrying the horn. Miss S. Bourns is secretary.

Lady Cusack-Smith, who is now the senior of four joint-Masters, has hunted the Bermingham and North Galway Hounds since 1946, when she and her husband, a former Master of Devonshire's Silverton (1937–9) and of the West-meath (1949–50), founded the hunt. Formerly Miss Mollie O'Rourke, Lady Cusack-Smith was Master of the Galway Blazers from 1939 to 1943. Hounds are kennelled at her home, Bermingham House, Tuam, and she is also hunt secretary. Her joint-Masters, all appointed in 1969, are Mrs Hyland and Mrs Merrick Coveney. John Pickering is huntsman.

Owing to the previous scarcity of foxes, no pack of foxhounds existed in Ulster until 1948. Although there is more plough—about 25%—than in Eire, the going is fairly light. It is closely fenced country, and, as in the south, there are walls, banks, drains and ditches to jump. Of Northern Ireland's three foxhunts, the oldest is the East Down, which lies in a radius of 15 miles around Seaforde, in Co. Down. The East Down descends from a harrier hunt started by the Forde family in the 1760s. The fox has been their quarry since 1947 when Lt-Col. Forde, who was then Master, decided to convert. Mr John Glover was appointed Master in 1970 and was afterwards joined by Mr P. M. D. Forde, who is also secretary, and Mr James Pooler. P. Dobbin has been huntsman since 1965.

The Dungannon, in Co. Tyrone, also formerly harriers, is now a foxhound footpack, the fox having been hunted unofficially here since 1939. Mr Henry Corr has been Master, huntsman and secretary since 1962. He was joined in the Mastership in 1975 by Mr S. H. McIvor; and north, in Co. Donegal and Tyrone, where there is a mixture of mountain, farmland and meadow to cross, we come lastly to the Strabane and Donegal, another hunt only founded in the late 1940s. Here Mr Smyth, who hunts hounds, and Mr Temple combine the Mastership with Mrs Eve Stafford.

The address of the Hon. Secretary of the Irish Masters of Foxhounds' Association, Mr Russell, is Seafield, Kilmacthomas, Co. Waterford.

Chapter 15

An American
Foxhunting Tour

(First published in *Country Life*, 1975)

HE FIRST TROOP, Philadelphia City Cavalry, the oldest military unit of the
United States, celebrated its 200th anniversary on 15 November 1974, the
night we flew into the 'Quaker city'; and, since that band of horse-soldiers
was formed from America's first substantial sporting organization, the Gloucester
Foxhunting Club, we could scarcely have chosen a more auspicious moment at
which to touch down for a hunting tour of five of the eastern and southern
states—a tour organized, through the generosity of a number of Masters, by
Col. John L. Hornor, Jr, M.F.H., with whom I first hunted in Virginia, in 1946.

The emergence of the Philadelphian clubmen, and their conversion to cavaliers
two centuries ago happened like this: in 1766 a group of prosperous young men,
hitherto enjoying their foxhunting privately and by mutual invitation, saw that
better sport might be had in combination; so, meeting that fall at a famous coffee
house, they agreed to build kennels by Gloucester Point Ferry, just across the
Delaware River from their 'city of brotherly love', and, with hounds imported
from England by the club's first president, Capt. Charles Ross, and another
member called Davies, they proceeded to hunt the fox on both the Jersey and
Pennsylvania sides of the Delaware, as energetically as they knew how.

In 1774 the members chose their dress: a dark-brown coatee, fringed with gold
and adorned with lapelled dragoon pockets, tan breeches and a black velvet coat
(the sombre colours being to appease their frivolity-deploring quaker elders).
When war with England loomed that December and they formed themselves
into the First City Troop, recruiting their own volunteers, the brown, gold-
edged club attire became the cavalry uniform. Samuel Morris, Jr, who commanded the troop throughout the War of Independence, with ultimate victory,
also became president of the hunt club, which he remained until 1812, the year
America went to war with England again, when the foxhunters lost their money
and within a few years the club closed down for ever.

Today, the spirit and character of all the Pennsylvania hunts stems from the
Gloucester Foxhunting Club, but only the Rose Tree, whose members wear
gold-edged brown collars with their scarlet coats, claims to be its direct descendant. The Rose Tree Hunt Club, which was founded in 1859 at the little stone-
built inn of that name, still standing on Route 252, finally succumbed to the

sprawl of Philadelphia suburbia in the 1960s, when the committee decided to move 80 miles west, into York County, and this, of course, resulted in a fresh clientele as well as a new country. Of the other pre-First World War hunts that are close to Philadelphia and still surviving, the Radnor (1883), which took on what was left of the old Rose Tree country, and the Pickering (1911) have both suffered serious territorial difficulties. Indeed the Pickering—with whom I hunted on 16 November at the invitation of Mr Harry Nicholas, who is President of the Masters of Foxhounds' Association and had then just retired from the joint-Mastership—only remained viable in recent years by absorbing two private hunts, the Whitelands and Eagles Farm.

Although the red fox is indigenous to the north-west and the central plains, he was not known along the eastern seaboard until 1730, when he was introduced from England into Maryland by foxhunters wearying of the little native grey, which invariably describes a circle like a hare. By the time the Gloucester Fox-hunting Club came on the scene, the European red was established in Pennsylvania, and Ross and Morris and their friends must occasionally have exulted in the long straight dash provided by 'Charles James'. But now—although the density of foxes is far less in America than in the British Isles—there are more reds than greys, and soon after the senior joint-Master, Mr Sylvester L. Quigley, led us away at 9.30 a.m. from Chester Spring, Phoenixville (a little under 30 miles from Philadelphia), a red fox was afoot in the forest by the famous Two Churches.

It was astonishing to see hounds hold his scent, for the air was as crisp and dry as you could imagine, the moisture on the ground fractional; but these pure Penn–Marydel hounds never lifted their heads nor quietened their tongues until 15 minutes later, when their quarry found a big drainpipe, and our horses were well lathered from traversing hills of white-green grass and parched earth fields, from which the maize had just been harvested; and—where in England there would have been more gates to open than hedges to cross—jumping panels and 'chicken coops' and post-and-rail fences. They left him in that drain: foxes are so scarce over there that Masters rarely, if ever, use terriers or dig; you never hear of 'vermin control', and American houndsmen set little store by 'blood'. ('Did you kill?' enquires the British countryman of the homegoing foxhunter, while 'Did you have a *good race*?' is what his American counterpart wants to know.)

Penn–Marydel? Founded in 1934, the Penn–Marydel corporation then stated its aim as follows:

> 'To preserve purity in the bloodline of a species of the American foxhound, which has been found to be most serviceable, and satisfactory for the club and pack hunting, and which has been bred and hunted for generations through the south-eastern sections of Pennsylvania, Maryland and Delaware. . . . '

Watching the Pickering pack more closely, with their light frames, long backs, low-set ears on high-domed heads and wide feet on sloping pasterns, as Albert

Crosson, their huntsman, lifted them from the drain, I was reminded of those pre-Meynellian paintings of English Northern beagles and Southern hounds; and, since the Penn–Marydels' ancestors were introduced into colonial America in the seventeenth and eighteenth centuries and the blood kept fairly pure, the resemblance surely goes even further.

Clearly, they are lower scenting than their modern English cousins; they have to be: the climatic conditions are much less favourable there. While they worked through the next forest, I wondered how they would fare in a tight-brambled English covert; for there is no such challenge in American woodland, where the bottom is never thicker than dogwood and hickory, entangled, perhaps, with wild grape and honeysuckle: the huntsman rarely pauses with his draw. Here they found again, and how their music, as deep and rich as I have heard anywhere (except, perhaps in Dumfriesshire), echoed through the valley, as they swung right round with him to the Two Churches, where the big green fruit of the Osage orange trees littered the avenues like a playground floor, and the still, moistureless air was filled, as it was nearly everywhere, with the faint subtle odour of bittersweet berries; but these Penn–Marydels are ponderous, they dwell on the line, and thus they lost him.

What a stimulating day it was, and what a contrast to my last foxhunting, three days previously, in Sussex, with mud up to the hocks, thronging at gates, cars at every junction of the close road network and long waits at covertside. And yet, for us, in America, some essential part of the scene is missing: is it a combination of soaking leaves, greenery and mist, hunting farmers and dedicated local foot followers, who in England help to 'tie the hunt to the land'?

Next day we visited the kennels of the Radnor hunt, whose hounds are Penn–Marydel–English crosses, and from there to the fine 1930s stone-built kennels at Unionville, where Mrs John B. Hannum, Master of Mr Stewart's Cheshire, keeps the largest pack in the United States: 63 couple of pure English hounds, with the blood of the Duke of Beaufort's, Garth and South Berks, Heythrop and South and West Wilts strongest in their veins. From these paragons, every one with their ears rounded, John Roche, the young kennel-huntsman (who had been carrying the horn since Mrs Hannum's last crippling fall), drew, for our admiration, Worry '72—by the Duke of Beaufort's Wafer—the bitch that won the 1974 Virginia championship.

What are the advantages in the western hemisphere of hound types from the 'old country' and what is the value of their blood in the American lines? At both the covertside and the dinner table these are among the great debating points and nowhere more than in Virginia, most famous of the foxhunting states—in which direction we now pointed.

On 19 November we reached Henchman's Lea, Orlean, Virginia, the home of Col. and Mrs Albert P. Hinckley, who have surely done more for British foxhunters during the past quarter century, especially for officers serving in Washington, than anyone else in the United States. Col. Hinckley, by whose house the Old Dominion hounds are still kennelled, succeeded to the Mastership of that hunt in 1947—during the season I first rode with them—and handed over to Mr William W. Brainard, Jr, the present Master, 21 years later.

Their country lies in the Piedmont section of Virginia, what is dubbed 'the Leicestershire of America', in north Rappahannock and west Fauquier Counties, at the foot of the Blue Ridge Mountains, which—always on the horizon—are sometimes lavender, sometimes indigo but never less than a striking blue. It is a rolling tract of grass, liberally interspersed with forest, the cattle country being enclosed rather less now with stake-and-rail and the traditional and picturesque chestnut-pole zigzag 'snake-fence', than with that woven 'American wire', which is so treacherous to hounds. Although the red-and-white Old Dominion strain, narrow, light and standing only 20 to 21 inches at the shoulder, can slip through the wire's 12-inch apertures more safely than most, even he sometimes gets himself hung in the mesh by a leg.

It was Ned Chadwell, formerly of the Orange County (a hunt established in Virginia, in 1903), who was put on as huntsman in 1924, when Mr Sterling Larrabee founded the hunt that was to become, in 1931, the Old Dominion; and it was Orange County hounds, whose blood goes back to the red hounds with white necks ('red ring-necks'), bred by William Early (1849–1934) and Burrell Frank Bywaters (1843–1922) and his son Hugh (1872–1952), that formed the basis of Larrabee's new pack. Early and the Bywaters bred theirs from hounds descended from those imported by settlers two or three centuries ago and sold them, as they sold their cattle, sheep and pigs—mostly to the night runners—the hunters, who still turn their hounds out into the hills after fox by starlight, listening for their cry through the dark and calling them in by horn in the morning.

These Early–Bywaters types were among the most quality-looking hounds I saw in the United States, and the compact and level Old Dominion their best representatives. Mr Brainard, a most successful breeder of animals generally, also keeps a pack of English hounds, which he usually hunts himself about once a fortnight.

From the meet, at Mr Joe Hume Gardiner's Cabin Branch Farm, for which I joined them on 21 November, the Old Dominion American pack drew through the rambling Bear's Den Forest, and there they remained for much of the day; like most American woodland in the east, it is composed largely of oak, not our oak, but the slim and lofty red oak, white oak, pin oak and chestnut oak, whose long, indented leaves, having the texture of maple leaves, form the backcloth of the Virginian fall's dazzling crimson and gold, but which, in this abnormally dry season, were now brown and tinder-dry on the forest floor. Yet, despite the dampless atmosphere, after 40 minutes blank, the red-and-white hounds found a fox, which they drove hard through the woods to a creek within half a mile of the Rappahannock River. There they threw up, and Ray Pearson, their huntsman, calling them to him with his 100-year-old cowhorn, lifted them away, because the coverts beyond are well-known deer havens and it was feared one of these might lead them into the swirling currents beyond. (After the Second World War the U.S. Government restocked several states with the nearly extinct Virginia white-tailed deer, and now, to the discomfiture of foxhunters, the forests are bristling with them.)

Soon they were on to another fox and made a picture of fleeting reddish-tan and white as they spoke to his line; but, although I was riding Col. Hinckley's sure-footed chestnut, Cracker, I could not watch them for long at a time as the ground was pock-marked with groundhog holes, which are so much more deadly than rabbit warrens, for they are secreted and scattered. The groundhog, or woodchuck, which has been responsible for many a broken cannon-bone or humerus, has one other significance in American hunting: his holes are legion, and the fox invariably improves on them, making them his own, which is one of the reasons why earth stopping is virtually pointless.

'Old Dominion'—that was colonial Virginia, so the name harks back to the state's first organized pack, that of the Sixth Baron Fairfax, who inherited huge estates there from his mother, a daughter of Lord Culpeper, Governor in the early 1680s. It was when he was employed as a surveyor at Fairfax's home, Belvoir, that George Washington, who was described by Thomas Jefferson as 'the foremost rider of his age', first developed his passion for foxhunting.

'Although a heavy man, he [Lord Fairfax] was a fine horseman', the future founder of the nation recorded, 'and, as I was never tired of the saddle, we were much engaged in the hunting of wild foxes. . . . ' Then, after the Revolution, Washington with the help of his ally, the Marquis de Lafayette, and various neighbours, established his own pack of hounds at his home, Mount Vernon.

Between Independence and the War between the states, the fox was hunted everywhere in charted America, and most of the plantation owners kept packs of hounds. The holocaust and social and economic upheaval of the 1860s reduced the sport to a miserable scale, lasting several decades, but one, at least, of the plantation hunts did survive—that established by the Confederate hero, Col. Richard H. Dulany, at Welbourne, Virginia, in 1840. The oldest hunt in the United States, this flourishes today as the Piedmont.

At the start of my day with the Piedmont, on 22 November, Mr Erskine Bedford, the Field Master—riding ex-champion steeplechaser, Bon Noval, the property of the Master, Mrs Archibald Randolph—faced us to stress the importance of keeping immediately behind him, in one body, reminding one of the sad fact that there is scarcely a hunt in the United States favouring followers who take their own line; this seems to be more because Americans hunt primarily 'for the gallop' and are all too prone to overrun the line, than to save the ranches. The Piedmont country is one of big landowners, with what they call 'well-manicured' farms: we rode from Mr Hubert Phipps' Rockbourn estate to Tan-y-Bryn, belonging to Mr Paul Mellon, the famous collector and a former Master of this hunt, and rarely have I experienced such a sense of open unblemished space; at certain times the plains swaggered, as nature designed them, to every horizon, without so much as a farmstead or a herd of cattle showing but only neat walls and spick stake-and-rail fences as evidence of man's presence.

Yet, alas, that is not typical of north Virginia, for many of the hunts are being pinched by the encroachment of new roads and suburbia; there is little, if any, building restriction in the open countryside; and the Orange County, I am told, will soon be divided down the middle by an inter-state highway. North Virginia, '*the* hunt country of America', as they boast it, so reputable, so convenient for Washington and still so beautiful, remains pre-eminent, but how long, one wondered, would it remain so?

Our first run, 15 minutes circularwise from find to finish, ended by Mr Mellon's celebrated sporting museum at Oak Spring, where hounds marked on a walnut tree. 'There he is!'—Mr Bedford pointed up with his whip—and I trotted forward, curious to see a grey (for only greys scale a tree of that height); but, instead, a wrathful figure, clad in black, white and ginger, gazed down. They had changed, in the final dash, from vulpine to feline, and looked, I thought, a little shame-faced as they sidled on towards Goose Creek and Black Forest. But then cats to seem do show an unhappy facility for getting involved in foxhunts in America. Perhaps their movements are a little too like those of the grey fox for their safety?

It was in this country that the famous Anglo-American Foxhound Match of 1905 took place. The challenge—that the American hound could be proved inferior, on its own soil, to the English—came from a name well known in British hunting circles, anglophile A. H. Higginson, Master of a pack coming mostly from Mr Fernie's—the Middlesex, of Massachusetts. The man who accepted the challenge—with 6½ couples from his American Grafton pack, bred in co-operation with B. F. Bywaters (and also from Massachusetts)—was one of the towering figures in the history of American foxhunting, Harry Worcester Smith, who had been recently elected Master of the Piedmont.

The contest began with a Middlesex meet at old Dulany's house, Welbourne, on 1 November, and, after 10 days, with huge fields at every outing, the match was decided in favour of Worcester Smith's lot. National pride reached high fervour and pack breeders soon came to put top faith in the likes of the Bywaters and Early. Nearly every follower at the 'great match' vouched, too, that the country was 'just as fine as Leicestershire' and that is how, by the First World War, northern Virginia became 'the hunt country'. Not only was it handy for Washingtonians but would soon become the mecca for New Yorkers and Long Islanders who were gradually to be squeezed from their home grounds.

Founded in 1887, with roots going back to 1807, the Warrenton, whose country lies east of the Old Dominion and south of the Orange County, are next oldest after the Piedmont. Mrs Tyler Wilson generously provided me with as fine a 'coop jumper and flyer as could be desired for my ride with this famous hunt on 23 November, and I was up with Mr Douglas Harcourt Lees, her joint-Master, throughout the day which was mostly spent on forest rides.

Mr Lees, like Mr Brainard, is a strong admirer of the English hound and a close observer of the English and Irish hunting scenes, but his pack are mostly By-waters, a well-matched tricolour lot; and very stylish they looked at 10 a.m. as they moved off from Rappahannock Farm under their huntsman, Fred Duncan.

Virginia was still dry and hot; they could not work out the line of the one that had been in the coverts around Canterbury, they drew blank in Brood Mare Barn Woods, but finding at 1 p.m. in Charlie Johnson pines, they gave us a good 30 minutes' race before they lost him by the cliffs of the Rappahannock River, and a straight spurt with another red fox which at length found sanctuary in a woodchuck hole in a field at Ashland.

Hacking 5 miles back to the horse-boxes before Mr Harcourt Lees' hunt break-fast, we crossed two roads, passed a dozen modern buildings and dismounted to unchain three gates, which made it the least 'natural' single ride in my American tour. For British foxhunters, that, in 5 miles, might seem nothing, but for Virginia it is bad. With such a precious heritage as theirs, one can only pray that if the country does get more 'tied up' and less 'opened up', it will do so by the slowest degrees.

Very early on the Monday morning, we drove 800 miles to southern Tennessee, whose foxhunters, as I shall tell, are faced by few such threats and who are, indeed, opening up fresh country year by year.

The forests became wilder and steeper as we drove south-west, mounting the high Appalachians for south Tennessee, and the open land grew browner, more prairie-like. That russet grass, feathery and waist high, called broomsedge, grows where the earth is sour and uncultivated, where rich grass cannot thrive; *en masse*, it gives the appearance of golden veldtland and looks very lovely as you are hacking home in the sunset. Where the ground rises, the deciduous woodland begins, and this is punctuated with the tall cones of juniper (Virginia red cedar), belying the presence of limestone outcrops, that make for rough riding. Broom-sedge and cedar are the hallmarks of wild Tennessee. The red and (more numerous) grey fox live there alongside the opossum, raccoon, coyote, woodchuck, bobcat and white-tailed deer, and the stark and lonely hunting landscape is frequently brightened by flocks of scarlet cardinals and lime-breasted meadow larks or by the dazzle of blue jays and silvery, red-crowned woodpeckers.

In the early 1800s the frontiersmen took this land from the Indians by treaty, and the new settlers cleared the trees from the plains and made them rich. With the War between the States, the agricultural boom ended, but tumbledown log cabins, occasional windowless verandah-style villas and long-abandoned churches, with graveyards overgrown with sumac and hickory, tell you that, up to the First World War, quite prosperous communities lived there, farming cattle, maize and cotton. Then the labourers, mostly negroes, went to the towns in

L

search of a living wage, and the countryside remains relatively deserted. Huge expanses have been bought by men with fortunes, whose limited aim may be to raise cattle but who, more ambitiously, develop it for gun, rod and horse. Although some of the remainder carries the soya bean, corn cob, pimento and sweet potato, and much more is wired up by beef and pig farmers, whose stock is their sole livelihood, it still constitutes a fine playground for the hunter.

In America, of course, hunting means duck shooting, coyote chasing or deer stalking, in fact more or less any pursuit with firearm or hound, and you carry the same sporting licence in your foxhunter's coat as you carry in search of black bear or bobwhite quail.

In Tennessee, the old tradition of foxhunting with packs of hounds expired with the Civil War, and its first new seed was not planted until 1930, when the great Joe Thomas brought his hounds there; then, in 1932, the Hillsboro emerged, under J. Mason Houghland, from the Harpeth Valley Country Club, near Nashville. The only other foxhunting legacy was that of the nightrunners, which, as it involves neither trampling men nor horses, in no way upsets the ranchers; but 'pack foxhunters', with their troop or so of riders in wake, are viewed with suspicion, and Masters opening up new territory have to work very hard to win the farmers' trust.

The first sign of a hunt country is a rash of 'chicken coops', and, under most coops in Tennessee, you will find barbed wire, for cattle thieving is rife there and no serious rancher regards an apron of wood, which can be simply pushed aside and put back, as defence against rustlers. To keep the cattle in, the coops need not be more than 2 feet 6 inches high, though most are nearer 3 feet 6 inches.

When the red fox invaded the southern states in the 1830s and 1840s, he was regarded as a menace by foxhunters. 'Whenever the grey fox was driven out', wrote that top authority of the last century, Col. F. G. Skinner, 'foxhunting was a labor instead of a pleasure, for the red devils, with far more speed and bottom than the natives, could easily outfoot the hounds . . . at last all sorts of devices were resorted to to improve the speed of the hounds.' Experiments with English hounds were mostly disappointing: 'Their noses were not cold enough', complained Skinner, 'and they were too fast and too silent.' Much as Virginian Masters and night hunters imposed their faith in the Bywaters, the southerners preferred the strains produced by John W. Walker, Col. G. L. F. Birdsong, Ben Robinson and Col. Miles Harris. Walkers are, perhaps, still the most popular in the South.

It was Thanksgiving weekend when we reached the quiet steep 'hillbillyland' of Tennessee; turkeys were being prepared for full-treatment hunt breakfasts, and, when the Hillsboro met at Cornersville, a sprinkling of children reminded one that the schools had closed until the Monday. The senior Master, Mr Vernon Sharp, who is also President of the Masters of Foxhounds' Association (founded in 1907), made me a nice speech of welcome at the meet; and it was his joint-

Master, Mr George Sloan (twice a Grand National rider), who carried the horn, because Bob Gray, their English huntsman, was in hospital, having driven a nail through his foot.

Here, with 40 years' tradition and the majority of land owned by hunt subscribers, there is scant trouble with access, and, in spite of a scorching day, with the yellow alfalfa butterfly out in force over the golden fields, the combination of a stout red fox and the tenacity of the Hillsboro's Walker-and-Fell-bred hounds provided the straightest run I had in the States—a quickly undulating 25-minute gallop.

I also enjoyed a Thanksgiving hunt, with the Mells, which was founded, in 1962, by our host, Col. Hornor. We started up the hill behind the kennels at Waco, and the Mells hounds, which are descended from a litter of Vale of Lune harriers—with Penn–Marydel, Bywaters and Walker outcrosses—soon found a red fox in a piece of woodland that made my memory of Virginian forest seem like ornamental parkland. We crouched low over the withers, screwing and ducking to avoid the 3-inch thorns of the honey locust tree and great loops of vine and honeysuckle, then slid down and clambered up near-vertical boulder-strewn gradients, before turning suddenly on to a majestic expanse of pasture, 1,000 yards across the ridge beyond. When I commented on the shortness of American hunting days—most of which amounting to no more than 3 hours in the saddle—Mr Richard E. Dole, Jr, who is now in his sixth season as Master, as though to modify my verdict, mounted me again, this time for a dripping wet 5-hour day in a 'new' woodland area, by no means properly panelled—the Mells country is a multiplicity of small estates—and we were forever dismounting in the rain, looking for passages over or round the barbed wire: no chicken coops, no free way.

My morning with Mr Buck Allison's private Cedar Knob Hunt helped me, more than anything else, to imagine what it was like to follow one of the old plantation packs, for Mr Allison has a charming southern take-what-you-please philosophy. He eulogized on the merits, as quarry, of coyote, and also bobcat, that tailless large-as-lynx native, one of which had recently given him a 4-mile point. Half-way through the morning he held up his hand to his friend, Mr William Carter and me—his only followers—for silence: he 'figured' that his hounds (like the Hillsboro, a Walker-and-Fell combination) were 'talkin' to barb cat on that ol' woodpile', but, despite his dismounting to lob on some boulders, nothing stirred. Within 10 minutes, hounds started a deer and did not return to kennels until the following day. But there was something especially exhilarating about following a 'one-man pack', with the silence of those nearly uninhabited hills broken that morning only by the Cedar Knob's grand music.

We now motored south, between the red cotton-fields, to Madison, Alabama, where Mr Harry Moore Rhett, Jr, Master of another private hunt, the Mooreland, kennels a very high-quality pack, established in 1961 and composed of about 65% American and 35% English. Mr Rhett's plantations, which came down to him from an equally sporting great-grandfather of pre-Civil-War days, form the nucleus of a country which is part flat cotton ploughland—admirable for seeing hounds work—and part woodland and pasture, at the tail-end of the Appalachians; and there cannot be many better examples of how foxhunting provides a principal winter recreation and initiates local interest in equitation than that shown by the Mooreland: few of the 40 followers out on my weekday had ever ridden before discovering the Mooreland, and a shrewd interest many took in the houndwork as two greys and a red were traced to ground.

My most spectacular days of all were still further south, with the Midland, which hunt not only Thursdays and Sundays from their Georgian kennels, south-east of Columbus, but also a new tract in Alabama, based on the old Fitzpatrick hunt centre. Their owner, Mr Ben H. Hardaway III, joint-Master and huntsman since 1950—a great-grandson of the founder of 'Hardaway's Rifles', that cele-brated unit whose guns first effectively defiladed the Union palisades in the War between the States—has fashioned a pack of 30 couples composed chiefly of American July, and of British Fell blood (coming from the West Waterford and College Valley), with occasional outcrosses of Penn–Marydel, Bywaters, the Duke of Beaufort's and the Heythrop. The Julys, descended from Irish importa-tions of the 1830s, gain their name from the foundation sire, *July '59*, bred in Maryland by Nimrod Gosnell and acquired, as a puppy, by Col. Miles G. Harris, of Georgia, in 1858. Mr Hardaway is the first to agree with the old hound expert, George Garrett, who advised a would-be breeder, 50 years ago, 'If you want music get the Walker hounds; however, if you want action and execution, get Julys by all means.' He was 15 when he acquired his first Julys from Garrett.

These narrow, long-legged, snipey-faced, and slightly broken-coated hounds are shy and temperamental but, crossed with the intelligent and similarly rangy Fell, produce—as the late Mr Ikey Bell suggested they would—wonderfully hard-driving fox catchers; and I never shall forget the way the Midland pushed their grey out of a slash pine and creeper entanglement on 7 December. They say the grey always describes a circle; but not this one; he ran straight as a dye into the open, across a great sweep of auburn grass where cotton once grew, and eventually into another conifer copse; here, vainly trying to shake them off, he twisted and turned a dozen times, from corner to corner of the covert, before they ran into him by our feet in a clearing, going 45 minutes from find to kill.

Straight after church next day, Mr Hardaway had 25 couples out from his Georgian kennels, and no whipper-in to turn them. *Harlot '70* (which he later presented to the College Valley) was first to speak to the line they hunted, and I wish the stalwarts of the Lake District, Northumberland and West Waterford could have heard the resounding Anglo-American chorus when the rest joined her, racing for half an hour on their grey's brush, and the dramatic silence after they took him in the creek, with 30 of us weaving through the hickory and rattan as we cantered up behind.

In my journey through the south, during which I was never less than royally

entertained and beautifully mounted, I was told everywhere that an increasing
number of people are taking up the sport, and I gained the impression that there
will be a proliferation of hunts here during the next decade. The southerners
certainly have a magnificently unspoilt arena for it.

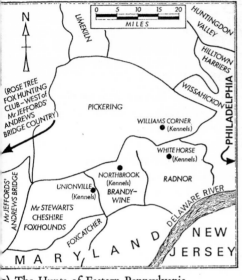

1) The Hunts of Eastern Pennsylvania.

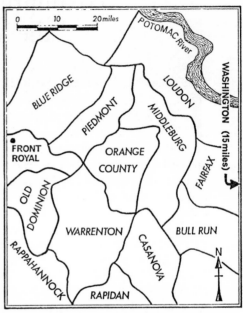

(2) Hunt boundaries of North Virginia.

(3) Approximate boundaries of
the Hunts of Tennessee, Alabama
and Western Georgia.

Courtesy Country Life.

Chapter 16

Foxhunting Around the World

AUSTRALIA. BY HEATHER B. RONALD

THE FOX IS not indigenous to Australia but has become thoroughly acclimatized since its introduction in the early days of settlement. Originally imported as the much sought-after quarry for packs of English-bred foxhounds, it was at first protected and was hunted in the style of 'carted deer'. In fact one well-known fox in the 1860s was trained to run for home when given a good start and was not caught by hounds for several seasons. Dingoes, kangaroos and emus were some of the native game hunted, but huntsmen considered that they did not compare with the red fox for giving a good run to hounds and followers. The love of the chase was deep-rooted in our British forebears and, wherever they settled, foxhounds were soon to be found.

It is difficult to ascertain just exactly when the first foxes arrived in Australia, but it would appear from contemporary newspaper reports that they could have come into New South Wales and Victoria at least from 1845 onwards. Eric Rolls, who did extensive research into this for his book, *They All Ran Wild*, stated that two successful releases of foxes were made in Victoria about 1871, one at Ballarat and the other near Point Cooke. The latter was one of several foxes imported by Thomas Chirnside, a keen follower of hounds, who, with his brother Andrew, was among the greatest of Australia's pioneer pastoralists and noted sportsmen. These foxes and others released near Adelaide at about the same time must have bred prolifically, for by 1880 they were not only well established in South Australia but had a 5,000-square-mile spread in Victoria.

There is no evidence to show whether foxes moved over the rest of Australia of their own accord or whether they were let go. They seem to do well in dry country, and it is recorded that, in 1937, in some of the driest country of South Australia, one grazier's stockmen killed 600 foxes in 12 weeks. Since the turn of the century the fox has been regarded as vermin in most parts of the continent, with a price on its head. It will kill and carry off poultry and lambs and has had a serious effect on reducing the native wildlife.

The hunting of foxes and other game with packs of foxhounds or beagles is still a popular sport in some parts of Australia, but, with the closer settlement in many areas, it is becoming increasingly difficult to find sufficient good open country to hunt within a reasonable distance of kennels. This has caused many packs to seek new country further out and can mean travelling 50 miles or more

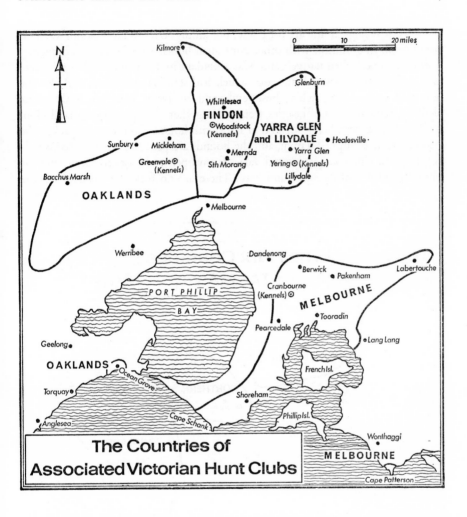

The Countries of Associated Victorian Hunt Clubs

to a meet, which presents few problems with the prevalence of towed horse floats. Some privately owned properties of several thousand acres are hunted up to 200 miles from kennels, and this entails at least an overnight stay.

New South Wales was the first part of Australia to become a British colony, and foxhounds were introduced there early. There are references to the Cumberland Hunt as far back as 1803, but mention of the Sydney hounds does not occur until 1833. The Sydney Hunt is the only pack of hounds in New South Wales and, after being disbanded for many years, was reformed in 1956, with hounds obtained from the Melbourne. It has the use of large tracts of country within 200 miles of Sydney, including some 7,000 acres 30 miles to the south-west. The usual obstacles are capped fences such as 'hogsback' over wire and plenty of natural obstacles in undulating country with plenty of creeks. Some meets are restricted to a drag. Some are for game, but killing foxes in New South Wales is now illegal. In common with other Australian hunts, a mixed pack is hunted.

Prior to 1840 when native game was abundant in Tasmania, foxhounds were used to hunt the forester kangaroo, which had stamina and speed, and also the imported deer. Later, when bushdevils and wallabies were the only game plentiful, several packs of beagles were put together. The present Midland Hunt is Tasmania's oldest, being formed in 1912 with hounds from the old packs. The kennels are at Campbell Town, and the hounds are predominately a foxhound–beagle cross. The country hunted varies from open paddocks to forest, and the game includes wallaby, deer and hare. There are no foxes in Tasmania. More

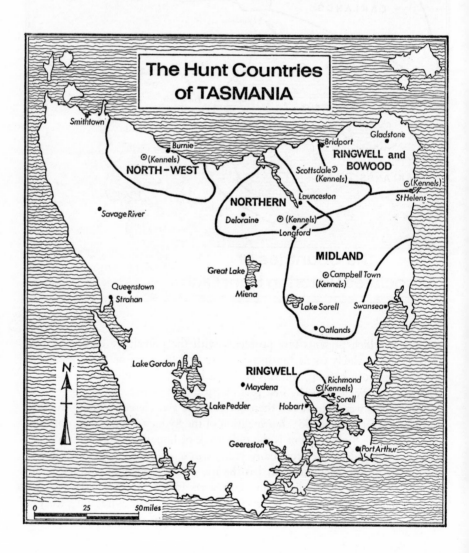

The Hunt Countries of TASMANIA

recently formed packs also have a large following: the Northern and North-West are drag-line clubs hunting north-west of Launceston; the Bowood and the Ringwell (a private pack) hunt native game in the north-east; and half the Ringwell pack is kennelled at Richmond for drag hunting in the Hobart area.

It is thought that the first foxhounds were taken across to Victoria from Tasmania about 1839, just 4 years after the founding of the colony. Hounds were sent out from Great Britain in several drafts to New South Wales, Tasmania and Victoria during these early years, and gradually Victoria became the main centre of foxhunting in Australia, a position it still holds today.

The Melbourne Hunt was formed by George Watson, a son of John Watson, of Irish fame. He arrived in Victoria in 1852, bringing with him a few couples of his father's foxhounds and an unequalled knowledge of hunting. By the 1890s the pack was acclaimed as the best outside Great Britain; this was due in no small measure to importations from the Duke of Buccleuch's pack in 1888, which had left outstanding progeny. Regularly over the intervening years English-bred foxhounds were secured for the Melbourne, and in 1930 some Welsh hounds from the leading packs in Wales. Some of these, and further importations in 1934 and 1940, came from the private pack bred by Sir Edward Curre. They were white hounds, bred to be easily seen from afar, and this colour still appears in the Melbourne pack today. In 1952 and 1956 hounds from the Duke of Beaufort's were sent out.

The Melbourne kennels are at Cranbourne, about 30 miles south-east of the city of Melbourne; and the hunts are on Saturdays, exclusively for the fox. The country is undulating and mostly open, with timbered creeks and some ti-tree coverts breaking the rich pasture land which has some fern-covered sandy ridges. This pack also hunts regularly at Cape Paterson and at Buffalo in Gippsland. Earths are not stopped, and a fox which goes to ground in the sand hills is almost impossible to dig out. Timber panels are built into the wire fences, or spars laid on top, and, whereas the nature of the country does not make for fast or long runs, the hound work is considered the finest in Australia.

Most Australian packs look for their outcrosses to the Melbourne, or to other southern hunts, but they import from England when possible.

The Findon Harriers in Victoria were founded in 1871 with hounds sent out from England, and the present kennels are at Woodstock, about 18 miles north of Melbourne. Stone walls are the main obstacles met, and it is usual during a run of some 3 to 4 hours' duration for about 25 fences to be jumped, and the pace is fast. Here both foxes and hares are hunted over the open plains. The Master, Noel Mason, has occupied this position for many years, longer than any other Master in Australia today, and is a very well-known and highly regarded figure. He was fortunate enough in 1972 to obtain a hound from the Puckeridge and Thurlow.

Oaklands Hunt Club is slightly north-west of Melbourne, with kennels at Greenvale, about 15 miles out. This pack was founded in 1888 with a few couples of hounds from the Melbourne and has the most recent importation, the stallion hound, Nelson, from the Heythrop. Meets are held during the season from May to September, and in their home country the pace is fast, and a good horse is required. It is mildly undulating, and both stone walls and timber over wire are encountered. This pack also hunts near Geelong, at Ocean Grove on the coast, and Anakie in the hills, where foxes abound in the rugged country.

Foxes are plentiful in the country belonging to the Yarra Glen and Lilydale pack—beautiful, undulating, grazing country some 25 miles east of Melbourne. The kennels are situated at Yering, not far from the property once owned by famous singer, Nellie Melba, whose son was a keen follower of the hunt. English-bred hounds have been introduced into the pack from time to time, and it is based mainly on Heythrop bloodlines. An average field of 30 to 40 riders attend the Wednesday hunts in this district, which have been held since 1900.

There is only one pack of hounds in South Australia, and that is the Adelaide Hunt Club, founded in the 1860s, which hunts mainly through the Adelaide Hills; and the Gillpark, established in 1972. The Adelaide kennels are at Cherry Gardens, about 17 miles south of Adelaide. Followers mostly encounter natural obstacles such as gorse hedges, capped fences or stone walls; and, when in fairly rough country, creek crossings are not infrequent. The only game hunted is fox, and every Saturday from May to August a different piece of country is hunted for about 7 or 8 miles, during which some 60 natural fences would be jumped. The most popular meet is that held on the Monday holiday for the Queen's Birthday, in June each year, at Buckland Park, a magnificent property 20 miles out of Adelaide.

The Freemantle Hunt Club, formed in 1896, was the forerunner of the present West Australian Hunt Club. The original hounds were sent out from England by the Duchess of Newcastle, whose brother, Major Cairns Candy, was the club's first Master. These were foxhounds, but later, because of the scrubby nature of the country, it was decided to change to beagles. Since 1958, when the kennels were moved north of the Swan River to Morley, where the country is more open, a slow breeding programme towards foxhounds has taken place. This has been accelerated by the addition of hounds from Victorian and South Australian packs. Hunts are through semi-forest and open country, on Wednesdays and Saturdays, with few if any fences being encountered by the average field of 30 to 40. The kennels are now at Wanneroo, 25 miles from Perth. The Pine Lodge Hunt Club, formed in 1963, has its kennels at Forrestfield, less than 20 miles from Perth and hunts three times a week. Foxes are abundant in the bushland nearby.

On the mainland, professional huntsmen are employed by most hunts, but the whippers-in are honorary; the Masters are usually landowners living in or adjacent to their hunting country. The larger packs provide some stabling for members' horses, as well as a huntsman's cottage, kennels and club rooms, but, where the Master hunts his own hounds, the hounds are often kennelled on his property. Subscriptions range from $2.00 to $15.00 in Tasmania and from $10.00 to $50.00 on the mainland for adult members of the various hunts. All packs try to encourage members of pony clubs to follow hounds, holding several special meets for them every season. Hunting is one of the most colourful traditions still retained in Australia and continues to attract numerous followers of all ages.

CANADA. BY LT-COL. A. BRITTON SMITH, MC, QC, MASTER OF THE FRONTENAC HUNT

The foxhound probably first came to Canada with United Empire Loyalists, particularly those families from Virginia, after the American Revolution. 30 years later as the Peninsula Campaign was concluded, many army units were sent to Canada direct from Spain and Portugal. Wellington encouraged foxhunting among units under his command, and it is assumed that foxhounds accompanied some regiments embarking for North America. Quite possibly some of the local deer hounds, owned by farmers, were pressed into service as brood-bitches.

The garrison packs were steadily upgraded. Quite often a new officer posted from England would be able to bring a stallion hound or puppy of good breeding. Since Confederation in 1867, the Canadian Army has supplanted British

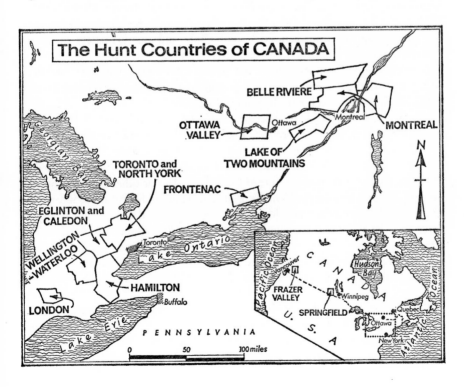

The Hunt Countries of CANADA

forces, and this source of new blood has been replaced by private importations. Several Canadian Masters bring out new blood from the best English packs from time to time. Running over the list of entries at the Canadian English foxhound show, it becomes apparent that English blood of recent importation predominates, chiefly through first generation progeny. This may not be a good thing, as Candian hunts should, perhaps, breed for the conditions encountered in the country.

The Canadian English foxhound show, established in 1965 by Mr William Bermingham, MFH, and Major Charles Kindersley, MFH, has done a great deal for the breed. Judges from England or Ireland are the rule. The show is held in mid-June, usually at Hamilton or Terra Cotta, Ontario. Lt-Col. Clifford Sifton, DSO, MFH, has bred some excellent hounds at the Toronto and North York kennels and has contributed to the establishment of several Canadian packs. His knowledge of kennel management and hound care has been incorporated in a handbook circulated to all Masters. Many special problems are dealt with, including the removal of porcupine quills. This hazard is particularly great for young entry.

There is no such breed as a Canadian foxhound. No classes for American foxhounds are included in the Canadian show, and those few kept by Canadian hunts are not shown. The Canadian Foxhound Club not only runs the annual hound show but also acts as an association of Canadian Masters. Most Canadian Masters are also members of the Masters of Foxhounds' Association of America, but all support the Canadian Foxhound Club, and many matters of purely Canadian interest are settled there. It has been suggested that the Canadian association might be independent, but strong bonds exist with the American Masters. Also the American foxhound stud book maintains excellent records which are important to hound breeding in Canada.

It is therefore impossible to describe a typical Canadian hound. A hound that would do well in a pack in Ireland, England or the United States would fit in any Canadian country. Perhaps because of the large coverts, some Canadian Masters favour hounds with prominent white markings, easily distinguished in the bush. One or two packs do breed for Belvoir Tan or other uniform, but the obvious aid to identification lent by a degree of individuality is recognized by most Canadian huntsmen and Masters. Good nose, good tongue and plenty of drive are the usual virtues sought. Apart from the import programme, the standard practice of sending bitches to a good stallion hound at another kennel is common. Smaller hunts are greatly aided by the well-established packs, as the service of the proven imported stallion hound is always available to recognized packs.

The Montreal Hunt was established in 1826 and is the oldest surviving hunt in North America. The Toronto Hunt dates from 1843, but changed its name about 1949, when the hunt country was moved to the north and the Eglinton and Caledon Hunt split off with part of the pack. The London Hunt, although formally established in 1885, has records going back also to 1843. The Ottawa Valley has existed since 1873 with some interruptions. Other hunts are chiefly traced to one or other of the above. In Montreal, foxhunting was popular with a somewhat restricted social group, and their activities were news. On 12 November 1860, the *Montreal Gazette* made mention of the history of foxhunting in that area:

> 'The Montreal Hunt was founded in 1829 and has been maintained from that date to this. Hunting in the Montreal area was reported in the press of Britain, with a comment that the country was more difficult owing to the high frequency of stiff timber fences.'

The Ottawa Valley Hunt traces its origin to the interest of the Duke of Richmond, Governor of Upper Canada in 1818. On a tour of inspecting the military garrisons, the duke was approached by an apparently tame fox, which he took to be a pet of the regiment he was visiting. The fearlessness of the fox was unfortunately due to rabies, and he promptly bit the governor, with ultimately fatal results. Another governor of Upper Canada, Lord Sydenham, was killed in a fall from his horse in the country west of Kingston, Ontario, but the circumstances are not recorded.

Foxhunting is referred to as the pastime of the élite in the days prior to Confederation. The popularity continued through the 1860s and 1870s, but the disappearance of the British garrisons, and with them their young bachelor officers, somehow made the sport less popular with the young ladies.

Foxhunting has felt the adverse effect of war on many occasions. In 1889, when the first contingent of 7,000 Canadian troops sailed from Quebec for South Africa, it included many members of Canadian hunts. The First World War took a heavy toll of the Candian foxhunting fraternity, and every hunt lost several of its most valued members. The story was repeated when the Second World War took place.

At the time of writing, there are thirteen active hunts in Canada, stretching from Quebec on the east to British Columbia on the west. These, reading from east to west, are as follows: Belle-Riviére, Lake of Two Mountains and Montreal, all in the Province of Quebec; Frontenac, Ottawa Valley, Toronto and North York, Eglinton, Hamilton, Wellington–Waterloo and London, all in the Province of Ontario; Springfield in Manitoba; and Fraser Valley in British Columbia. Several new hunts are in the process of organization. The season for most runs from August until freeze-up, which can occur anywhere between late November and early January. If it does not actually freeze, the fall and winter rains usually render country so deep that hunting is stopped to avoid damage to ground. Most hunts meet several times in the spring when weather permits. Quite often there are dry spells in April, May and June, which permit hunting, but this is usually confined to drag on high ground. Cub hunting in August and early September is very casual and in many hunts is simply an excuse to initiate horses and members and to permit huntsmen to expose their young entry to strange horses. As the fox population is presently reduced by rabies, it is a rare Master who will risk destruction of any cubs.

Customs regarding clothing for hunting in Canada vary little from those prevailing in England and the United States. All Canadian hunts follow the basic patterns, but it is very rare to see anyone in a 'shadbelly' or 'cutaway'. The black coat is standard wear with the usual sprinkling of red. Staff all wear red, with the exception of lady members who in Canada invariably stick to black. This includes both lady Masters and lady whippers-in. The general practice is three-button coats for members, four for Masters and five for professionals. Square-cut coats are worn by Masters and staff, rounded for members. The hunt cap is no longer the prerogative of staff, ex-Masters and farmers. Most hunts permit all members to wear a conventional hunt cap. Of course, silk hats are not uncommon, and the hunt bowler is frequently worn by both sexes, with black coats. Every hunt has a distinctive button and collar.

The usual practice is to incorporate the hunt as a limited company with president and directors. The company holds title to any hunt land and is responsible for insurance and hunt business generally. The Master, of course, retains his usual prerogatives and authority, and has full charge of all hunt arrangements, kennels and hunt staff. Most hunts do have a hunt committee, but, in some cases, this function is to an extent assumed by the board of directors. Hunt annual meetings are usually held in mid-winter and often involve some films on hunting or a visiting speaker. The hunt ball is a standard fixture and invariably produces good fun for the members and some money for the treasurer. The spring horse show and the hunter trials in October do the same. A few hunts also have a point-to-point. Hunt race meets in recent years have become very rare, however. The Ottawa Valley has reverted to the old fashioned point-to-point with some success.

There is always a considerable degree of social activity associated with hunting, and an eager body of social members and car followers help to support every hunt. One custom which may be peculiarly Canadian is a mobile bar, which turns up at the end of the hunt or as soon thereafter as convenient for the refreshment of the field. In the Ottawa Valley and the Frontenac, this is known as 'the green box'—this term is said to have originated with the lugging of the essential ingredients around in a container of that colour. However, the post-hunt festivities in the Toronto Hunt in 1909 were held at an old hotel leased by the hunt at Steel's Corner, near Thornhill, which was called 'Green Bush Lodge', and it is believed by many that the term 'going to the green bush' was corrupted to 'green box'. It is also possible that the term antedates the hotel and that the hotel was in fact named after the custom, and the drinking may well have been done in the bush in the early days!

Quite frequently the field hack back to the meet location after the hunt to collect their trailers, and, at this time, once horses are cooled and loaded, the green box is a welcome relaxation. If the meet should chance to be at the home of a member, crackers and cheese are forthcoming. The same member has probably also produced a quantity of sherry as a stirrup cup before hounds move off. The tendency these days is to serve sherry or an alternative in paper cups, a regrettable departure from tradition. Hunt revenue is derived from the sale of drinks out of the green box to a considerable degree, although the legality of charging money has been questioned more than once.

Rolling farm country is general throughout eastern Canada. Fields and pastures are found in all sizes, but most are 10 or 20 acres in extent. Wire fences are now the general rule in the more prosperous areas. However, there are many less fortunate townships where rails and stone walls still predominate. These are much the best countries. The walls are of dry stone, either rock slabs or hardheads piled to a height of about 3 feet and a width of 4 feet. Many have cedar rails along the top, but a good horse will change feet on the top stones. The timber fences are found in various patterns. The most common is the snake-rail, loosely stacked in a zig-zag fashion. This is a waste of land, and the better farmers have replaced snake-fences with a post-and-rail, using two posts with the rails dropped between and tied part way down with wire. Occasionally, stump fences or solid log fences are encountered in remote areas.

All hunts have a panelling committee, charged with the construction of 'chicken coops' or 'tiger traps' over wire fences. Quite often, two of these will be found in one corner of a field. Rough slabs or old planks are the favourite materials. Cattle will not cross such panels, but a loose rail is added to the top for security of livestock. Hunt gates are quite often put in by the committee where conditions require. Coverts are generally large and may run to 40 acres. Brush is thick around the edges, but mature trees provide open avenues in the interior. Landowners are generally friendly and co-operative, particularly in the old settled areas. A fair number of farmers hunt.

As everywhere, the growth of towns and villages, and the widening of roads, is causing problems for Masters. In Canada, however, there is no lack of room, and it is a simpler matter to meet somewhat farther afield as urban development spreads.

The native fox is the common red fox, *Vulpes fulva*, with a white tip on the brush and black feet. The occasional individual is encountered with some black markings on the shoulders. (Perhaps because a blue fox has escaped from a fur farm.)

The principal enemy is rabies which sweeps back and forth in epidemics but never seems to die out. This disease has plagued Canadian foxes for at least a century. Many foxes die as a result of encounters with porcupines. The spiny quills of this slow-moving animal penetrate mouth, tongue and sometimes eyes, resulting in infections or blindness. Surprisingly, some foxes can skilfully kill and eat a porcupine with impunity! The method is to seize the nose of the porcupine and worry it to death.

ITALY. BY COUNT CIGALA FULGOSI, MASTER OF THE ROME HUNT

'See Chesterfield advance with steady hand,
Swish at a rasper and in safety land.
Who sits his horse so well? Or at a race
Drives four-in-hand with greater skill or grace?
And when hounds really run, like him can show
How fifteen stone should o'er the country go.'

These verses of an old song of the Belvoir Hunt refer to George Stanhope, Sixth Earl of Chesterfield, a famous horseman and a very keen foxhunter. At the end of 1835 he came to Rome with his wife, who was suffering from tuberculosis and had been ordered by the doctors to spend the winter in a mild climate; but, although the Italian climate improved the health of her ladyship, the Roman life was very dull for Lord Chesterfield, who greatly missed his hunting in Leicestershire.

One day, however, riding along the Appian Way, a fox happened to cross the road in front of him, and he immediately realized what perfect hunting country the Roman countryside could make. He quickly sent home for hounds, hunters, huntsman and whipper-in and, within a few months, was hunting the Campagna Romana, followed by a group of Italian friends, enthusiasts of a sport entirely new to Rome.

When, in 1837, after 2 seasons as Master, Lord Chesterfield returned to England, Prince Odescalchi took over and officially founded the Società Romana della Caccia alla Volpe (the Rome Hunt). Since then, hunting in the Campagna Romana has continued without a break, with the exception of during the two world wars.

Since Lord Chesterfield's day, the huntsmen of the Rome Hunt have always been English or Irish, except for two periods, the first from 1895 to 1907, when Marchese di Roccagiovine, then the Master, had an Italian huntsman, and the present day, when I have been hunting hounds myself. Perhaps also for this reason the English organization has always been carried on, and the establishment is run on English lines. Hounds are fed with raw meat and pasta, instead of meat and oatmeal as in England. They are spoken to in English, and a sort of pidgin Roman–English is the *lingua franca* in the kennels.

Every year, since its inception, the hunt has organized a point-to-point at the end of the season; and the Grand Steeplechase of Rome, which has now become an open race held at the Capannelle race-course, originated from the hunt point-to-point. The hunt point-to-point continues today on the estate surrounding the kennels with all races (members, ladies, officers and children) strictly reserved for horses which have hunted regularly throughout the season.

The hounds are English foxhounds, all bred in Italy for many generations, derived from drafts of the best packs in England and in Ireland. Since 1960, when I took over the breeding of the hounds, in order to improve the pack and to avoid inbreeding, every couple of years I imported one or two dog hounds to be used as stallions: nearly all these hounds came from the Kilkenny, from the Flint and Denbigh and from Sir Watkin Williams-Wynn's, having been kindly given to me by the Masters, Major Victor McCalmont, Captain Simon Lloyd and Sir Watkin Williams-Wynn Bart., all of whom have a great reputation as hound breeders.

Normally the hunting pack is about 30 couple. The kennels are on the Appian Way, about 8 miles from the centre of Rome. They were built especially for the

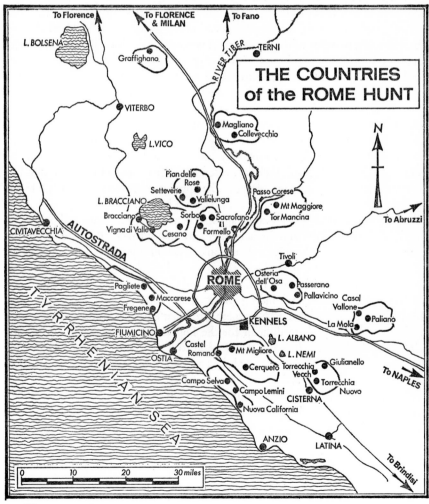

THE COUNTRIES of the ROME HUNT

purpose in 1923, with large rust-coloured stones from local quarries. The horses and hounds are housed on the ground floor, and above them are flats for the hunt servants. The ceiling of the boxes and of the kennels are about 15 feet high, with two windows to each and ventilation is good, even in the height of summer.

The Roman hounds hunt the Campagna Romana, which includes the territory north and south of Rome between the foothills of the Apennines and the Tyrrhenian Sea. The countryside has changed enormously in recent times, with the growth of the city, new residential areas going up everywhere, land reform, the breaking up of the old estates and the introduction of intensive farming. Sadly, the Campagna Romana is no longer the ideal hunting ground that Lord Chesterfield knew, with its miles and miles of open grassland. However, though divided from each other, there are still several large areas of grassland, usually centred in one or other of the few remaining large estates. The countryside consists of gentle bare hills, interrupted occasionally by stone walls. Until the last war, the main resource of the large estates was cattle and horse breeding, and the countryside was strongly fenced with timber, two or three bars of thin chestnut, the famous Roman *staccionata*. Now these are found only on the estates where cattle and horses are still kept, as sheep are the most common livestock now, and these are never fenced in.

Usually at least one side of the hills is covered with thick Mediterranean vegetation; these coverts, usually not too large, are called *spallette*. Some large woods are encountered near the sea. Foxes are usually found in the *spallette* and in the *marrane*, high steep-banked ditches covered by a dense mass of thorn bushes. No horse can get across a *marrana* except at the appointed crossings, and it is difficult working ground even for the most experienced hound.

In spite of the ruthless war waged against them with guns, traps and poison by shepherds, gamekeepers and farmers, there are many foxes (all red foxes) in the Campagna Romana. There is rarely a blank day, hunting 5 days a fortnight; but, although it is quite easy to find a fox, it is more difficult to catch one. Owing to the climate, the scent is usually rather poor, and the wild country hunted provides so many earths, holes and hiding places that proper stopping is impossible. Regarding the climate, it must be remembered that Italy has a milder climate than England, and it is perhaps difficult for the English to realize that even in mid-winter, say in January, it is not uncommon to have dry spells of 2 or 3 weeks' duration: the ground becomes very hard and rather dusty, and scent under these conditions is extremely bad.

The field on Saturday usually numbers between 60 and 80: on a weekday between 25 and 40. All are well mounted, often on Irish horses, and smartly dressed. As the country is mostly open (we never hunt over plough, and the going is seldom heavy), the best type of horse, which is generally used, is an Irish or Italian one, almost thoroughbred, as it is necessary to have good speed to follow the hounds. Even if, in the Campagna Romana, there are no longer as many fences as before the land reform, it is still advisable to have a good bold jumper to negotiate the remaining timber and the high and wide stone walls. Ladies are few, compared with English and American hunts.

There are always several cavalry officers in the field, hunting in uniform. Since the foundation of the famous Cavalry School of Tor di Quinto, its connection with the hunt has been very close. The school was founded in 1891: all cavalry officers, after the main course at the Cavalry School of Pinerolo, near Turin, were sent to Rome for a supplementary course at Tor di Quinto in cross-country riding. The first instructor, the Marchese di Roccagiovine, was chosen by King Umberto I himself who, having regularly hunted for many years when he was crown prince, remembered him as a superb rider across country. The first thing the Marchese asked, and obtained, from the War Office was a subscription to the hunt, so that all the officers of the school and of the mounted regiment in Rome could hunt regularly. The tradition still survives today. When Marchese di Roccagiovine took over as Master of the Roman Hounds in 1895, Captain Frederico Caprilli, who had been a pupil of the first course at Tor di Quinto and then his assistant, succeeded him as instructor of the school.

The Rome Hunt is mainly a city affair: nearly all the subscribers, including those who own land in the hunting country, live, during the winter, in town and keep their horses at livery in one of the many riding clubs or livery stables of Rome.

There is an excellent organization of large horse-boxes which, on request, collect the horses from the stables, take them to the meet, and, at the end of the day, take them back.

This state of affairs reflects also on the Pony Club. Rome has a very lively Pony Club which is well connected to the hunt: however, it is a different sort of organization from the English Pony Club. Children go to day-school 6 days a week, and, as they all live in town, they keep their horses and ponies at livery at the Rome Pony Club—where there is stabling, a club house, indoor and outdoor schools and two good instructors. Every day, after school, the children go there to have riding lessons and exercise their horses. Whenever possible (for instance when they have a holiday from school on a hunting day) they have a day out with the hounds, and they also compete in point-to-points, horse trials and show-jumping events organized by the hunt or by other Roman riding clubs on Sundays.

La Società Romana della Caccia alla Volpe is the oldest sporting association in Rome and has always been the centre of social life, in particular for all sportsmen interested in horses. The subscribers of the hunt in 1869 founded the Circolo della Caccia, 'the best club in Rome', which had the honour of having among its other royal members, their Majesties King George V, King Edward VIII and King George VI, and now the Duke of Edinburgh.

King Umberto I who, as I wrote above, while he was Crown Prince, was a regular follower of the hounds, when he ascended to the throne became the honorary chairman of the hunt. All the succeeding kings of Italy also granted the hunt this honour, and today, King Umberto II in exile in Portugal, heads the hunt list. In the last century Empress Elizabeth of Austria followed the Rome hounds as well as hunting in England and Ireland, as did Prince Napoleon of France and many of the Bonaparte family when in Rome.

The Roman hunt is very popular with English, Irish and American sportsmen, and foreign visitors are very often seen out with us. A few years ago, when hunting was banned in several parts of England due to foot-and-mouth disease, several English enthusiasts flew to Rome at the weekends to hunt with the Roman hounds, and we gave them a very warm welcome.

I resigned as Master, after 14 seasons, in 1976, handing over to Prince Colonna. He engaged Bob Parker (formerly of the Curre and the Tickham) as huntsman.

PORTUGAL
(First published in *Country Life*, February 14, 1974)
Twice a week, each Portuguese winter, a bright cavalcade of 30 horsemen and women, following a level and handsome pack of rather large English foxhounds, may be seen winding through the cork and conifer forests, a few miles across the River Tagus from Lisbon. This is the Equipagem de Santo Huberto, 'the sporting club of the patron saint of hunting'. A dozen of these cavaliers are dressed more or less in the style of English huntsmen, while the other men and the women wear black coats with their velvet caps.

Their mounts are less stereotyped; some are pure Arab, a few Irish, others barb, two or three of the *rejeonador*'s sort, and one, unmistakably, of English thoroughbred strains. They have learned to tread very carefully, these horses, for below the scented undergrowth of mimosa, rosemary, oleander, wild olive and gorse, the sandy ground is pock marked with rabbit burrows and other traps.

The shadows, first of cork, then of eucalyptus, then of pine, dapple softly over the equestrian figures, and the forests are so quiet, so lightly touched by the hand of man, that you imagine the scene belongs closer to the eighteenth century than the present day. The procession rarely stops, for, if they do not find, hounds draw on and on, pausing only momentarily for a fuller investigation of, say, a tangle of bramble and bracken or a broom thicket.

Then it is 'Leu in, my bee-ooties!' carefully modulated on the lips of huntsman José Nogueira. Riding just behind, are the two joint-Masters, Baron Frederic de Beck, who came from Austria to Portugal 25 years ago and has since been the moving spirit of the hunt, and Professor Belo de Moraes who was elected in 1972. A discreet distance behind these are the followers, including, on the day I am riding, the American Chargé d'Affaires and the British Embassy's Counsellor, and led by the Field Master, Senhor Antonio de Brito e Cunha. One young Lisbon blade, impatient with the trot, is giving his Arab a zig-zagging pipe-opener over the gorse and mimosa clumps. If he rides too far forward on the flank, Brito e Cunha breaks off the native-tongue chat he is enjoying with his neighbour, for a caution of 'Hold hard!' or 'I say, sta-idy there!' in linguaphone Leicestershire.

This English affectation has its roots in the Peninsular War: for the first fox-hounds the Portuguese saw were those followed by Wellington's officers and led by his huntsman, Tom Crane, who was fired upon more than once when his pack led him behind the French lines. Wellington's hunt became a shining legend in the country, and when, later in the nineteenth century, the Portuguese first established their own pack expressly to hunt the fox, it was the English pattern that was insisted upon. Up to the Second World War, there flourished three equipagem or hunting clubs, whose leading lights were Carlos I, Count Palava and Senhores Roque de Pinho, Count of Alto-Mearim, and Coelho da Cunha. In 1908, Carlos, the last but one King of Portugal, and his son were assassinated on their return from hunting at Vila Voçosa, once a great hunting centre, now only famous for its marble quarries and as the home of the dukes of Braganza.

A revival of the combination of those clubs, the Santo Huberto owes its birth in 1950 to three keen equitators: the Countess of Barcelona, wife of the Spanish pretender, who is now honorary Master, the Marques de Graciosa, the hunt's first Master, and Senhor Ing. Moniz Galvao. They imported drafts from the Albrighton, the Bramham Moor, Duke of Beaufort's and the Pytchley and hired a series of Englishmen to hunt them: John Long, Richard Farquhar-Thompson, Bob Kemp, Frank Bishop, Ted Fitzpatrick and John Kirkham. From these, José Nogueira learned a good deal more than the difference between 'Who-op!' and 'Get away bike!'

'Yeet-tray, hay, hay!' urges José, as the trotting phalanx threads through a fresh pattern of cork, whose trunks and lower limbs are showing the stark cocoa-coloured underbark, where the cutters have removed the precious commodity. There seems to be no end to the silence of this unenclosed wilderness. Until gun-shots ring out. Then you know the forests are shared by other weekend hunters. Baron de Beck leans across from his Irish chestnut to let you know how much he 'hopes they only intend to shoot the birds'. He implies 'and not us'. For these game-shots have a reputation for popping off at anything that flickers; but, when the hunt goes by, they call their dogs and gaze up, delighted at the unexpected pageantry. Their display of pleasure is not reciprocated: the sight of the guns reminds the foxhunters that, here, increasing areas of land are fenced off as shooting reserves, to which horses and hounds are forbidden entry and to which the hunted fox escapes, probably to be shot, to be poisoned or to be trapped by the gamekeepers.

A hound speaks. 'Hake to Playmate, hake!' (None of your Isabel nor Rosario; these are *English* hounds making *English* sport.) The frost that lay in the open during the early hours and the dew in the woody fastnesses have long since dried, and you wonder how the scorching sand can hold any trace of scent; but they are all on now, and the trotting retinue gathers into a canter, permeating through the eucalyptus to the fir. A check. 'Hold hard, I say!' The line is retraced; the hunt proceeds for 2 miles. Then, 'He has certainly gone to ground', explains the young Count of Monsaraz, Director of Portugal's Turf Club and an amateur whipper-in; but hounds will not mark; they are held back. . . . What measures do you now take in England? A terrier? We could not do that; it might catch him. Foxes are too scarce here to allow any killing except in the open. You ride up to exa-mine the earth. Strange: there are so many foxes' padmarks around the entrances; it looks as though half a dozen chose this retreat.

They hunt two more across 3 miles with scarcely a serving scent. You are told that conditions are 'quite abnormal'. Never mind, it is a rare privilege to follow hounds through these lovely evergreen woods with their scents of gorse and thyme and eucalyptus in the crisp air. At two o'clock Baron de Beck decides it is time for luncheon. He gives José the signal. The cavalcade race back, without a pause, and it is advisable for you to keep well up at this moment, for they canter nearly all the way, and, without the music of hounds to guide you, it is easy to get lost. In a trice these hounds with the old English look are home in the capacious and beautifully kept kennels at Santo Estevao which were built in 1962 by Baron de Beck, with Senhor Brito e Cunha as architect.

The pre-prandial scene at the adjacent club-house reminds you of the players' section of a polo pavilion; muddy white breeches and sweat-stained boots lie outside the steaming showers, from which pour excited talk of horses and the sport they provide in general. For the Equipagem is more than a hunt: it is an equitation club. Next door, below walls hung with foxes' masks and Leech's paintings from Surtees, whisky is ordered and glasses are raised towards the photograph of the Countess of Barcelona, who, if she will never be a queen in name, has reigned where St Hubert's spirit now moves in Portugal, from the beginning.

Chapter 17

Point-to-Point
Racing

by G. B. Fairbairn, *Sometime Chairman of the Point-to-Point Secretaries'*
Association

MOST PEOPLE are aware that the names steeplechase and point-to-point
arose from the fact that our forefathers decided to race from one
church steeple to another church steeple, or from one prominent
point or landmark to another. Those days are long past, except in a few instances
where hunts or hunt clubs organize what today is called a cross-country race.
There are not many of these races left, and they are usually run over 3 miles, or
more, of natural hunting country, taking place prior to hounds meeting and the
day's foxhunting, lightweights, heavyweights and ladies all riding against each
other, with individual prizes given for different sections, usually a cup and a
bottle of champagne.

These courses are across true hunting country, with the wire removed from
fences and with each person able to take his or her own line. It is almost impossible to find a point-to-point horse in these cross-country races; they are regarded
as being far too precious to risk in such a hurly-burly. These hunt races, from
which the modern point-to-point arose, were, for a while, controlled by the
Masters of Foxhounds' Association. Then, gradually, the National Hunt Committee took over, and the control has remained in their (now the Jockey Club's)
hands, ever since. For a period things just seemed to drift along with, to all
appearances, the controlling body not really interested in point-to-points, and
those involved were left with the feeling that they were a nuisance—the unwanted
poor relation of National Hunt racing.

The Jockey Club set up a Committee in 1971, under the chairmanship of Lord
Leverhulme, to look into all aspects of point-to-point racing. The recommendations of this committee were accepted, and, while the Jockey Club still retained
the final say in the guidance of point-to-point races, they brought back the
Masters of Foxhounds' Association into the controlling organization, as well as
giving those concerned, through another Committee called the Point-to-Point
Secretaries' Association, the means by which the people involved with these hunt
races could put forward their views and recommendations. The theory of the
consultation was sound, but, in practice, it has many weaknesses, which, I am
sure, will gradually be overcome. This is the structure as it has evolved over the
years for the control of point-to-points. The one anomaly is the fact that point-

to-points racing is controlled by persons not immediately involved in the sport, and those really involved and knowledgeable have little say in its control or development.

So much for the control of point-to-points. What of the races and the competitors? The courses are virtually miniature race-courses with fences built to standards set out by the Jockey Club, usually on a circuit of 8 or 10 fences, most of which are jumped twice, very different indeed from the old original races from 'point to point' but very much better for the spectators, who can usually see all the fences. In consequence this makes a much more satisfactory spectator sport and of course helps to encourage betting. This is vital to the sport, as the bookmakers donate varying sums to the funds, and the Levy Board make generous payments to help with the upkeep and improvements to all point-to-point courses. The latest step, in the endeavour to see that fences and courses are fair, is a series of 'teach-ins' under the guidance of the Jockey Club course inspectors. This can do nothing but good, and perhaps the criticism of too much standardization can best be overcome by the variation in the terrain at individual meetings, while the local course inspectors will have a common standard to see that the fences are fair to horse and rider.

What of the modern point-to-point horse? A glance at sale results from Ascot or Doncaster, or one of the several other National Hunt sale organizations, would scarcely be believed by someone returning to the point-to-point scene after an absence of 10 or 15 years. The better point-to-point horses are now valued in several thousands of pounds. If you look at the breeding of runners as printed in the race card at any hunt meeting, you wonder as to the viability of the horse breeding industry, with horses by Derby winners and top stallions regularly featured and running for a prize of £40. If an owner has a nice young horse and can win a few races, then he has a very valuable asset, as this type of horse which can gallop and jump a genuine 3 miles, with 12 stone or more on its back, is popular with professional trainers and can command a very high price. This is not surprising when one reads of horses such as The Dickler (Cheltenham Gold Cup 1973 with Charlie Potheen) as having started their racing careers in the point-to-point field.

These horses have attracted a new type of owner, particularly in the south and the Midlands, owners who possibly do not even hunt or ride themselves. The horse is kept at livery—in order to comply with the rules—and some of these professional point-to-point livery yards even have their own stable riders— usually the most competent jockeys in the area. There was at least one such livery stable with a reported twenty-plus point-to-point horses in it for the 1974 season. In view of this attitude to point-to-point racing, it is not surprising that the stewards of the Jockey Club have had to revise the rules governing point-to-point racing and that these have increased in number from 58 to 172 and are so complex that a special summary has had to be included, so that they can be more easily understood. Before castigating the stewards for this action, it should be remembered that extra rules need only to be made when the old ones fail to control the situation.

One of the amazing facts in point-to-point racing is the number of owners prepared to run horses for the maximum permitted cash prize of £40. Possibly one of the more significant remarks was made by Mr Richard Miller (the 1973 champion point-to-point rider) at the annual point-to-point dinner—when he said he did not wish to see any great increase in prize money, as he felt it would lead to the 'fun' going out of point-to-pointing, and after all, 'We do it for "fun".'

This leads me onto the subject of why point-to-points have such great support. Possibly there can be no hard and fast answer, but my own suspicion is that many of those involved as riders, owners, trainers—not to mention the public—prefer the informality of the point-to-point meeting rather than the rigid protocol, the herding into different enclosures, the paper work and the formalities involved in running a horse at, or attending, a proper race meeting. This is possibly understandable from the owner–rider viewpoint; but what is the attraction to the public in a point-to-point meeting? Is it this lack of formality: knowing many people there, access to all and any part of the course, close proximity to horses and riders? For the amenities are nothing to compare with those available on most race-courses. The bars are usually located in a draughty tent, and the car park is a muddy field, all this in February or March. There are several popular hunt meetings in the south and the south Midlands where the crowds are the envy of many race-course executives with the tote takings alone running into five figures, or close to it.

Where does this leave point-to-pointing in the 1970s? Gone are the days when the good hunter could be asked to go round and give a respectable performance—he would be galloped off his legs in no time today. Yet, at the same time, it is somewhat unfair to term these meetings, as some critics have, as third-rate steeplechases. Possibly, they fall into a category entirely of their own. Sufficient of the old original hunt race spirit and tradition is left and handed down to keep them that little bit informal and friendly, so it is to be hoped that this spirit is strong enough to stand up to the pressures of new rules and regulations, so that these hunt point-to-point meetings can retain this, their own particular flavour.

What of the future? If this account so far gives the impression that this form of hunt racing is too beset by rules and troubles, that was not the writer's intention. Rules there have to be, as well as changes, and there is little to be gained by looking back on the point-to-point meeting as a means by which the hunt could provide its own members, and those of adjacent hunts, with the opportunity and fun of riding over fences, and at the same time a chance to entertain the farmers. Few Masters of Hounds are really interested in the point-to-point as such—even though, by the Jockey Club rules, they are directly responsible for running their own meeting. In most cases they delegate this responsibility, merely turning up on the appointed day.

The Master or joint-Masters and the hunt now look to the point-to-point as a source of finance towards the hunt funds, and, in consequence, the meeting has to be viable. This financial side has been helped enormously by local firms sponsoring the prize money. The trend now goes even further, with sponsors for each individual fence. This sponsorship often has little direct commercial viability to the donors, but sponsors are generous, in the name of goodwill in their support of the local hunts. Besides this local sponsorship, there are a series of area and national championships, for which riders, horses and owners are allocated points for wins and places, with various trophies being presented at dinners organized at the close of the season. These contests have added certain extra competition, but whether this has been to the good of the spirit of point-to-point racing is doubted in some quarters. A large proportion of these generous national and area sponsors are connected with the drink trade, presumably backing the theory that the winners will be celebrating victory and the losers drowning their sorrows!

How regrettable it is that the stewards found it necessary (in 1974) to introduce dope testing at point-to-points, but there is no doubt that this form of cheating has been resorted to in the past. Further, the local stewards have now to be provided with an up-to-date form book (hunterguide) to check on the running of horses, if need be. Both these actions are an indication that hunt racing has changed and that harsh realities must be faced; but at the same time there have been changes and improvements which help to keep point-to-point racing in a form and tradition of its own. The approach to the preparation for both horse and rider is professional and will become more so unless restrictions are placed on the type of horse we see running today, possibly in the shape of allowances for home-bred horses or horses by premium stallions. If something on these lines could be framed, it might possibly give the local boy or girl a much better opportunity of getting a first ride over fences, which seems to become more and more difficult every year.

In some areas there is a definite shortage of competent riders, but, with women playing a larger part in the horse world each year, it is only right that there should be more opportunities for them to ride at point-to-point meetings. Until recently they were confined to the ladies' race at each meeting. Then, a few years ago, they were invited to ride in members' races with the men—really to help swell the runners in these races. In 1974, for the first time, they could ride in the adjacent hunt race. Possibly it will not be long before the ladies are riding against the men at level weight in all the races at point-to-point meetings. There are already a few ladies' races under the rules of flat racing, and, at the time of writing, ladies' hunter chases are said to be coming in. Who knows, we may soon be having to frame 'men only' races.

The hunts will always wish to encourage and support point-to-points, not only for their direct financial help but for their indirect contributions, in the form of subscriptions for the horses being qualified and subscriptions from would-be jockeys, and, without a doubt, there is considerable local goodwill from which the hunts benefit by these meetings.

It is not without a smile that one reads of hunt race problems at the beginning of the last century. There was no central control, so that each hunt made up its own rules, and, as could be expected, these races were thoroughly corrupt. Surtees, not a lover of steeplechasing, went as far as to say, '... but the bevy of scamps and vagabonds it brought into the field was enough to drive all respectable competitors out of it and to leave the sharks to eat each other. ...' Nimrod wrote of them as 'men who rode as if spare necks were to be had as easily as spare stirrup leathers'. Point-to-pointing has progressed far from those days, and it will surely adapt to changing conditions and will provide a great deal of pleasure to many people in the countryside for a long time to come.

Chapter 18

The Future of Foxhunting
in Britain

I N MOST OF Britain, foxhunting is the countryman's primary traditional and
recreational pursuit. It is really the only integral pageantry he owns. For
him it is at once healthy and honourable, thrilling and beautiful; but there
are other men and women who view the sport less indulgently. Indeed there is a
faction pressing for the abolition of all forms of hunting, not those farmers, smallholders and shepherds, who are concerned about damage, but ordinary citizens
who believe it to be a cruel practice. Let us quieten their objections.

Firstly we refer to man's obligation to keep all animals at a reasonable level,
especially those that destroy livestock, deplete vegetable and cereal crops,
damage trees and spread disease. Bark-eating grey squirrels are trapped by the
forester; corn-eating woodpigeons are shot by the farmer; turnip-loving hares
are slain by the thousands in the February drives; rats are poisoned by the poultry
keeper and caught by his terriers; and egg- and chicken-stealing crows are sniped
whenever they can be induced within range.

The fox, too, during lambing he is a menace to the shepherd. When he
invades a hen-run or a duck enclosure, he goes much further than killing for food;
he kills all within range; he kills for the lust of killing; but he also does good.
He helps, for instance, to keep rodents in check and he is one of the most attractive
creatures that has so far survived the hand of man. It would be a tragedy if we
were to lose the fox.

But, if his numbers must be kept at a reasonable level how is it to be done?
With poison? That way promises a lingering death. Trapping? Snaring? It is still
an acknowledged method of control even if the gin trap is prohibited. But how
many foxes are killed outright by the trap? How many wrench a noose away on
their necks and keep it tight for the remainder of their days, or gnaw through a
trapped foot and go through life on three legs and a stump? Shooting? With the
shot-gun, except at close range, the fox takes a deal of hitting to kill. Many are
wounded by non-hunting game shots and angry farmers and keepers. Such foxes
die slowly, if they die at all, either directly from their injuries or from gangrenous
wounds. Should whole families of foxes simply be dug out and knocked over the
head in the spring and early summer? If that became the accepted means, then
foxes would soon disappear from many areas of Britain. Gassing? The same
applies. How? . . .

Once, the fox population of Britain was less than half its present scale. Men had no cause to control foxes in those days. Wolves and, to a lesser extent, lynxes were the key to that situation. Then the weak fox and the old fox rarely died of old age or starvation. They were taken by their predators. Such was nature's way; but the wolf and the lynx became extinct in Britain more than two centuries ago. During that period man's substitute for the wolf pack has been the hound pack. So hunting plays a true, if small, part in the ecosystem, in the balance of nature. The hunts take the sickly and the senile first; they do not often catch the quick cunning fox, the fox in his prime. Hunting with hounds implies a clean death—a snap across the back from the leading hound or two and oblivion, or a humane killer, or a clean escape.

A few years after the Second World War a body called the Scott Henderson Committee, set up by the then Labour government and composed of seven people, well informed on country matters and including a naturalist, a vet, a trades unionist, a medical practitioner and a zoologist, made an enquiry into 'practices or activities which may involve cruelty to British wild mammals'. The committee concluded that, of all forms of fox control, hunting with hounds was certainly the most humane method. When a bill against hunting was then debated under the same government, the then Minister of Agriculture, Tom Williams, put his view before the house like this:

'All the evidence available to me shows that humanitarian interests are better served by an organized effort, under the control of responsible, experienced people, who are all animal lovers themselves. . . . There is, in hunting, very much less chance of cruelty than by indiscriminate trapping or snaring, or, indeed, in expert shooting. I have seen traps which had caught animals, which have then escaped, leaving a leg behind. . . . I also know about snaring, which means slowly choking to death. And I know something about shooting, which certainly produces a much higher rate of prolonged suffering than does the instantaneous kill of the hunt. . . . '

Foxhunters do not pretend their way is the most *effective* form of control; that it could never be, for foxes avoid detection, or they escape so often that only a few thousand are killed by the hunts each season; but they do believe it is the kindest way.

Hunting with hounds occasionally—all too occasionally these days—involves a long run, which exhausts the fox (just as he was exhausted by the wolf pack); but no well-informed naturalist will say that it *terrifies* him, as is often suggested. Those with a sound understanding of animal behaviour know that a hunted animal cannot anticipate death, cannot suffer as we would suffer in those circumstances. Time and again close observers of the hunted fox have seen him look calmly back and, if hounds do not seem to be too close, begin to search along a hedgerow or covertside for rodents and insects. All through the history of the sport, huntsmen have noticed that foxes, when not too severely pressed, often appear to treat the performance as a game, while the more closely hunted ones give the impression of animals accepting a challenge, as if they were saying, 'I'm neither elderly nor frail, you picked the wrong one this morning.' And would this not have been the fox's attitude to the wolf pack? Far better for the fox born in those days than in our age of shot gun, snare and strychnine.

'How would you like to be chased across the country by hounds, then caught, killed and eaten?' the anthropomorphic 'anti' asks the foxhunter. 'I should hate it,' counters the hunting man or woman, 'but then I am not a fox; I do not live in a hole in the ground, nor eat rats and beetles, nor slaughter lambs, nor raid hen runs; I do not kill or maim as a way of life. I should find a fox's life positively revolting, just as he would find my rarefied life as dull as ditchwater. You cannot compare my instincts with his.'

Having swayed a few of the more open-minded critics with his arguments, the foxhunter is often asked, 'Why then do you make a ritual of it? Why must you dress up and make sport of the hounding to death of one of God's creatures?' The foxhunter replies with a question, 'Is there greater sin in human atavism as such than there is in animal atavism?' The eyes of man, like the eyes of tigers, of apes, of wolves, of foxes, are in front: they are predator's eyes. Our remote ancestors were possessed of certain survival instincts, prompting them to hunt to eat. We have not lost those instincts. Some people sublimate them, channel them into a variety of vigorous pursuits, while a number satisfy them by following hounds and indulging in other field sports, nor are they less civilized than their neighbour for that.

Ferocity there is in the wild—we know it from the death screams of predator and prey in the woods and waysides by night, if we have no other direct evidence. But there is no sadism; the lion is not cruel, the falcon is not cruel, the stoat is not cruel, the hunting man is not cruel; only, in the case of vulpicide, is the irresponsible vermin destroyer, with gun, poison, spade and trap, cruel.

Although it may or may not be a primitively aggressive streak in the psyche of some foxhunters that prompts them to *follow hounds*, they certainly do not sacrifice time and money and physical effort for the pleasure of seeing foxes killed. Far from it, foxhunters are animal lovers. Nearly all endeavour to avoid being present at the kill. They hunt for the pleasure of seeing hounds work, to experience the incomparable sights and sounds and smells of a hunting day, for the exhilaration of riding cross-country in an uncertain direction and for that other invaluable, if intangible, ingredient, the 'fraternity of the chase'.

The foot follower, as we have seen, gets much of this and, in some subtle ways, more.

'But why,' the mounted enthusiast is asked, 'dress up in scarlet and silk hat, white breeches and top boots, carefully tied stocks and coats of fine Melton, coloured waistcoats and laundered gloves?' Some hunting folk beg the question with the answer, 'This is a free country, isn't it?' True; and yet hunting dress is more a matter of conformity than freedom. Some items of it could hardly be described as practical. It is worn from a sense of parade and tradition, from a desire to contribute to the pageantry of the hunt in the smartest way one knows; from a sense of sharing in a unique and classless brotherhood.

That, they admit, is a reason why foxhunters are readier targets for the objectors than other field sportsmen. They present a stark target. At the animal end of the scale, it is perfectly evident that people who are against hunting tend to rush to the defence of creatures in the order of their charm and size: deer, foxes and others; then hares; then birds; and fish not at all. Foxes are never wounded by hounds, but rabbits and woodpigeons and pheasants are wounded by gunshot, and it would be naive to think that they do not suffer pain; foxes are not played by the mouth on a hook for long periods before being knocked on the head, but the fisherman's catch is thus played, and let no man declare that a creature with the delicate senses of a fish feels less discomfort with a hook on his lip than a rat or a squirrel or a pigeon can feel with gun pellets under their skin. Apart from the smaller size and degree of attractiveness of the creatures involved, for the ardent 'anti-blood-sports' campaigner to make a stand against the wildfowler or the angler would, of course, be poor politics. Indeed it would be rather a waste of time: for neither fishers nor shooting men look down from horses, nor wear scarlet, nor parade in villages. Anyway there are far far too many of them to challenge; and so it is the smaller, hunting community—a mere 250,000 of them —who take the brunt of the criticism against country sports.

But behind the bright shield of the British Field Sports Society, fishermen, hunting folk, stalkers and game shots club together in mutual support.

All through the present century, the army of foxhunters has shown a steady increase, and many of the hunts are more and more embarrassed by the size of their fields. Some see fit to confine their membership and following to those who live and keep horses in the hunt country concerned. For, besides the sport itself, it is the land that inevitably suffers from too many horses; but, ironically and gratifyingly, these enlarged fields owe their growth largely to the expanding prosperity of the farmers and their families, who contribute perhaps 80 to 90% of the mounted strengths of many hunts. Owing to busy roads and intensive agriculture, there is a great deal less opportunity for riding far and fast across country, and more people 'ride to hunt' rather than 'hunt to ride': they take more interest in watching hounds work, the truer purpose of hunting.

Membership of hunt supporters' clubs—the foot, car and bicycle brigade—also swells, and, while the hunts are anxious to encourage this enthusiasm, the growing number of cars out on hunting days does put hounds at a considerable disadvantage. The hunts accept this, while encouraging car followers to switch off their engines whenever they can and to avoid heading the fox.

Foxhunting becomes more popular and so does pheasant shooting. Guns pay high prices for their place in a syndicate. Keepers kill a huge number of foxes annually. The shoots do not welcome disturbance of their carefully nurtured coverts, particularly in October, November and December, and many shoot owners ban the hunt from those coverts until the pheasant season ends. Thanks, however, to a series of joint trials carried out in recent years by the Game Conservancy and the British Field Sports Society, it has been demonstrated that hounds disturb game coverts and disperse pheasants far less than was hitherto supposed, and we may hope that the shooting fraternity will, in future, turn a more indulgent eye towards foxhunters and foxhounds.

However, nothing much is likely to alleviate Britain's unrelenting march of urbanization and road-building. The reasons underlying the many hunt amalgamations that have taken place since the 1960s give the most convincing examples of how huntable country is irrevocably lost. They also point an ominous finger to the future. The Garth and South Berks, for instance, joined forces in 1962 on account of the spread of built-up areas, especially around Bracknell and because of roadbuilding, notably the M4. (The Masters of Foxhounds' Association have requested that no draws shall take place within 2 miles of a motorway.)

It was also the menace of the M4, coupled with the new areas around Basingstoke, that drew the Vine and Craven together. The Meynell and South Staffs merged in 1970 following the spread of the Birmingham, Lichfield, Derby and Burton-on-Trent suburbs and the link up of the M4. ('Although vast on the map', Dermot Kelly, their joint-Master and huntsman, told me at the time, 'the combined area is really quite small in terms of genuine huntable country.') The Vale of Aylesbury came into being principally because the M1 and M5 carved up what used to be the Hertfordshire's country, the M404 and A40 divided the plough-ridden South Oxfordshire, while the Old Berkeley were afflicted with ever-sprawling townships and industrial areas.

Many more hunts must be looking very anxiously at the pronouncements of the town and country planners and the rural district schedules. How long, one wonders, before the Enfield Chace, whose country lies on the north fringe of London, must seek marriage or stoop to an aniseed trail. And how long before the Old Surrey and Burstow, whose northern sector has been chopped off by the M25 and their western end threatened by the M23 and a new railway, must seek amalgamation with, say, the West Kent?

England's rideable country and copses recede each year: a snippet here, an enclave there, private, public, agricultural. Ventures like open-range chicken farms, pony studs and many other specialized units, neatly enclosed with electric-fenced paddocks, are on the increase; holdings whose owners would not dream of allowing a single horseman through, let alone a charging hunt; and great stretches of farmland, selected for intensive seed dressing and manuring, have to be circumvented because scent is annulled. In many parts of Britain the coverts are falling to agriculture like ninepins. (Capt. MacAndrew, of the Zetland, wrote to me recently saying that his country have lost as many as 31 fox-holding copses since the 1950s.)

In the face of our countryside showing more fertilizer and diesel, increased plough and wire, heavier traffic and crowds, will the foxhound's qualities need to

31 Count Cigala Fulgosi (centre), Master and Huntsman, Marchese Napoleone Roccagionine (right), Honorary Whipper-in, and Cesare Cialli with the Rome Hounds near Pantano Borghese

32 Equipagem de Santo Huberto with Huntsman Jose Nogveina leading hounds

33 A typical Canadian obstacle, zigzag
'snake-rail' fence of split cedar

34 A characteristic fence of split chestnut rails
laid in the 'snake' pattern, jumped by Harry
Worcester Smith, Master of Grafton (Loudoun
Country, Virginia)

United States

35 A grey fox on a feeding rock in full sunlight
at midday

36 Jumping a fence made out of the stumps
pulled out of the ground when the first settlers
cleared the land, Battle Creek Hunt, Michigan

Champion-ridden hunter   Stone-wall country

37   Mr Robert Irwin's five-year-old 'Kit-Chin'
ridden by Rosemary McVeigh, Dublin 1974

38   Cotswold followers, near Chedworth,
Gloucestershire

Derbyshire and Yorkshire hunts

39 On steaming horses as hounds check are (left to right) Miss Ann Perkins, Major Tom Hanbury, Mrs Freddie Barker and Lady Margaret Fortescue (Meynell Hunt)

40 Mr Tom Oldfield (left) and Mr Keith Preston with the Sinnington terriers

Jumping together

41 The Adjacent Hunts Moderate Race at the
Tweseldown Point-to-Point

42 Jumping a thorn fence with a ditch beyond
in the Quorn Hunter Trials in Leicestershire

All set for a day on the lakeland fells

43 Opening meet of the Ullswater at Dockray, Cumberland, (from left to right) Mr J. A. Bulman (Joint-Master), Joe Wear (Huntsman, 1932–40 and 1945–70), Dennis Barrow (Huntsman) and Capt. the Hon. A. G. Lowther (Joint-Master)

44 John Nicholson (left) with the Lunesdale hounds, near Sedburgh, Yorkshire

Foxhunting for young and old

45 Three-year-old Linda Savage with the Chiddingfold Farmers Hunt near Newlands Corner, Surrey

46 Octogenarian Mr Joe Bond out with the Stevenstone, near Abbot's Bickington, Devon

be more accentuated in the future? Since foxes are continually headed, we need hounds that turn ever more tightly on their quarry. Clearly they must have a superlative nose, for no hounds can run faster than their noses. They must have, too, a good strong voice so that both hunt staff and followers, who find it more difficult than ever to keep up, will know just where they are. Also, perhaps, they will need greater pace and drive and determination to keep on terms with their fox. Close breeding from the Beaufort–Heythrop hound has produced a type that, if not quite as standardized as the 'old Belvoir', is one that has, perhaps, become just as conventional. Albeit the Peterborough award-winning hunts are the most adept at catching foxes, some experts believe that fresh blood will be wanted. Where would they turn? To the College Valley, perhaps, or the Cotley? Or to pure Welsh?

How about rising prices and the cost of the sport? At present, foxhunters pay less for their 6 months' fun than syndicate game-shots who may have, perhaps, as little as a dozen Saturdays in 3 months to look forward to; and, although one hopes that it will always be possible for those, besides farmers, of moderate means, to hunt, there is little doubt that the foxhunter will be required to dig deeper into his pocket as the years go by. In these difficult times, why should Masters be asked to pay £1,000 a year for the honour of making their self-sacrifice? Besides, Masters who are required to find the whole of the difference between the guarantee and the total bill are all too inclined to run out of cash after a few years. Then a new Master has to be found. Far better to have the best man for the job, regardless of his purse, and to pay the hunt expenses through increased subscriptions. Long Masterships are very important for the health of any hunt. They imply stability and long vision; they mean continuity when hunt servants come and go.

But what about immediate problems? Every year, each hunt, each foxhunter is full of anticipation. Will the harvest be late? Shall we have a dry autumn? How soon will Bluebell recover from that tendon that went at the hunter trials? How will X, our new huntsman, just in from Ireland, get along in our knee-deep plough country? Is it true that the farmer who's moved into Absolam's threatens to lock his gates on hunting days? How are those puppies shaping, the ones we walked? Did you know there's a new livery stables opening up at Westham? Is it confirmed that, as a result of Little Dinton becoming an overspill area for Newton, there'll be no more hunting there next season but one? How do you think Fanciful and Fearless will enter? . . .

Some of these questions are serious challenges, others happy anticipation. Although no sport has been threatened as seriously as foxhunting, and still survived, in the past century and a half, the echo of its votaries' first cry sounds through as clearly as ever, 'Be with them we will!'

Why do they set such a high premium on their sport? John Masefield, Poet Laureate, knew why, 'Hunting makes more people happy than anything else I know', he wrote in the introduction to *Reynard the Fox*, 'When people are happy

N

together, I am quite certain that they build up something eternal, something both beautiful and divine, which weakens the power of all evil things upon this life of men and women.'

Therein lies the real significance of foxhunting's survival.

Chapter 19

The Literature
of the Sport

'In that word 'unting
what a ramification of knowledge is compressed.' JORROCKS

BRITAIN

SINCE I could not hope to present the whole broad rich scope of foxhunting's literature in a single chapter, I shall compromise by giving short biographies of those I consider to be the greatest contributors to that literature, with flavours of their writings, followed by a list of books for the foxhunters' shelves. Since Beckford was the first writer to express genius on modern foxhunting let us begin with him; and from Beckford to Surtees, Nimrod, Whyte-Melville, Trollope, Bromley-Davenport, Somerville and Ross, Masefield and Sassoon.

PETER BECKFORD   Born in 1740, son of Julines Beckford, who bought Steepleton Iwerne, Dorset, from Thomas Fownes, the first man in the west of England to hunt fox deliberately. Peter was educated at Westminster School. He kept harriers, then foxhounds, in Dorset. He made a detailed study of the science of hunting. He published anonymously *An Essay on Hunting* in 1733. He sat as an M.P. for Morpeth in 1768. He married Louisa, daughter of Lord Rivers in 1773. He travelled in Italy in 1789 and wrote an account of it. He was a distinguished scholar, of whom a contemporary wrote:

'Never had fox or hare the honour of being chased to death by so accomplished a huntsman, never was the huntsman's dinner graced by such urbanity and wit. He could bag a fox in Greek, find a hare in Latin, inspect his kennels in Italian, and direct the economy of his tables in excellent French.'

He died in 1811.
Beckford's *Thoughts upon Hunting*, a series of letters, printed in 1798, is still regarded as the greatest authority on hunting ever written. Here he is on casting and lifting (Letter XX):

'In my seventeenth letter I gave you the opinion of my friend—*"that a pack of foxhounds, if left entirely to themselves, would never lose a fox"*. I am always sorry when I differ from that gentleman in anything; yet I am so far from thinking they never would lose a fox that I doubt much if they would ever kill one. There are times when hounds should be helped, and at all times they must be kept forward. Hounds will naturally lie on a cold scent, when stopped by sheep or other impediments; and when they are no longer able to get forward, will oftentimes hunt the old scent back again, if they find that they can hunt no other. It is the judicious encouraging of hounds to hunt, when they cannot run, and the preventing them from losing time by hunting too much when they might run, that distinguishes a good sportsman from a bad one. Hounds that have been well taught will cast forward to a hedge, of their own accord; but you may assure yourself that this excellence is never acquired by such as are left entirely to themselves. To suffer a pack of foxhounds to hunt through a flock of sheep, when it is easy to make a regular cast round them, is, in my judgement, very unnecessary; it is wilfully losing time to no purpose. I have, indeed, been told that hounds at no time should be taken off their noses: I shall only say, in answer to this, that a foxhound who will not bear lifting is not worth the keeping; and, I shall venture to say, it should be made part of his education.

Though I like to see foxhounds cast wide and forward and dislike to see them pick a cold scent through flocks of sheep to no purpose; yet I must beg leave to observe that I dislike still more to see that unaccountable hurry, which huntsmen will sometimes get themselves into the moment their hounds are at fault. Time ought always to be allowed them to make their own cast. . . . '

ROBERT SMITH SURTEES Born at Hamsterley Hall, near Newcastle, in 1805, younger son of Squire Anthony Surtees, who was described by Nimrod as 'every inch a sportsman'. Son, grandson and great-grandson of Masters of Foxhounds, he hunted from an early age with his father's hounds and those of his neighbour, Ralph Lambton. He was educated at Ovingham and Durham Grammar Schools and then was articled to a Newcastle solicitor's clerk in 1822 and 'further articled' to Mr Bell of Bow Churchyard, London, in 1825. However, he showed no interest, his 'taste for scribbling', as he called it, taking precedence; he wrote for the *Sporting Magazine* till 1831 and was co-founder, with Rudolph Ackemann the younger, of *The New Sporting Magazine*, in 1831; he published the *Horseman's Manual* in 1831. His elder brother, Anthony, having died in 1831, Robert succeeded to Hamsterley on his father's death in 1838. His first action there was to form a pack of hounds. He collected and published a pick of his fugitive sketches under the title, *Jorrocks's Jaunts and Jollities*, in 1838. He stood unsuccessfully as Conservative candidate for Gateshead in 1837. He married Elizabeth Jane Fenwick, daughter of Mr Addison, J.P., in 1841. He was J.P. and D.L. for Durham County in 1842 and was a Major in the Durham Militia. He published *Analysis of the Hunting Field*, with illustrations by Henry Alken Jr. in 1846 and published nine novels in the years 1845–65. High Sheriff of Durham in 1856. He died at Brighton in 1864.

Robert Surtees saw English country life of the 1820s, 1830s, 1840s and 1850s principally through a foxhunter's eyes. A satirist with an inimitable sense of the ridiculous, his caricatures stand right out in front on the stage of hunting literature. Surtees hated the regular army and was contemptuous of the aristocracy. He was both admirer and detractor of Nimrod, whom he burlesques as Pomponius Ego, the smart hunting correspondent, who, in *Handley Cross* (or Jorrocks), is invited by the cockney tea merchant, turned Master of Foxhounds, for a day's hunting. This passage from Ego's report on the day well illustrates Surtees' view of Nimrod's style and attitudes:

'From the appearance of the early morning, I feared we should not have been able to hunt, so keen was the frost at the dawn; but the general influence of an extremely powerful sun dispelled all fears, and, before we reached the place of meeting, the country had quite laid aside its coat of white. I thought what language can elevate the charms of nature, and exclaimed, with the Tuscan poet, *"Difficile est propria communia dicere."*

Prior to throwing off, Mr Jorrocks presented the principal members of his hunt to me, by all of whom I was received with marked respect, and I am sorry to add that he was also thrown off himself, by his horse pitching him over his head—an accident which I saw once occur to my friend, Count Pitchinstern, at his château one morning, when I was chatting, with the charming countess on my arm. I also remember, many years ago, as my readers may suppose it is, when I say it was in the days of Mr Corbet, in Warwickshire, seeing Will Barrow, his huntsman—and a better never cheered hound—get precisely a similar fall. . . . '

Except as a tool for his cynical wit, Surtees had little time for the snobbish or pompous; but he loved the likes of his invention, John Jorrocks. This is how he portrays him toward the end of the famous 'Cat and Custard-Pot' day:

'To increase our worthy Master's perplexities, a formidable flock of sheep now wheel semi-circularly over the line, completely obliterating any little scent that remained, and though our finest huntsman under the sun, aided by Charley as whip, quickly got the hounds beyond their foil, he was not successful in touching upon the line of the fox again.

"Humph", grunted our Master, reviewing his cast, "the ship must ha' heat 'im, or he's wanished into thin hair"; adding, "Jest put 'em on to me, Charley, whilst I makes one o' Mr Craven Smith's patent all-round-my-'at casts, for that beggar Binjimin's of no more use with a pack o' hounds than a hopera-box would be to a cow, or a frilled shirt to a pig." So saying, Mr Jorrocks out with his tootler, and giving a shrill blast, seconded by Charley's whip, proceeded to go down wind, and up wind, and round about wind, without, however, feeling a touch of his fox. At length scarce a hound would stoop, and old black Lucifer gave unmistakable evidence of his opinion of matters by rolling himself just under Jorrocks's horse's nose, and uttering a long-drawn howl, as much as to say, "Come, old boy! Shut up! It's no use bothering: let's off to dinner!"

"Rot ye! ye great lumberin' henterpriseless brute!" roars Jorrocks, cutting indignantly at him with his whip, "rot ye! d'ye think I boards and lodges and pays tax 'pon you to 'ave ye settin' up your 'olesale himperance that way? G-e-et-e away, ye disgraceful sleepin' partner o' the chase!" continued he, as the frightened hound scuttled away with his tail between his legs. . . . '

CHARLES JAMES APPERLEY NIMROD   Born 1777 at Plasgronow in Denbighshire, son of a scholarly country gentleman who is said (by Nimrod) to 'have corresponded with Dr Johnson and read Greek before breakfast', he was educated at Rugby. He was commissioned in Sir Watkin Wynn's Ancient Light British Dragoons in 1798, with whom he served during the suppression of the Irish rebellion of that year. He was squire of Beaupaire in the Vine country. He married Miss Wynn, a cousin of Sir Watkin's, resigned from the Army, settled first in Leicestershire, in 1801, and then in Warwickshire. He turned to writing for financial reasons at a time when foxhunting had recently become established as England's premier sport. Nimrod was first famous through a series of articles, 'Foxhunting in Leicestershire', which appeared, in 1822, in the Sporting Magazine, which, with further Nimrod publications, doubled its circulation in 2 years. He was quickly acclaimed as 'the best writer on foxhunting since Beckford'. Nimrod possessed an excellent sense of history and was the foremost authority on both the British hunting and coaching scenes. Consorting familiarly, and on nearly equal terms, with the great, he travelled in exorbitant style and made heavier and heavier financial demands upon his editor, Mr Pittman. Nimrod was dropped from the magazine on the succession of a new editor, in 1829. He accepted Surtees' hostility without rancour. He wrote several books and contributed articles to the Quarterly Review but spent most of the remainder of his life in penury at Calais and died in London, in 1843, aged 65.

Although his snobbishness and conceit made him unpopular with many people, Nimrod was also an immensely attractive personality and much loved. One intimate wrote this:

'A more delightful companion was never met with. His works were a reflection of himself—abounding in anecdote and quick observation; his knowledge of men and horses being coupled with a certain simplicity of manner which has been well said to be an attribute of true greatness. . . . '

His gift for anecdote is well proved, for example, in his description of a day with the Quorn, attended by what he described as 'a snob just arrived from a very rural country', a person with whom he, in some part, doubtless identifies:

'Our Snob is amongst them. . . . Two horses are seen loose in the distance—a report is flying about that one of the field is badly hurt, and something is heard of a collar-bone being broken, others say it is a leg; but the pace is too good to enquire. A cracking of rails is now heard, and one gentleman's horse is to be seen resting, nearly balanced, across one of them, his rider being on his back in the ditch, which is on the landing side. "Who is he?" says Lord Brudenel to Jack Stevens. "Can't tell, my Lord; but I thought it was a queerish place when I came o'er it before him." It is evidently a case of peril, but the pace is *too good* to afford help. . . .

"Now for the timber jumper", cries Osbaldeston, pleased to find himself upon Ashton. "For heaven's sake, take care of my hounds, in case they may throw up in the lane." . . . Snob is here in the best of company, and that moment perhaps the happiest of his life. . . .

"Hold hard, Holyoake!" exclaims Mr Osbaldeston (now mounted on Clasher), knowing what double-quick time he would be marching to, with fresh pipes to play upon, and the crowd well shaken off, "Pray don't press 'em too hard and we shall be sure to kill our fox. Have at him there, Abigail and Fickle, good bitches—see what a head they are carrying." . . . "We shall have the Whissendine brook", cries Mr Maher, who knows every field in the country. . . . "And a bumper, too, after last night's rain", holloas Capt. Berkley, determined to get first to four stiff rails in a corner. "So much the better", says Lord Alvanley, "I like a bumper at all times." "A fig for the Whissendine", cries Lord Gardner, "I am on the best water jumper in my stable." . . . "Who is that under his horse in the brook?" enquires that good sportsman and fine rider, Mr Green, of Rolleston, whose noted old mare had just skimmed the water like a swallow on a summer's evening. "It's Middleton Biddulph", says one. "Pardon me", cries Mr Middleton Biddulph; "Middleton Biddulph is here, *and here he means to be!*" "Only Dick Christian", answers Lord Forester, "and it is nothing new to him." "But he'll be drowned", exclaims Lord Kinnaird. "I shouldn't wonder", observes Mr William Coke. But the pace is *too good* to enquire. . . .

The fame of Snob and his little bay horse reaches Melton before he walks in himself. . . .

. . . Further enquiries are made, and satisfactory information obtained. On the fourth day, a nod from one—a "How do you?" from another—"A fine morning", from a third—are tokens good humouredly bestowed upon him by some of the leading men; and, on the fifth day, after a capital half-hour, in which he again distinguished himself, a noble *bon-vivant* thus addresses him, "Perhaps, sir, you would like to dine with me to-day; I shall be happy to see you at seven." . . .

GEORGE JOHN WHYTE-MELVILLE Born in 1821, son of John Whyte-Melville, laird of Mount Melville, Fife, he was educated at Eton. He had a Regular Army Commission in 1839, was gazetted to the Coldstream Guards in 1846 and retired in 1849; he re-joined for the Crimea campaign, throughout which he served with the Turkish Cavalry, retiring again at the end of the war in the rank of Major. He wrote 28 books in 26 years and was known by his contemporaries as 'the poet laureate of the hunting field'. His *Market Harborough* is one of the great novels of foxhunting, and *Riding Recollections* is a classic on horsemanship and riding to hounds. He was not a brilliant horseman himself, but immensely brave. Major Whyte-Melville had a huge circle of friends and was universally liked. He died out hunting with the Vale of White Horse in 1878.

Here is part of his description of a run with the Pytchley over the battlefield of Naseby, the prelude to his Civil War romance, *Holmby House*:

' ... "Tally ho!" shouts our friend, Jack, erect in his stirrups. "Twang" goes Charles Payne's horn from the middle of the gorse. Already the owner of the covert is coming best pace round the corner. Trust him not to lose his start, and to make good use of it when he has got it. In twos and threes the hounds are pouring through the boundary fence; 10 or 12 couple are settling to the scent; the rest, with ears erect, are flying to the cry. Now they stoop together with collective energy and drive along over the grass in all the mute ecstasy of *pace*. A burst such as this is pastime for the gods.

It sobers our imaginary steed, our pen-and-ink Pegasus; he drops quietly to his bridle, and a turn in our favour enables us to pull him into a trot and to look about us. Seven or eight men are in the same field with the hounds; half a dozen stiff fences and a couple of miles of grass have shaken off the larger portion of the field, but they are even now coming through a bridle gate not far distant in the rear, and, should a check unfortunately occur at this critical moment, they will be up in plenty of time to do lots of mischief still. But no; the pack is streaming on. "Forward", says Charles Payne, cramming his horn into its case, and gathering his horse for an "oxer". "Forward!" echoes Mr Villiers, "doubling" it neatly on his right. "Forward!" adds Mr Cust, cracking the far rail as he swings over the obstacle in his stride. "Line!" shouts a Meltonian at an unfortunate aspirant, whose horse is swerving to the thickest part of the fence. "Serve him right!" remarks the Meltonian to himself, landing safely in the next field, while the aspirant rolls headlong to the earth. Jack Woodcock, with an amused smile, slips quietly by to the front. ...

The fox is not travelling so straight now. Up and down yonder hedgerow the pack turn like harriers, and we think we must be very near him. But see: the crows are stooping yonder over a low black object in the distance. 'Tis the hunted fox, pointing straight for the coverts of Althorpe. He will never reach them, for the hounds are now close upon his track, and they run into him in the large grass field by Holmby House under the old oak tree.'

ANTHONY TROLLOPE Born in 1815. His father was a bankrupt lawyer and his mother, Frances, a quite successful writer. Educated at Harrow and, briefly, at Winchester. He secured clerkship in the General Post Office in 1834. He hunted, with huge enthusiasm, on horses allotted for the post, mostly with Galways Blazers, when Postmaster in Ireland, 1841–9, and, subsequently, in England. He served in Egypt and the West Indies in 1859. He is credited with the invention of the post box. He retired in 1859. Then he travelled in Australia, Egypt and the West Indies. His first three books were all failures. He made his name with the Barsetshire novels. Wrote eight 'Hunting Sketches' for *The Pall Mall Gazette*, which were printed in a volume in 1865. He adored foxhunting and wrote vivid accounts of the mid-Victorian scene. He was a very self-disciplined writer, committing himself to a precise daily stint. He died in 1882.

In *The American Senator*, John Morton plays host to Elias Gotobed, senator for Mickewa, and is at pains to explain to him the mysteries of English foxhunting. Morton's task, generally awkward, is rendered almost impossible when a dead fox, suspected to be poisoned, is found, during a day's hunting, on Lord Rufford's land:

'The Senator and Morton followed close on the steps of Lord Rufford and Captain Glomax (the Master) and were thus able to make their way into the centre of the crowd. There, on a clean sward of grass, laid out as carefully as though he were a royal child prepared for burial was—a dead fox. "It's pi'son, my lord; its pi'son to a moral", said Bean, who, as keeper of the wood was bound to vindicate himself, and his master and the wood. "Feel of him, how stiff he is." A good many did feel, but Lord Rufford stood still and looked at the poor victim in silence. "It's easy knowing how he came by it", said Bean.

The men around gazed into each others faces with a sad tragic air, as though the occasion were one which at the first blush was too melancholy for words. ... The dreadful word "vulpicide" was heard from various lips with an oath or two before it. "It makes me sick of my own land to think it should be done so near", said Larry Twentyman, who had just come up. Mr Runciman declared that they must set their wits to work not only to find the criminal but to prove the crime against him and offered to subscribe a couple of sovereigns on the spot to a common fund to be raised for the purpose. "I don't know what is to be done with a country like this", said Capt. Glomax, who, as an itinerant, was not averse to cast a slur upon the land of his present sojourn.

"I don't remember anything like it on my property before", said the lord, standing up for his own estate and the country at large.

"Nor in the hunt," said young Hampton. "Of course, such a thing may happen anywhere. They had foxes poisoned in the Pytchley last year."

"It shows d— bad feeling somewhere", said the Master.

"We know very well where the feeling is," said Bean, who had by this time taken up the fox, determined not to let it fall into any hands less careful than his own.

"It's that scoundrel Goarly", said one of the Boseys. ...

"Do they know all the foxes?" asked the Senator. In answer to this Morton only shook his head. ... '

WILLIAM DAVENPORT BROMLEY DAVENPORT   Born in 1821, son of a West Country landowner, he was educated at Harrow and Christ Church, Oxford. He travelled extensively. He was attached Coldstream Guards during the Crimean War. He married Miss Campbell of Islay in 1858. His early years of marriage were spent at Melton Mowbray. He was Conservative M.P. for North Warwickshire, for 20 years from 1864. He was J.P., D.L., Yeomanry Colonel and an amateur actor, musician and artist. He devoted much of his life to the Society for Relief of Distress and the Charity Organization Society. He was a brilliant all-round sportsman and had a reputation for extraordinary courage and nerve in the hunting field. He possessed great graphic power as writer. His book, *Sport* (the 1933 edition has a useful introduction by Lord Newton), was widely acclaimed a century ago, and its chapter on *Foxhunting* still reads very well today. He was more famous as a versifier than a writer of prose. In *The Dream of the Old Meltonian*, he falls asleep in the House of Commons, and his reverie is of a great Leicestershire run. Here are verses 3–7:

'Last night in St Stephen's so wearily sitting,
(The Member for Boreham sustained the debate,)
Some pitying spirit that round me was flitting
Vouchsafed a sweet vision my pains to abate.
The Mace, and the Speaker, and House disappearing,
The leather clad bench is a thoroughbred horse,
'Tis the whimpering cry of a foxhound I'm hearing,
And my "seat" is a pig skin at Ranksboro' Gorse.

He's away! I can hear the identical holloa!
I can feel my young thoroughbred strain down the ride,
I can hear the dull thunder of hundreds that follow,
I can see my old comrades in life by my side;
Do I dream? All around me I see the dead riding
And voices long silent re-echo with glee;
I can hear the far wail of the Master's vain chiding,
As vain as the Norseman's reproof to the sea.

Vain indeed! for the bitches are racing before us,
Not a nose to the earth—not a stern in the air,
And we know by the notes of that modified chorus,
How straight we must ride if we wish to be there!
With a crash o'er the turnpike, and onward I'm sailing,
Released from the throes of the blundering mass,
Which dispensed right and left, as I topped the high railing,
And shape my own course o'er the billowy grass.

Select is the circle in which I am moving,
Yet open and free the admission to all,
Still, still more select is that company proving,
Weeded out by the funker and thinned by the fall!

Yet here all are equal—no class legislation,
No privilege hinders, no family pride—
In the image of war shew the pluck of the nation,
Ride, ancient patrician! democracy ride!

Oh! gently my young one—the fence we are nearing
Is leaning towards us—'tis hairy and black,
The binders are strong and necessitate clearing,
Or the wide ditch beyond will find room for your back.
Well saved! we are over! now far down the pastures
Of Ashwell the willows betoken the line
Of the dull flowing stream of historic disasters,
We must face, my bold young one, the dread Whissendine! . . . '

SOMERVILLE AND ROSS   Edith Oenone Somerville and her cousin, Violet Martin (pseudonym, Martin Ross), collaborated to write 29 books. Edith, eldest of what was to be a family of eight, was born in 1848, in Corfu, where her father, Col. Thomas Somerville, an Irish landowner, was then serving. She studied art in Düsseldorf, Paris and London and exhibited very successfully during her life. She was also a considerable philanthropist, active and knowledgeable farmer and famous hostess. Edith was the first woman Master of Foxhounds (West Carbery, 1903–8 and 1912–19). She wrote in *The Smile and the Tear*:

'Hunting literature has never, or so it seems to me, dwelt sufficiently on the charm of foxhounds. Their purely professional qualities are extolled—nose, tongue, speed, endurance—but nothing is said of their social gifts. Of, for example, the charm of the reception that, in their own domain, the bitch-pack will accord to a friend. . . . '

She died in 1949

Martin Ross was born in 1862. She was neither as talented nor as prolific as Edith, but she was thought to be the guide and leader of the partnership and to have written the love scenes, which Edith could not handle. Ross was a clever short-story teller. She was crippled by a hunting accident in 1898 and died in 1915.

Most of their joint endeavours contain at least a generous ration of foxhunting. Arnold Bennett wrote that their novel *The Silver Fox* 'is, within its limits, a perfect novel. Their style exhibits a meticulous care not surpassed by that of Henry James. It actually repays a technical analysis. It is as carefully worded as good verse. There is a reason for every comma, and the place of every preposition and conjunction. All prose which pretends to be artistic should be as meticulous as this. . . . ' Lord David Cecil graded *The Real Charlotte* as 'a masterpiece, a classic, one of the very few novels of the first rank that has appeared in England during this century'. In the following scene from 'The Pug-nosed Fox', a chapter of

Experiences of an Irish R.M., Major Sinclair Yeats, the resident magistrate of the book's title, has temporarily assumed command during the absence of Flurry Knox, M.F.H., and a hunt photograph has been organized:

'... "The dogs are not in the picture, Whip!" said Mr McOstrich, the photographer, in the chill tone of outraged dignity.

I perceived that the hounds, much demoralized, had melted away from the slope in front of us and were huddling in a wisp in the intervening hollow. Blandishments were of no avail; they wagged and beamed apologetically but remained in the hollow. Michael, in whose sensitive bosom the term "whip" evidently rankled, became scarlet in the face and avalanched from the hilltop upon his flock with a fury that was instantly recognized by them. They broke in panic, and the astute and elderly Venus, followed by one or two of the young entry, bolted for the road. They were there met by Mr McOstrich's carman, who most creditably headed the puppies with yells and his driving whip but was outplayed by Venus, who, dodging like a football professional, doubled under the car horse and fled irrevocably. Phillipa, who had been flitting from rock to rock with her Kodak, and unnerving me with injunctions as to the angle of my cap, here entered the lists with a packet of sandwiches, with which, in spite of the mustard, she restored a certain confidence to the agitated pack, a proceeding observed from afar with trembling indignation by Minx, her fox terrier. By reckless expenditure of sandwich the hounds were tempted to their proper position below the horses, but, unfortunately, with their sterns to the camera and their eyes fastened on Phillipa.

"Retire, Madam," said Mr McOstrich, very severely, "*I* will attract the dogs!"

Thus rebuked, Madam scrambled hastily over the crest of the hillock and sank in unseemly laughter into the deep heather behind it.

"Now, very quiet, please", continued Mr McOstrich, and then un-expectedly uttered the words, "Pop! Pop! Pop!" in a high soprano.

Michael clapped his hand over his mouth, the superseded siren in the heather behind me wallowed in fresh convulsions; the hounds remained unattracted.

Then arose, almost at the same moment, a voice from the wood behind us, the voice of yet a third siren, more potent than that of either of her predecessors, the voice of Venus hunting a line. . . . Before Michael had got out his horn, the hounds were over the wall, before the last stern had disappeared the leaders had broken into full cry.

"Please God it might be a rabbit!" exclaimed Michael, putting spurs to his horse. . . . '

JOHN MASEFIELD   Born in 1878, he ran away to sea in his youth. He travelled in the United States. On his return to England, he joined *The Manchester Guardian* editorial, he wrote poems, short stories, novels and plays. He was appointed Poet Laureate in 1930 and died in 1967.

Masefield took a keen interest in hounds and the science of hunting. As a regular foot follower, he was, too, a close observer of the hunting field's social scene. His one great contribution to the literature of the sport, his epic narrative verse, *Reynard the Fox*, which is quoted below, was published, with drawings by G. D. Armour, in 1921:

'There they were coming, mute but swift,
A scarlet smear in the blackthorn rift,
A white horse rising, a dark horse flying,
And the hungry hounds too tense for crying.
Stormcock leading, his stern spear-straight,
Racing as though for a piece of plate,
Little speck horsemen field on field;
Then Dansey viewed him and Robin squealed.

At the View Hallo the hounds went frantic,
Back went Stormcock and up went Antic,
Up went Skylark as Antic sped
It was zest to blood how they carried head
Skylark dropped as Maroon drew by,
Their hackles lifted, they scored to cry.

The fox knew well, that, before they tore him,
They should try their speed on the downs before him,
There were three more miles to the Wan Dyke Hill,
But his heart was high, that he beat them still.
The wind of the downland charmed his bones
So off he went to the Sarsen Stones.

The moan of the three great firs in the wind,
And the Ai of the foxhounds died behind,
Wind-dapples followed the hill-wind's breath
On the Kill Down Gorge where the Danes found death. . . .

Then Leu Leu Leu went the soft horn's laughter,
The hounds (they had checked) came romping after,
The clop of the hooves on the road was plain,
Then the crackle of reeds, then cries again.

A whimpering first, then Robin's cheer,
Then the Ai, Ai Ai; they were all too near;
His swerve had brought but a minute's rest,
Now he ran again, and he ran his best.

With a crackle of dead dry stalks of reed
The hounds came romping at topmost speed,
The redcoats ducked as the great hooves skittered
The Blood Brook's shallows to sheets that glittered
With a cracking whip and a Hoik, Hoik, Hoik,
Forrard, Tom galloped. Bob shouted "Yoick"
Like a running fire the dead reeds crackled
The hounds' heads lifted, their necks were hackled.

Tom cried to Bob as they thundered through,
"He is running short, we shall kill at Tew".
Bob cried to Tom as they rode in team,
"I was sure that time that he turned up-stream.
As the hounds went over the brook in stride
I saw old Daffodil fling to side,
So I guessed at once, when they checked beyond."
The ducks flew up from the Morton Pond.
The fox looked up at their tailing strings,
He wished (perhaps) that a fox had wings. . . . '

SIEGFRIED SASSOON   He was a poet. He was born in 1886, son of a Sephardic Jew, was orphaned and brought up by an aunt. His youth included education privately and at Marlborough. Foxhunting was then, apparently, his principal interest. He fought in the First World War, gallantly, but wrote outspokenly against it. He became a Labour politician, a Roman Catholic convert and the biographer of Meredith. He died in 1967.

Sassoon's works include *The Old Huntsman*, 1917, *Memoirs of a Foxhunting Man*, 1928, and *Sherston's Progress*, 1936. This passage is from the description of cub-hunting with Denis Milden* his young hero, a Master of Foxhounds, in autobiographical *Memoirs of a Foxhunting Man*, in which Sassoon features as George Sherston:

'. . . Not many minutes afterwards we were out by the range of loose-boxes under the rustling trees, with quiet stars overhead and scarcely a hint of morning. In the kennels the two packs were baying at one another from their separate yards, and, as soon as Denis had got his horse from the gruff white-coated head-groom, a gate released the hounds—25 or 30 couple of them, and all very much on their toes. Out they streamed like a flood of water, throwing their tongues and spreading away in all directions with waving sterns, as though they had never been out in the world before. Even then I used to feel the strangeness of the scene with its sharp exuberance of unkennelled energy. Will's hearty voice and the crack of his whip stood out above the clamour and commotion which surged around Denis and his horse. Then, without any

*Based on Norman Loder, Master of the Southdown, 1911–13.

apparent lull or interruption, the whirlpool became a well-regulated torrent flowing through the gateway into the road, along which the sound of hoofs receded with a purposeful clip-clopping. . . .

The mornings I remember most zestfully were those which took us on to the chalk downs. To watch the day breaking from purple to dazzling gold while we trotted up a deep-rutted lane; to inhale the early freshness when we were on the sheep-cropped uplands; to stare back at the low country with its cock-crowing farms and mist-coiled waterways; thus to be riding out with a sense of spacious discovery—was it not something stolen from the lie-a-bed world and the luckless city workers. . . .

It is possible that even then, if I was on a well-behaved horse, I could half forget why we were there, so pleasant was it to be alive and gazing around me. But I would be dragged out of my day dream by Denis when he shouted to me to wake up and get round to the far side of the covert; for on such hill days we often went straight to one of the big gorses without any formality of a meet. There were beech woods too, in the folds of the downs, and lovely they looked in the mellow sunshine, with summer's foliage falling in ever-deepening drifts among their gnarled and mossy roots.' . . .

Beckford, Surtees, Nimrod, Whyte-Melville, Trollope, Bromley-Davenport, Somerville and Ross, Masefield and Sassoon—if these produced the cream of the cream of foxhunting literature, many more have shown rich milk. Here is my selection of authors and titles for the foxhunter's shelves.

ACTON, C. R.
    The Modern Foxhound 1935
    The Foxhound of the Future Ebenezer Baylis 1953

ALDIN, CECIL
    Ratcatcher to Scarlet Eyre & Spottiswoode 1926
    Scarlet to MFH Eyre & Spottiswoode 1933
    Time I was Dead (autobiography) Eyre & Spottiswoode 1934
    Hunting Scenes Eyre & Spottiswoode 1936

APPERLEY, CAPTAIN W.
    A Hunting Diary Nisbet 1926

APSLEY, LADY
    Bridleways through History Hutchinson 1936
    The Foxhunter's Bedside Book Eyre & Spottiswoode 1949

ARMITAGE, MARIGOLD
    A Long Way to Go Faber
    A Motley to the View Faber 1961

ARMOUR, G. D.
    Bridle and Brush Eyre & Spottiswoode 1937

BATHURST, EARL
   The Breeding of Foxhounds   Constable   1926
   The Charlton and Raby Hunts   Constable   1938
'B.B.'
   Wild Lone (The Story of a Pytchley Fox)   Eyre & Spottiswoode   1938
BEACH THOMAS, SIR WILLIAM
   Hunting England   Batsford   1936
BEAUFORT, THE DUKE OF, and MORRIS, MOWBRAY
   Hunting   Longmans Green   1885
BECKFORD, PETER
   Thoughts on Hunting (with introduction and notes by J. Otho Paget)
      Methuen   1899
BELL, ISAAC
   Foxiana   Country Life   1929
   A Huntsman's Log Book   Eyre & Spottiswoode   1947
BENSON, C. E.
   Crag and Hound in Lakeland   Hurst & Blackett   1902
BENTINCK, LORD CHARLES
   Goodall's Practice   1871
BERKELEY, GRANTLEY F.
   Reminiscences of a Huntsman   1897
BERRY, MICHAEL F.
   Foxhunting from the Times   Office of The Times   1933
   More Foxhunting   1937
BERRY, MICHAEL, and BROCK, D. W. E.
   Hunting by Ear   H. F. & G. Witherby   1937
BOOTH, J. B.
   Bits of Character (The Life of 'The Druid')   Hutchinson   1936
BOVILL, E. W.   *The England of Nimrod and Surtees (1815–1854)*
      Oxford University Press   1959
BOWEN, MURIEL
   Irish Hunting   The Kerryman   1955
BRADLEY, CUTHBERT
   The Foxhound of the Twentieth Century   George Routledge,   1914
   British Hunts and Huntsmen (4 volumes)   Bibliographical Press   1911
BROCK, D. W. E.
   The ABC of Foxhunting   Philip Allan   1947
   The Foxhunter's Week-end Book   Seeley Service
   Foxhunting (Beaufort Library)   Seeley Service   1954
   To Hunt the Fox

BROMLEY DAVENPORT, WILLIAM DAVENPORT
Sport—Foxhunting, Stalking, Fishing and Covert Shooting (introduced by Lord Newton) 1933
The Dream of the Old Meltonian
Lowesby Hall

'BROOKSBY' (CAPT. E. PENNELL ELMHIRST)
Collected Letters—The Cream of Leicestershire 1883
The Best Season on Record
The Best of Fun (1891–7) 1903

BUCHANAN-JARDINE, SIR JOHN
Hounds of the World Methuen 1937

BUDGETT, H. M.
Hunting by Scent Eyre & Spottiswoode 1933

BURROWS, GEORGE T.
Gentleman Charles—A History of Hunting Vinton 1951

CARR, RAYMOND
English Foxhunting, A History Weidenfeld & Nicolson 1976

'CECIL'
Records of the Chase Longman 1854

CHALMERS, PATRICK
The History of Hunting (Lonsdale Library) Seeley Service 1930
The Horn Collins 1937

CLAPHAM, RICHARD
Foxhunting on the Lakeland Fells Longmans Green 1920
The Book of the Fox Herbert Jenkins 1936

CLAYTON, MICHAEL
A Hunting We Will Go Pelham Books 1967

CONYER, DOROTHEA
Peter's Pedigree Hutchinson 1904
The Strayings of Sandy Hutchinson 1908
Lady Elverton's Emeralds Hutchinson 1909
Sporting Reminiscences E. P. Dutton 1920
Sally Hutchinson 1912
The Boy, Some Horses and a Girl Edward Arnold 1914
A Mixed Pack Hutchinson 1915
A Scratch Pack Hutchinson 1916
B.E.N. Hutchinson 1919
Follow Elizabeth Hutchinson 1929

COOK, COLONEL JOHN
Observations on Foxhunting Edward Arnold 1922

COOPER, LEONARD
R. S. Surtees Arthur Baker 1952

O

CUMING, E. D. (editor)
A Foxhunting Anthology Cassell 1928

DALE, THOMAS F.
A History of the Belvoir Hunt Constable 1899
The Eighth Duke of Beaufort and the Badminton Hunt Constable 1901

DAVIES, E. W. L.
Memoir of the Rev. John Russell 1902

DAWSON, LIONEL
Lonsdale 1939

DELME RADCLIFFE, F. P.
The Noble Science Ackermann 1839

'THE DRUID' (H. H. DIXON)
Post and Paddock Piper Stephenson 1857
Silk and Scarlet Rogerson & Taxford 1859
Field and Fern Vinton 1912

EARDLEY-WILMOT, J. E.
Reminiscences of Thomas Assheton Smith John Murray 1860

EDWARDS, LIONEL
Famous Foxhunters 1932
Sketches in Stable and Kennel 1933
Huntsmen Past and Present Eyre & Spottiswoode
My Hunting Sketch Book Eyre & Spottiswoode
Seen from the Saddle Eyre & Spottiswoode 1937
My Irish Sketch Book Collins 1938
The Fox Collins 1949

EGERTON-WARBURTON, R. E.
Hunting Songs Scribners 1925
Cheshire Ballads
Poems, Epigrams and Sonnets
Warburton's Hunting Songs 1951

FANE, LADY AUGUSTA
Chit Chat Thornton Butterworth 1926

FEVERSHAM, THE COUNTESS OF
Strange Tales of the Chase Godfrey Bles 1972

FITZPATRICK, B. M.
Irish Sport and Sportsmen 1878

FORBES, COMMANDER W. M. ('MAINTOP')
Hounds, Gentlemen, Please! Hodder & Stoughton 1910

FREDERICK, C. E. (et al)
Foxhunting (Lonsdale Library) Seeley Service 1930

GARLE, HUBERT
Hunting in the Golden Days 1896

GREAVES, RALPH
Yonder he Goes Collins 1935

HARE, C. E.
The Language of Sport Country Life 1939

HAYES, M. HORACE
Riding and Hunting 1901 (7th edition, 1961)
Veterinary Notes for Horse Owners 1877 (latest edition, 1973)

HIEOVER, HARRY
Stable Talk and Table Talk 1846
The Stud 1849
The Hunting Field 1850

HIGGINSON, A. H.
Advice from an Old Foxhunter 1929
The Meynell of the West—A Biography of J. J. Farquharson Collins 1936
Peter Beckford Esquire Collins 1937
Hunting in the United States and Canada (with Julian Ingersoll Chamberlain)
Try Back Huntingdon Press 1931
The Fox that Walked on the Water Collins
A Tale of Two Brushes Collins 1943
The Perfect Follower Collins 1944
The Hill Vixen Collins 1945
Two Centuries of Foxhunting Collins 1946
Foxhunting, Theory and Practice Collins 1948

IVESTER LLOYD, T.
Hounds 1934

JAMES, DAVID, and STEPHENS, WILSON (editors)
In Praise of Hunting Hollis & Carter 1960

LANIER, CHARLES D.
We go Foxhunting Abroad—An American's first Venture with Irish Banks and English Downs 1924

LEGER GORDON, DOUGLAS ST
The Way of the Fox John Murray 1951

LEWIS, ERNEST
A Hill Fox

LEWIS, PETER (editor)
A Foxhunter's Anthology Lovat Dickson & Thompson 1934

LINDSAY GORDON, ADAM
Sporting Verse 1927

LONDONDERRY, THE MARCHIONESS OF
  Henry Chaplin—A Memoir 1926

LONGRIGG, ROGER
  The History of Foxhunting Macmillan 1975

LUCAS, MAJOR SIR JOCELYN
  Hunt and Working Terriers Chapman & Hall 1931

MACHIN GOODALL, DAPHNE
  Huntsmen of a Golden Age Witherby 1956

MARCH, EARL OF
  Records of the Old Charlton Hunt Elkin Matthews 1910

MARCH PHILLIPS, GUS
  Ace High Macmillan 1938
  Sporting Print Bell

MASEFIELD, JOHN
  Reynard the Fox, or The Ghost Heath Run Heinemann 1921

MOLYNEUX, J.
  Thirty Years a Hunt Servant Hutchinson 1935

MOORE, DAPHNE
  The Book of the Foxhound J. A. Allen 1974

'NIMROD' (C. J. APPERLEY)
  Hunting Tours Pittman 1835
  Northern Tour Walter Spiers 1835
  Memoir of the Life of the Late John Mytton 1837
  The Chase, the Turf and the Road Edward Arnold 1843
  Hunting Reminiscences Rudolph Ackermann 1843
  The Life of a Sportsman Downey 1901
  Remarks on the Condition of Hunters Bodley Head 1908
  My Life and Times (editor E. D. Cuming) W. Blackwood 1927

OGILVIE, WILL
  Galloping Shoes Constable 1922
  Over to Grass Constable 1925
  Scattered Scarlet Constable 1923
  Collected Sporting Verse Constable 1932

OSBALDESTON, GEORGE
  Squire Osbaldeston (editor E. D. Cuming) 1926

OTHO PAGET, J.
  Hunting J. M. Dent 1900

PAGE, ROBIN
  The Hunter and the Hunted Davis-Poynter 1977

PAGET, MAJOR GUY
The Melton Mowbray of John Ferneley, 1782–1860 Backus 1931
Bad 'Uns to Beat Collins 1936
The History of the Althorp and Pytchley Hunt, 1634–1920 1937
Mr Silas P. Mowbray returns to Melton Backus 1940
The Life of Frank Freeman Backus 1948

PITT, FRANCES
Hounds, Horses and Hunting Country Life 1948

POLLARD, HUGH B. C.
The Mystery of Scent Eyre & Spottiswoode 1937

RICHMOND AND GORDON, THE DUKE OF
Records of the Old Charlton Hunt

ROOK, DAVID
The Ballad of the Belstone Fox Hodder & Stoughton 1970

ROSS, MARTIN
Some Irish Yesterdays 1906
Strayaways 1920

SASSOON, SIEGFRIED
The Old Huntsman Faber 1917
Memoirs of a Foxhunting Man Faber 1928
Sherston's Progress Faber 1936

SCARTH DIXON, WILLIAM *The Hunting Year* Ham-Smith 1912

'SCRUTATOR'
Letters on the Management of Hounds Bell's Life 1852
Horses and Hounds Routledge 1858
The Master of Hounds 1859

SHEDDEN, LADY DIANA, and APSLEY, LADY
To Whom the Goddess Hutchinson 1932

SMITH, THOMAS ('CRAVEN')
Extracts from the Diary of a Huntsman 1841 (with an introduction by
    Frederick Watson, 1933)
The Life of a Fox Whittacker 1843

SOMERVILLE, E. O. (editor)
Notes on the Horn 1934

SOMERVILLE, E. O., and ROSS, MARTIN
The Real Charlotte Longmans 1894
Some Experiences of an Irish R.M. Longmans 1899
An Irish Cousin Longmans 1903
Further Experiences of an Irish R.M. Longmans 1908
Mr Knox's Hounds Longmans 1915
Irish Memories Longmans 1918

SOMMERVILLE, E. O., and ROSS, MARTIN—*Cont.*
  Mount Music   Longmans   1920
  French Leave   Heinemann   1928
SOMERVILLE, WILLIAM
  The Chace   1735
SPARROW, WALTER SHAW
  British Sporting Artists   Lane & Bodley Head   1922
STEEL, ANTHONY
  Jorrocks's England   Methuen   1932
SUMMERHAYS, R. S.
  Elements of Hunting   Country Life   1938
  Encyclopaedia for Horsemen   Frederick Warne   1952
SURTEES, R. S.
  The Horseman's Manual   1831
  The Analysis of the Hunting Field   1845 (Edward Arnold, 1923)
  Hawbuck Grange   Bradbury Agnew   1847
  Young Tom Hall   Blackwood   1852
  Mr Sponge's Sporting Tour   Methuen   1853
  Handley Cross   Methuen   1854
  Ask Mamma   Methuen   1858
  Plain or Ringlets   Methuen   1860
  Mr Facey Romford's Hounds   Methuen   1865
  Hillingdon Hall   Nimmo   1899
  Jorrocks's Jaunts and Jollities   Downey   1901
TROLLOPE, ANTHONY
  Hunting Sketches   1865 (with an introduction by James Boyd, 1934)
  The Eustace Diamonds   1873
  The American Senator   1879
UNDERHILL, G. F.
  A Century of Foxhunting   R. A. Everett   1900
VINER, R. T.
  Noticia Venaticia   Rudolph Ackermann   1841
WATSON, ALFRED E. T.
  Sketches in the Hunting Field   Chapman & Hall   1895
  Fur, Feather and Fin   (*The Fox*)
  English Sport   Macmillan   1903
WATSON, FREDERICK
  Hunting Pie   H. F. & G. Witherby   1931
  In the Pink   H. F. & G. Witherby   1932
  R. S. Surtees   Harrap   1933
WELCOME, JOHN, and ORCHARD, VINCENT (editors)
  Best Hunting Stories   Faber   1954

WHYTE-MELVILLE, MAJOR G. J.
  Holmby House Chapman & Hall 1860
  Riding Recollections Chapman & Hall 1878
  Market Harborough Ward Lock 1899
  Hunting Songs and Verses and The True Cross Longmans Green 1899

WILLOUGHBY DE BROKE, LORD
  Hunting the Fox Constable 1920
  The Sport of our Ancestors E. P. Dutton 1921
  The Passing Years Houghton Mifflin 1924

WYNDHAM-QUINN, COLONEL
  The Foxhound in County Limerick 1919

'YOI-OVER'
  Hold Hard! Hounds Please! Scribners 1925
  Bells of the Chase Hutchinson

YORK, EDWARD, 2ND DUKE OF
  The Master of Game Ballantyne Hanson 1904

YOUNG, J. R.
  Foxhunting Longmans Green 1934

AMERICAN FOXHUNTING BIBLIOGRAPHY

GARRETT, GEORGE J.
  Fifty Years with Fox and Hounds Hobson Book Press, New York 1947

HIGGINSON, A., and CHAMBERLAIN, J.
  Hunting in the United States and Canada Garden City, New York 1928

HOUGHLAND, M.
  Gone Away Blue Ridge Press, Berryville, Va. 1949

HULL, DENISON B.
  Thoughts on American Fox-Hunting David McKay, New York 1958

MACKAY-SMITH, A.
  The American Foxhound, 1747–1967 American Foxhound Club, Millwood,
    Virginia 1968
  American Foxhunting, An Anthology American Foxhound Club Millwood,
    Virginia 1970
  The Songs of Foxhunting American Foxhound Club, Millwood, Virginia
    1974

MADDUX, BOB LEE
  History of the Walker Hound B. L. Maddux, Cookeville, Tennessee 1961

MADDUX, SID (editor)
  Hill Topping Cookeville, Tennessee 1976

ROSSELL, COL. J. E.
  Organized Hunts of America The Sporting Press, Baltimore, Maryland 1955

ROSTAD, THURSTON J.

The American Foxhound   T. J. Rostad, Spring Valley, Wisconsin   1905

SMITH, H. W.

Sporting Family of the Old South   J. B. Lyon, Albany, New York   1936

THOMAS, J. B.

Hounds and Hunting Through the Ages   The Derrydale Press, New York   1928

TRIGG, H. C.

The American Fox-Hound   H. C. Trigg, Glascow, Kentucky   *c.* 1895

VAN URK, J. BLAN

Story of American Foxhunting, Vol. I, 1650–1861, Vol. II, 1865–1906   The Derrydale Press, New York   1940, 1941

VISCHER, P. (editor)

Horse and Horsemen   Van Nostrand, Princeton, New Jersey   1967

WADSWORTH, W. P.

Riding to Hounds in America   Berryville, Virginia   1959

WALKER, W.

Walker Hounds, Their Origin and Development   The Hobson Book Press, Cynthia, Kentucky   1945

The Locations of the American Hunts

Alabama
Mooreland Hunt, Madison

Arizona
Grass Ridge Hounds, Sonoita

California
Los Altos Huht, Woodside
Santa Fe Hunt, El Cajon
West Hills Hunt, Chatsworth

Colorado
Arapahoe Hunt, Littleton
Roaring Fork Hounds, Carbondale

Connecticut
Fairfield County Hounds, Newtown
Mr Haight, Jr, Litchfield County Hounds,
 Litchfield
Middlebury Hunt, Middlebury

Delaware
Vicmead Hunt, Middletown

Florida
Two Rivers Hunt, Zephyrhills

Georgia
Belle Meade Hunt, Thomson
Midland Foxhounds, Midland
Shakerag Hounds, Fulton County
Tri-County Hounds, Milner

Illinois
Fox River Valley Hunt, Barrington
Mill Creek Hunt, Wadsworth
Oak Brook Hounds, Naperville
Old Stonington Hounds, Taylorville
Southern Illinois Open Hunt, Carbondale
Wayne–DuPage Hunt, Wayne
Wolf Creek Hounds, Goreville

Indiana
Hound and Horn Hunt, Schereville
New Britton Hunt, Spencer
Romwell Foxhounds, Romney
Traders Point Hunt, Zionsville

Kansas
Fort Leavenworth Hunt, Fort Leavenworth
Mission Valley Hunt, Stilwell

Kentucky
Iroquois Hunt, Lexington
Licking River Hounds, Carlisle
Long Run Hounds, Simpsonville

Maryland
Antietam Hunt, Burkittsville
De La Brooke Foxhounds W,
 Mechanicsville
Elkridge–Harford Hunt, Monkton
Foxcatcher Hounds, Elkton
Goshen Hunt, Derwood
Green Spring Valley Hounds, Glyndon
Howard County Hunt, Glenelg
Mr Hubbard's Kent County Hounds,
 Chestertown
Marlborough Hunt, Upper Marlboro
Middletown Valley Hunt, Middletown
New Market Hounds, New Market
Potomac Hunt, Potomac
Wicomico, Salisbury
Wye River Hounds, Easton

Massachusetts
Myopia Hunt, South Hamilton
Nashoba Valley Hunt, Pepperell
Norfolk Hunt, Dover
Old North Bridge Hounds, Concord

Michigan
Battle Creek Hunt, Augusta
Metamora Hunt, Metamora
Waterloo Hunt, Grass Lake

Minnesota
Long Lake Hounds, Long Lake

Mississippi
Austin Hunt, Lake Cormorant

Missouri
Bridlespur Hunt, New Melle

Nebraska
North Hills Hunt, Omaha

New Jersey
Amwell Valley Hounds, Ringoes
Essex Foxhounds, Peapack
Monmouth County Hunt, Allentown
Spring Valley Hounds, Mendham

New Mexico
Juan Tomas Hounds, Sandia Park

New York
Genesee Valley Hunt, Geneseo
Golden's Bridge Hounds, North Salem
Hopper Hills Hunt, Victor
Limestone Creek Hunt, Manlius
Millbrook Hunt, Millbrook
Old Chatham Hunt, Old Chatham
Rombout Hunt, Staatsburg
Smithtown Hunt, Stony Brook, L.I.
Windy Hollow Hunt, Florida

North Carolina
Mecklenburg Hounds, Matthews
Moore County Hounds, Southern Pines
Sedgefield Hunt, Brown Summit
Triangle Hunt, Durham
Tryon Hounds, Tryon

Ohio
Camargo Hunt, Indian Hill Village
Chagrin Valley, Gates Mills
Lauray Hunt, Bath
Miami Valley Hunt, Spring Valley
Rocky Fork Headley, Gahanna

Oklahoma
Lost Hounds Hunt, Edmond

Pennsylvania
Beaufort Hunt, Harrisburg
Brandywine Hounds, West Chester
Chestnut Ridge Hounds, New Geneva
Dutch Fork Hunt, West Alexander
Harts Run Hunt, Ajlison Park
Huntingdon Valley Hunt, Furlong
Mr Jeffords' Andrews Bridge Hounds,
   Christiana
Limekiln Hunt, Reading
Pickering Hunt, Phoenixville
Radnor Hunt, Malvern
Rolling Rock–Westmoreland Hunt,
   Ligonier
Rose Tree Foxhunting Club, York
Sewickley Hunt, Sewickley
Mr Stewart's Cheshire Foxhounds,
   Unionville

Rhode Island
Bradbury Foxhounds, West Greenwich

South Carolina
Aiken Hounds, Aiken
Camden Hunt, Camden
Greengille County Hounds, Gowensville
Woodside Hounds, Aiken (inactive)

Tennessee
Cedar Knob Foxhounds, Cornersville
Hillsboro Hounds, Brentwood
Longreen Foxhounds. Collierville
Mells Foxhounds, Lynnville
Oak Grove Hunt, Germantown

Texas
Hickory Creek Hunt, Corinth

Vermont
Green Mountain Hounds, Morrisville
Windsor County Hounds, Woodstock

Virginia
Bedford County Hunt, Bedford
Blue Ridge Hunt, Boyce
Bull Run Hunt, Manassas
Casanova Hunt, Casanova
Deep Run Hunt, Manakin
Fairfax Hunt, Ashburn
Farmington Hunt, Charlottesville
Glenmore Hunt, Staunton

Virginia—*cont.*
Keswick Hunt, Keswick
Loudoun Hunt, Leesburg
Middleburg Hunt, Middleburg
Montpelier Hunt, Montpelier Station
Old Dominion Hounds, Orlean
Orange County Hunt, The Plains
Piedmont Foxhounds, Upperville

Princess Anne Hunt, Virginia Beach
Rapidan Hunt, Rapidan
Rappahannock Hunt, Sperryville
Rockbridge Hunt, Glasgow
Warrenton Hunt, Warrenton

Washington
Woodbrook Hunt, Tacoma

Foxhunting Terms

AT FAULT
: When hounds check, they are said to be at fault.

BABBLER
: This is a hound which throws its tongue too much, when it is uncertain of the scent or when it is a long way behind the leading hounds.

BAG FOX
: Any fox which is turned out especially for hounds to hunt. This was a common practice in the old days but is now not recognized.

BILLETT
: A fox's excreta.

BOB-TAILED
: Applied to a fox which has no brush, or only a very short one.

BOLT
: To bolt a fox is to force him out of a drain or earth.

BREAK
: A fox 'breaks' when he leaves a covert.

BREAK UP
: Hounds 'break up their fox' when they tear apart and eat its carcase.

BRUSH
: The fox's tail.

BULLFINCH
: A high uncut fence, to be jumped through rather than over.

BURST
: The first part of a run, if quick, is called a sharp burst.

CARRIES A SCENT
: Good scenting land is said to 'carry a scent'.

CARRY THE SCENT
: Those hounds which are actually working out with their noses the fox's line when the pack is running are said to 'carry the scent'.

CAST
: An effort made by the pack, or by the huntsman with his pack, to recover the scent at a check.

CATCH HOLD
A huntsman 'catches hold' of hounds when he lifts the pack. The term is also used of a horse that pulls.

CHALLENGE
A hound that 'opens' is said to 'challenge', or to 'challenge on a fox'.

CHARLEY
A slang term for fox.

CHECK
Hounds check when they stop running and temporarily lose the fox's scent.

CHOP
Hounds are said to chop a fox when they kill one asleep or when they surprise one before he has time to escape.

CLEAN GROUND
Ground which is neither foiled nor stained.

COUPLE
Two foxhounds. A pack is, for instance, 16½ couples (but a single hound is referred to as one hound).

COUPLES
Two leather collars joined by steel links, used for coupling two hounds together.

COURSE
To course a fox is to run it 'in view'.

COVERT
All woods or thickets that might hold a fox.

CRY
The music of a pack. When the whole pack are running hard and throwing their tongues, they are said to be in 'full cry'.

CUB
A young fox. They become 'foxes' on 1 November.

CUB HUNTING
Carried out in September and October in the early mornings with the object of moving foxes and teaching hounds and young foxes their duty.

CUR DOG
Any dog other than a foxhound.

DOG FOX
A male fox.

DOPED FOXES
Foxes whose natural scent has been increased by some means. Bag foxes are sometimes doped.

DOUBLE
A fence or bank with a ditch on both sides.

DOUBLE THE HORN
A huntsman is said to do this when he blows a succession of quick sharp notes, for example when a fox is holloaed away.

DRAFT

A collection of hounds which have been drafted. To draft a hound is to get rid of it from the pack. Drafts may be 'entered' or 'unentered'.

DRAG

The line of a fox leading to his kennel. It is also the name of an artificial line, made by laying some strong-smelling substance over a certain line of country. It is not done in foxhunting.

DRAW

Hounds 'draw' for a fox in covert.

The day's draw is the area of country which the Master has planned to draw in a day's hunting, and the earths of which have been stopped.

When a huntsman takes one hound away from the rest of a pack, he 'draws' it.

EARTH

A fox's underground home.

EARTH STOPPER

One who goes out during the night before a day's hunting to block the entrances to the earths, while the fox is abroad. He may be paid by the hunt.

ENTER

Teaching young hounds to hunt a fox is to enter them.

FEATHER

A hound 'feathers' when it is not certain that it owns the scent, driving slowly along the line and waving its stern.

FIELD

This is the body of mounted men and women hunting with a pack.

FLAGS

The floor of the kennel courts. One visits hounds in kennels to see them 'on the flags'.

FOIL

Any smell which obliterates the fox's scent, for example when horses, sheep, etc., pass over the line of the fox the ground is foiled.

A fox is said to 'run his foil' when he doubles back on his tracks.

GONE TO GROUND

When a fox has got into an earth or drain.

HACKLES UP

When a hound is angry, the hair along its back and top of neck stands on end, and its stern is curved stiffly over its back.

HEADED

A fox which has been caused to turn aside from his original line is said to have been headed.

HEADS UP

Hounds which have stopped feeling for the scent have 'got their heads up'.

HEEL (HEEL-WAY)
Hounds run heel (or heel-way) when they run the line of a fox the opposite way to which he was going.

HIT THE LINE
Used of a hound, or a huntsman in his cast, when they strike the line of the fox.

HOICK. HUIC
Hunting cheers, meaning 'Hark', pronounced 'Hike', 'Ike' or 'Ark'.

HOLD
A huntsman, in making his cast, is sometimes said to 'hold hounds round'.

HOLD HARD
A huntsman's, or Master's, rate to riders who press hounds too closely.

HOLD UP
One can hold up a litter or a covert by surrounding it to prevent foxes leaving.

HOUND JOG
The normal pace, about 6 miles an hour, that hounds travel on a road.

HUIC HOLLOA
A cheer to draw attention to a holloa.

IN AND OUT
Two fences close together, but too far apart to be negotiated in one jump.

KENNEL
A fox's bed in a covert, etc., above ground.

LIFT
A huntsman lifts hounds when he holds them on to a place where he thinks the fox may be, or where one has been seen.

LINE
The trail of a fox.

MAKE A PACK
To count hounds.

MARK
Hounds are said to 'mark the fox to ground' when they gather round and bay outside an earth or drain into which the hunted fox has gone.

MASK
A fox's head.

MOB
To mob a fox is to surround it or to hunt it without giving it a fair chance.

MUSIC
The cry of hounds.

MUTE
A term to describe a hound which does not throw its tongue when on the line of a fox.

MUZZLE
A hound's nose.

NOSE

The ability of a hound to smell.

OPEN

Hounds 'open' on a fox when they first speak to a line in covert. An open *earth* is one which has not been stopped.

OWN THE LINE

Used of a hound which is on the fox's line.

OXER

Thorn fence with a guard rail. A double oxer is a fence with a rail on each side.

PACK

A collection of hounds.

PAD

A fox's foot. To track a fox is to 'pad' him.

PICK

To pick hounds up is to lift them.

PIPE

A branch or hole in an earth.

POINT

The distance, measured as the crow flies, between two points in a run. The actual distance is described 'as hounds ran'.

PROVINCES

Any hunting country in England, Scotland and Wales, less the Midlands and Shires.

PUDDING

The meal porridge as fed to hounds.

PUT DOWN

The expression used when a horse or hound is killed on account of old age, etc.

PUTTING TO

Earths are 'put to' when they are closed, on a hunting morning, with the fox inside them.

RASPER

Any big fence.

RATE

To reprove or scold a hound is to 'rate' it.

RIDE

A path through a covert.

RINGING FOX

One which runs in circles, close to its home covert.

RIOT

Any animal, other than a fox or bird, hunted by hounds. When hounds so hunt they are said to riot.

RUNNING

Hounds are running when they are actually in pursuit of a fox.

SCARLET

The colour of a hunting coat. The terms 'red' or 'pink' are also used. One can say, 'He hunts in scarlet (or pink)', but with 'red' it must be, 'He hunts in a red coat'.

SCENT

Scent is said to be 'breast high' when hounds race and do not stoop their heads. When hounds lose the scent they 'throw up' their heads. Scent is 'ticklish' when it varies from good to bad. Hounds run almost mute when there is a 'burning scent'.

SHIRES

Cover parts of Leicestershire, Rutland and Northamptonshire. The Shire packs are Belvoir, Cottesmore, Fernie, Pytchley and Quorn.

SINKING

When a fox is very tired at the end of a run, he is said to be sinking.

SKIRT

A hound which cuts off corners, while other hounds are following the true line of the fox, is a 'skirter'.

SPEAK

This is the term for a hound when it barks.

STAIN

Foil.

STALE LINE

The line of a fox which has been a long time gone.

STERN

A hound's tail.

STOPPING

Or stopping out, that is closing earths when the fox is abroad during the night.

STUB-BRED

Applied to foxes which are born above ground.

TAIL HOUNDS

Hounds which are right behind the rest, when running. When hounds do not run abreast it is called 'tailing'.

TALLY O!

A hunting cry made when one has viewed a fox. If the huntsman is a long way off, a shrill cry (known as a 'View holloa') is given instead.

TIMBER

Post and rails.

TONGUE

Cry of hounds, which are said to 'throw the tongue' when they speak to a line.

TOUCH THE HORN

To blow the horn.

UNENTERED

An unentered hound is one which has not finished one cub-hunting season.

P

VIEW

The sight of a fox. To see a fox is to view it.

'VIEW HOLLOA' or 'HOLLOA'

Pronounced 'Holler'. The scream given when one has viewed a fox.

VIXEN

A female fox.

WALK

Hound puppies are out 'at walk' when looked after at farms, etc.

WATTLE

A hurdle.

WHELPS

Unweaned puppies.

WIND

A hound is said to wind a fox, that is to smell it.

WOODLAND

A very large covert, or a large area mostly woods.

A Simple Guide for Hunter Trials

by The British Horse Society

Introduction

The British Horse Society and the Hunters Improvement Society, having received many complaints as to the running and judging of hunter trials, formed a joint committee to suggest a simple guide to encourage unification in organizing and judging these events. A number of suggestions were studied from various organizers of hunter trials and the following recommendations were made, which will be included in the British Horse Society's new leaflet *Rules for Hunter Trials*.

Recommendations

It was generally agreed that the chief cause of complaint was that out of a number of clear rounds, unless decided on speed, few had any idea of how the winners were selected. The committee were against speed being the deciding factor for obvious reasons. It was considered that the ideal method was to have a second and shortened course of approximately ½ mile and consisting of 8 to 10 bigger and more complicated fences. This course to be judged by one judge with style taken into account. A competitor having gained a clear round on the ordinary course should immediately report to the starter of this jump-off course. Alternatively, if the necessary ground is not available, a few fences, preferably those that are the more tricky and knock-down, can be judged on style. This will mean that one judge, in each class, must judge these fences entirely. Competitors must be told which fences will be judged on style.

The course

The course should be about 1½ miles in length with approximately 20 fences, and these should be capable of being judged from the least possible number of positions. The start and finish should be adjacent to assist timing and control.

Fences

They should be similar to those in the surrounding country, and they should be strongly built. Any fences capable of being knocked down should be constructed so that they are not easily dislodged. A top timber rail or pole must be of at least 5 inches in diameter.

Suggested dimensions of fences in a novice class are given below. They should be adjusted for an open class or a class for ponies. Normally a team's class will use the novice course.

(a) Obstacle with height only 3 feet 6 inches.
(b) Obstacle with spread only 9 feet.
(c) Obstacle with height and spread:
    (i) Spread should not exceed 4 feet at top, 6 feet at base.
    (ii) When maximum spread is used at top, height should not exceed 3 feet 3 inches.

Organization of a class and scoring

Competitors should go in flights of two, the higher number wearing a sash. In the first round of any class, time should only be used to decide the 'time allowed, for the course. Penalties should be awarded as shewn below. Horses with clear rounds or equal first will qualify for a jump-off. A British Showjumping Association score card can be used for recording the results (obtainable from the British Showjumping Association, price 40p per dozen, at the National Equestrian Centre, Kenilworth, Warwickshire, CV8 2LR).

Penalties

Knocking down an obstacle (other than one classified as fixed)	10 faults
First refusal, circle or run-out at an obstacle	10 faults
Second refusal etc., on the course	10 faults
Third refusal on the course	Elimination
Fall of horse or rider anywhere on the course	30 faults
Jumping wrong panel when in a flight	Elimination
Jumping own panel that has already been knocked down by another competitor	No penalty
Error of course not rectified	Elimination
Every commenced period of 5 seconds in excess of 'time allowed'	1 fault
Exceeding time limit which is twice the 'time allowed'	Elimination

Speed

Subject to the nature of the going and the local terrain the 'time allowed' should be based on a speed of 450 yards per minute for all classes except the open, which should use a speed of 500 yards per minute.

Style

This is for a smooth performance and manner of going of horse and rider at a fair hunting pace, for which extra marks are allotted. In a team or pair class, style should include the competitors going together for which 20 marks can be allotted.

The novice class

A 'novice' is a horse or pony which has not previously gained a money prize in a hunter trial or similar event, that is horse trial, working hunter, showjumping.

Index

Accidents and First Aid, in the hunting field,
    128–32
Acton, C. R., 207
    on kennel cleanliness, 81
    on hound diet, 82
    on hound condition, 83
    on hound hysteria and diet, 85
    on getting to know hounds, 87
    books, 207
Adelaide Hunt Club (Australia), 170
Ainsworth, Sir Thomas, M.F.H. (Tipperary),
    150
Alabama, hunting in, 163–4
Albrighton hounds in Portugal, 181
Aldin, Cecil, 207
Alexander, Major John, M.F.H. (Kilkenny), 150
Alexander, Mrs, of Lilford (Carlow Hunt Club),
    150
Alexander the Great, 15
Alken, Henry Sr, sporting artist, 25
Alken, Henry Jr, sporting artist, 25, 196
Allison, Buck, M.F.H. (Cedar Knob), 163
Althorp, Lord, M.F.H. (Pytchley), 26
Alto-Mearim, Senhor Roque de Pinho, Count
    of, Portuguese Master, 181
Ambleside, 142
American Foxhound Club, 35
American Hunts, locations of, 217–19
American Senator, The (Trollope), 201
Analysis of the Hunting Field (Surtees), 196
Annaly, Lord, M.F.H., 92–3
Anne, Queen of England, 20
Appalachian Mountains, 161, 164
Apperley, C. J. (Nimrod), 1777–1843, 198–9
    describing 'The Melton Style', 25
    on 'bagmen', 26
    disliked by Surtees, 197
    books, 212
    steeplechasing, 187
Apperley, Captain W., 207
Appian Way, 177
Apsley, Lady, 207, 213
Aristotle, 15
Armitage, Marigold, 207
Armour, G. D., 205
    book by, 207
Arrian, 16
Arundell, Lord, of Wardour, 21, 23
Ascot sales, 184
Austin, Sir William, M.F.H. (Ormond), 150

Austria, Elizabeth, Empress of: Foxhunting
    visits to England and Ireland, 28; in Italy,
    180
Avent, James M., of Hickory Valley,
    Tennessee, 33
Avondhu Hunt, 152
Azoturia, 131

Bakewell, Robert, pioneer of modern farming,
    23
Ballymacad Hunt, 148
Barcelona, Countess of, Hon. Master,
    Equipagem de Santo Huberto, 181, 182
Barclay, Captain C. G. E., M.F.H., 11
    quoted on hound-breeding today, 56
Barrow, Dennis (Ulswater), 144
Barton, William, of Grove, founder of
    Tipperary Hunt, 150
Bassenthwaite, 137, 142
Bathurst, 7th Earl
    on hound breeding, 52, 53
    on Welsh cross, 66
    books by, 207
'B.B.', author, 208
Beach Thomas, Sir William, 208
Beamish family (Co. Cork), 152
Beatty, David, M.F.H. (Wexford), 151
Beaumont, Major Michael, M.F.H. (Kildare),
    149
Beaufort, 5th duke of, turns from deer to fox,
    21
Beaufort, 8th Duke of, 208
Beaufort, 10th Duke of, 19
    as breeder of hounds, 30
    on hunt staff, 94–5
    hounds, 193
    hounds in Portugal, 181
    blood of hounds, in Australia, 169
    blood of hounds, in U.S.A., 157, 164
    Leveller 10, 66
Beck, Baron Frederic de, M.F.H. (Equipagem
    de Santo Huberto), 11, 180–2
Beckford, Peter (1740–1811), 18, 22, 195–6
    on scent, 42
    on whippers-in, 98
    on treatment of hounds, 105
    as author, 208
    hound discipline in his day, 86–7
    on hunting heel-line, 196

on hunting through foil, 196
on hounds at fault, 196
Bell, Isaac, M.F.H., 153
  as breeder of hounds, 30
  on line breeding, 52, 53
  on the Belvoir-type, 55
  uses Welsh outcrosses, 56
  on Sir Edward Curre's hounds, 66
  with Sir Alfred Goodson, 68
  as Master of the Kilkenny, 151
  on July–Fell cross, 164
  as author, 208
Bell-Irving, Captain John (Dumfriesshire), 73
Bell-Macdonald, Miranda, of Dumfriesshire,
  74
Belle-Rivière Hunt, Canada, 173
Belo de Moraes, Professor (Equipagem de
  Santo Huberto), 180
Belvoir Hunt, 26, 177, 193
  hounds in Canada, 172
Belvoir Weaver '06, 66
Belvoir Watchman '07, 66
Bennett, Arnold, 203
Benson, C. E., 208
Benson, John (Melbreak), 141
Bentinck, Lord Charles, 208
Bentinck, Lord Henry (Old Burton), 54
Beresford family (Co. Waterford), 152
Berkeley, 5th Earl of, 21
Berkeley, Grantley F., 208
Berkeley Hunt, 56
Bermingham, William, M.F.H., founder of
  the Canadian English Foxhound Show,
  172
Bermingham and North Galway Hunt, 154
Berry, Michael F., 11
  on scent, 45–6
  as author, 208
Berry, Oliver (Central Committee of Fell
  Hunts), 144
Beveridge, J. C., M.F.H., 148
Birdsong, Col. George L. F., M.F.H., of
  Georgia, 60, 162
Bishop, C. J., M.F.H. (East Galway), 154
Bishop, Frank (Portuguese huntsman), 181
Black-and-Tans, see Scarteen
Blencathra Hunt, 140, 141–2
Bobcat, hunting of, in Tennessee, 163
Bolton, William, M.F.H., founder of the
  Island Hunt, 151
Bonaparte family, hunting in Italy, 180
Booth, J. B., 208
Boothby, Thomas, first Master of the Quorn,
  21
Border Hunt, 67, 71
Borwick, Col. M.
  on hound exercise, 79–80
  on vitamins in hound diet, 81
  on bitches in whelp, 85–6
  on fairness to hounds, 87
Bourns, Miss (East Galway), 154
Bovill, E. W., 208
Bowe, Loughlin, M.F.H. (North Kilkenny),
  150
Bowen, Muriel, 208

Bowles, Charlie (Ballymacad), 148
Bowman, Joe (Ullswater), 143–4
Boyd, A. J. B. (Wexford), 151
Bradley, Cuthbert, 208
Brainard, William W. Jr, M.F.H. (Old
  Dominion), 158, 161
Bramham Moor hounds in Portugal, 181
Brecon Whipcord, 73
Bree Hunt, 151
Briscoe, Henry, M.F.H., 151
British Field Sports Society (B.F.S.S.), 29, 191,
  192
British Horse Society, 11, 229
British Show Jumping Association, 230
Brito e Cunha, Senhor Antonio (Equipagem
  de Santo Huberto), 180, 182
Britton Smith, Lt-Col. A., MC, QC, M.F.H.,
  11, 171
Brock, D. W. E., 208
Brocklesby Hunt, 21, 26
Brocklesby Rallywood, 26, 54
Bromley Davenport, W. D., 29, 201–3, 209
Brook, Col. Charles, M.F.H. (Dumfriesshire),
  73
Brooke, Robert, 17th-century Maryland
  settler, 30
Brooksby (Capt. E. Pennell-Elmhirst), hunting
  correspondent, 209
Bryan, Rev. Leslie (Muskerry), 152
Bryn Mawr hound show, 58, 62
Buccleuch's, Duke of, Hounds, 60
Buchanan-Jardine family, 72
Buchanan-Jardine, Sir John, Bt, M.F.H.
  breeder of Dumfriesshire hounds, 72–3
  on foxhounds' feet, 51
  on College Valley hounds, 68
  on Gascon-Ariegeois hounds, 74
Buchanan-Jardine, Major Sir Rupert, Bt, MC,
  M.F.H., 11, 73–4
Buckingham, George Villiers, 1st Duke of, 21
Budgett, H. M., M.F.H., author of *Hunting by
  Scent*, 42f
Bulman, John, M.F.H. (Windemere Harriers
  and Ullswater), 144
Burke, Richard, M.F.H. (Tipperary), 150
Burrows, George T., 209
Buttermere, 137
Byrne, Kevin, M.F.H. (Island), 151
Bywaters, Burrell F., American hound
  breeder, 34, 158, 160
Bywaters, Hugh, American hound breeder, 158
Bywaters, strain of hounds, 161, 162, 163

Caesar, Julius, 16
Cairns, Candy, Major (Freemantle Hunt Club),
  170
Calahan, J. F. Jr (Ormond), 150
Cameron, Mrs C., M.F.H., 148
Campagna Roma, hunting in the, 177, 178
Canada, foxhunting in, 171f
  dress, 174
  organization, 174
  social, 174
  country, 175
Canadian Foxhound Club, 172

Canute, King, 17
Capannelle racecourse (Rome), 177
Capel, Rev. Hon. William. In case of Essex v.
  Capel, 1809, 24
Capell, Ben, huntsman to the Kilkenny and
  Belvoir, 151
Caprilli, Frederico, Italian riding instructor, 179
Caps, 89–90, 94
Carbery Hunt, 153
Carlos I, King of Portugal, 181
Carlow Hunt and Carlow Hunt Club, 149–50
Carrigan, J., Secretary to the Tipperary, 150
Carter, William, of Tennessee, 163
Casting, 101–4
Cats, and hunting in U.S.A , 160
Cecil (Cornelius Tongue), 52, 209
Cedar Knob Hunt (Tennessee), 163
Chadwell, Ned (Orange County and Old
  Dominion), 158
Chalmers, Patrick, 209
Chamberlain, J., 215
Chaplin, Col. Frank, M.F.H. (Kilkenny), 151
Chapman, Anthony (Coniston), 143
Chapman, G., M.F.H. (Island), 151
Chapman, Tom (Coniston), 143
Chard, Jack (Forestry Commission), 138
Charlemagne, 17
Charles I, King of England, 20
Charles II, King of England, 20
Charlton Hunt, 21
Checks, 101–2
Cheshire, Mr Stewart's, *Worry '72*, 157
Chesterfield, George Stanhope, 6th Earl of, in
  Italy, 176–7
Chicken-coop jumps in U.S.A., 125, 160, 162
  in Canada, 175
Childe, William, of Kinlet (The Flying
  Child), 23
Cholmondeley, Thomas, of Cheshire, 26
Christian, Dick, 199
Chronicle of the Horse, 11, 127
Circolo della Caccia (Rome), 179
Clapham, Richard, 209
Clarke, Capt. S. T., M.F.H., 11
Clayton, Harry (Dulhallow), 153
Clayton, Michael, hunting correspondent, 209
Clonmel Hound Show, 151
Clonmell, Earl of, M.F.H. (Kildare), 149
Clowes, A. S., 95
Cockayne, Sir Thomas, author of *The Short
  Treatise on Hunting*, 19
Co. Clare Hunt, 153
Coelho de Cunha, Senhor, Portuguese Master,
  181
Colic, 131
College Valley Bellford '58, 71
College Valley Hunt, 67–9, 71, 141, 142, 164,
  165, 193
College Valley Ruffian, 71
Collingwood, William (Melbreak), 141
Colonna, Prince, Master of Rome Hunt, 180
Coniston Hunt, 140, 142–3
Conolly, Thomas, founder of the Kildare
  Hunt, 149
Conolly-Carew, Capt. Hon. Patrick, 149

Control of hunting, 89
Conyer, Dorothea, 209
Cook, Col. John, 28, 209
Coollatin, 151
Cooper, Leonard, 209
Corr, Henry J., M.F.H. (Dungannon), 154
Costs of hunting, 89
Cotley harriers, 69–71, 193
Country Life, 11
Courcy-Parry, C. N. de ('Dalesman'), 67, 68, 151
Coverts, 96
Coyote hunting in Tennessee, 163
Craig, Dr R. N., M.F.H. (East Devon), 71
Crane, Tom, huntsman to the 1st Duke of
  Wellington, 181
Cromwell, Oliver, 149
Croome Clansman, 73
Crosson, Albert (Pickering, Pennsylvania), 157
Crotty, E., M.F.H. (Galway Blazers), 154
Crozier, John (Blencathra), 142
Crummock, 137
Cub-hunting, 104–7
Culham, David, M.F.H. (Dumfriessshire), 73
Cumberland, History of, by Hutchinson, 138
Cumberland Hunt (N.S.W.), 167
Cuming, E. D., 209, 212
Cunningham-Jardine, Capt. Ronald
  (Dumfriesshire), 73
Cruraghmore, 151
Curre, Sir Edward, of Itton, M.F.H., 56
  how he founded his strain of hound, 65–6
  hounds in Australia, 169
Curre Hunt, 65–7
  author with, in 1973, 66–7, 71
Cusack-Smith, Lady, M.F.H. (Bermingham
  and North Galway), 154

Daily Telegraph, hunting reports, 29
Dale, Thomas F., 210
Dalton, Jim (Blencathra), 142
Daly, Major Bowes, M.F.H. (Galway Blazers),
  153
Daly, D. J. (United Hunt Club), 152
Daresbury, Lord, M.F.H. (Belvoir and
  Limerick), 153
Darley Arabian, 20
Darlington, 2nd Earl of, 21
David Davies Hunt, 66
Davies, E. W. L., 210
Dawnay, Major Hugh, M.F.H. (Waterford),
  152
Dawson, Lionel, 210
Dean, Thomas (Cotley Harriers), 69–71
Dempsey, M., M.F.H. (East Galway), 154
Dene, Lt-Col. J. A. (North Tipperary), 150
Derwentwater, 137
Dickler, The, Cheltenham Gold Cup winner,
  184
Dillon, Michael, M.F.H. (North Kilkenny), 150
Dixon, H. H. ('The Druid'), 27
  quoted, 72
  books, 210
Dobbin, P. (East Down), 154
Dobson, Tommy, M.F.H. (Eskdale and
  Ennerdale), 143

Dole, Richard E. Jr, M.F.H. (Mells), 163
Donaghue, Peter (Ballymacad), 148
Doncaster Sales, 184
Doubling the horn, 100
Drag-hunting, in U.S.A., 126
Drag, fox's, 99
Dress, 121

Eagles Farm Hunt (Pennsylvania), 156
Eames, Lt-Col. R. F. P., M.F.H. (Cotley), 11,
    70-1
Eames family, of Devon (Cotley harriers), 70
Eames, Thomas Palmer, M.F.H., 70
Eardley-Wilmot, J. E., 210
Early, William, American hound breeder, 158,
    160
Earth-stopping, 90, 96-7
East Down Hunt, 154
East Galway Hunt, 154
Edinburgh, H.R.H., The Prince Philip, Duke
    of, 179
Edward II, King of England, 18
Edward VIII,
    hunting in the Shires when Prince of Wales,
    29; in Italy, 179
Edwards, Lionel, 210
Egerton-Warburton, R. E., 210
Eglinton and Caledon Hunt, 172
Eglinton hunt, 100
Elizabeth I, Queen of England, 20
Enfield Chace Hunt, 192
Ennerdale, 137
Equipagem de Santo Huberto (Italy), 180f
Eskdale and Ennerdale Hunt, 143
Essex, 5th Earl of. In case of Essex v. Capel
    (1809), 24
Eton Beagles, 56
Evans, Gerald W., 11
Experiences of an Irish R.M. (Somerville and
    Ross), 204
Eyre, Giles, M.F.H. (East Galway), 154
Eyre, Lord, M.F.H. (East Galway), 154

Fairbairn, George (Point-to-Point Association),
    11
Fairfax, Thomas, 6th Baron, pioneer of
    foxhunting in U.S.A., 31, 58, 159
Farquhar, Lt-Col. Sir Peter
    as breeder of hounds, 30
    with Sir Alfred Goodson 68
Farr Yeatman, Rev. Harry,, West Country
    Master, 70
Fell Hounds, 68
    Conformation of, 140
    cry of, 140-1
    blood in U.S.A., 164, 165
Fell Hunting, 137-45
Feversham, Countess of, M.F.H., 210
Filgate, William, M.F.H., 149
Filmore, Sir Edward, of East Sutton, Kent,
    provides hounds for Lord Fairfax, 31
Finbar, Barry Ryan, M.F.H. (West Carberry),
    153 a
Finding a fox, 100
Findon Harriers (Australia), 169

Fingall, 11th Earl of, 148
Fitzgerald, Edward (Waterford), 151
Fitzpatrick, B. M., 210
Fitzwilliam, Earl, M.F.H. (Island), 151
Fitzwilliam family, 149
Field Masters
    qualifications of, 92-3
    during hunt, 101
Field Trials in U.S.A., 32, 59-60, 124
Firestone, Bertram, M.F.H. (Kildare), 149
Fleming, William, of Kentucky, donor of
    silver collar for field trials, 32
Flint and Denbigh blood in Italy, 177
Following on foot, 133-6
Forbes, Cdr W. M. ('Maintop'), 210
Forde, Lt-Col., M.F.H. (East Down), 154
Forde, P. M. D., M.F.H. (East Down), 154
Forestry Commission, 138
Forward, Rev. E. C., Devonian Master, 70
Four Burrow Whipcord '05, 66
Fownes, Thomas, 21
Fox, Charles
    on cooking hound food, 81
    on health of hounds, 85
Fox Destruction Societies, 138
Fox, natural history of, 36-40
    habitat, mode of living and diet, 37
    skill as hunter, 37
    range and movement, 38
    mating and breeding, 38-9
    causes of death, 39
    importance of hunting to fox popluation,
    39-40
    American, 57-8, 162
    Grey, 124, 160, 161, 162, 164
    Movements of the European Red Fox in
    America, 59
    Lakeland, 146
Foxes, in Italy, 178
    in Canada, 175
    in Australia, 166
Foxhound, The, 47f
    discipline, 86-7
    drafting, 89
    entered and unentered, 48, 89
    importance of balance and symmetry in, 51
    exercise, 48
    feeding and condition, 82-5
    in kennels, 77-81
    puppies, 47-8
    qualities required in, 49
    points of, 50-1
    Mendelian principles, 51-2
    pedigree and line-breeding, 52-4
    evolution of, 54-6
    introduction of Welsh blood, 56
    modern type, 56-7
    whelps, 86
Foxhound, The, in U.S.A.
    18th-century and Penn-Marydel strains,
    58-9
    new hound needed to hunt the imported red
    fox, 59
    field trial strains, 59-60
    hunting countries, 60-1

Foxhound, The, in U.S.A.—*cont.*
  how pack-hounds are hunted, 61–3
  the future, 63–4
  English blood, 157
Foxhound Kennel Studbook
  of America, 34
  of Great Britain, 54, 89
Foxhunter's Licence, in U.S.A., 162
Foxhunting in Italy, 176f
  history of, in the U.S.A., 30f
  in Australia, 166–71
  obstacles, 167
  in the U.S.A., hunting countries, 60–1
  in Canada, 171–5
  in Portugal, 180–2
Foxhunting, Early History of
  Ancients, 15–17
  Normans, 17–18
  Plantaganets, 18–19
  Tudors, 19–20
  First packs entered to fox only, 21
Foxhunting, Post Meynellian History of
  Meynell and the first scientific breeding, 21–3
  Enclosure Acts, 23
  Hunt Boundaries, 24
  Golden Age, 24–9
  Effects of railways and metalled roads, 24
  Tap-roots of foxhound blood, 26
  Pheasant shooting versus foxhunting, 26
  Leadenhall bagmen, 26
Foxhunting, Modern History of
  planting of foxcoverts, 27
  relaxation of Game Laws, 27
  women in the hunting field, 27–8
  attitudes to farmers, 28
  Lord Willoughby de Broke on the end of
    'the Golden Age', 29
  effects of motor-cars, 29
  effects of the Great War, 29
  Scott Henderson Committee, 29
  changing character of land in the 20th
    century, 30
Fraser Valley Hunt (Canada), 173
Frederick, Sir Charles, M.F.H.
  on converts and earths, 96
  author, 210
Frontenac Hunt (Canada), 171, 173, 174
Froude, Parson, West Country Master, 70
Fulgosi, Count Cigala, Master of the Rome
  Hunt, 11, 176
Fund-raising, 93

Galls, girth and saddle, 132
Galway Blazers, 153–4
Game Conservancy, 192
Garle, Hubert, 211
Garrett, George, American breeder of hounds,
  164, 215
Garth and South Berks Hunt, 157, 192
Gascon-Ariegeois hounds, 74
Gascony hounds, 17, 19
Gaskarth, Anthony, M.F.H. (Coniston), 142
Gaunt, John of, Duke of Lancaster, 18
Genesse Valley Hunt, New York State, 33
George V, King, 179

George VI, King, 179
Gibson, Michael, 11
Glover, John, M.F.H. (East Down), 154
Gloucester Foxhunting Club (New Jersey), 31
Gloucester Foxhunting Club (Pennsylvania),
  155–6
Goathland Rosebud '21, 68
Gone away, 100
Gone to ground, 102
Goodall's Practice (Bentinck), 208
Goodson, Sir Alfred, Bt, M.F.H., 11, 142
  and the College Valley, 67–8
  and Sir J. Buchanan-Jardine, 72
Gosnell, Nimrod, American breeder of hounds,
  164
Graciosa, Marques de, M.F.H. (Equipagem de
  Santo Huberto), 181
Grafton, Dukes of, hunting in Norfolk,
  Northamptonshire and Surrey, 21
Grafton, 2nd Duke of, 21
Graham, Sir Bellingham, M.F.H. (Pytchley),
  28
Graham, Joe (Dumfriesshire), 72
Grand Steeplechase of Rome, 177
Greaves, Ralph, 211
Gregory, Anne (West Waterford), 152
Grey of Werke, Ford, Lord, 21
Grogan, W. E., M.F.H. (Carlow), 149
Groundhog holes, hazard of in U.S.A., 159
Gwyn-Jones, T., M.F.H. (East Galway), 154

Hall, Mrs, M.F.H. (Carlow), 149
Hamilton-Stubber family (Leix), 150
Handley Cross (Surtees), 197
Hannum, John B., M.F.H. of Maryland and
  Pennsylvania, 58
Hannum, Mrs John B., M.F.H. (Mr Stewart's
  Cheshire, Pennsylvania), 157
Harcourt Lees, Douglas, M.F.H. (Warrenton),
  161
Hardaway, Ben H. III, M.F.H. (Midland), 11,
  164–5
Hare, C. E. 211
Harrington, Earl of, M.F.H. (Limerick), 153
Harris, Col. Miles, American breeder of
  hounds, 162
Harpeth Valley Country Club Tennessee, 162
Hartigan, Jack (Kildare), 149
Hartley Edwards, Capt. E., 11
Hartropp, Col., M.F.H. (Kilkenny), 151
Harvey, James, M.F.H. (Wexford), 151
Hawkes family (Muskerry), 152
Hayes, M. Horace, 211
Hays, W., of Duns, Berwickshire, 72
Heart and lump, equine, 131–2
Heel-line, 98
Hemphill, Lord, M.F.H. (Galway Blazers), 154
Henry, Dr Thomas Y., Virginian M.F.H., 60
Hertfordshire Hunt, 27
Heythrop hunt, 157
  blood in Australia, 170
  hounds, 193
Hickman, Anne, M.F.H. (West Waterford),
  152
Hieover, Harry, 211

Higgens, M. R. C., M.F.H. (Tipperary), 150
Higginson, A. H., M.F.H. in England and
    U.S.A., and author, 33
  on puppies at walk, 47
  on Sir Edward Curre's hounds, 66
  on kennel cleanliness, 81
  on feeding hounds, 82
  on hound hysteria, 85
  on whelping, 86
  on hound discipline, 87
  on responsibilities of M.F.H., 91
  on Masters hunting hounds, 92
  on the Anglo-American Foxhound match,
    160
  on Huntsmen, duties of, 94, 97–104
  author, 210, 215
Hillsboro Hunt (Tennessee), 162
Hill-toppers, in U.S.A., 125
Hilton-Green, Major C., M.F.H., 148
Hinckley, Col. Albert P., M.F.H., 11, 157–8
Hitchcock, Thomas Sr, and the Meadow Brook
    Hunt, 33
Hoare, Major Robert, M.F.H., 11
  on hound breeding, 53
Holloas, 100
Holmby House (Whyte Melville), 200
Holroyd Smith family, founders of West
    Waterford, 152
Honey Locust tree
  in U.S.A., 164
  hazard of, 163
Horgan, P. St A., M.F.H. (Macroom), 153
Hornor, Col. John L. Jr, M.F.H., 11, 155, 163
Horse (see also 'Hunters')
  Arab stallions imported, 18
  Darley Arabian, 20
  performance of, 132
  Points of, 110
  treatment of, after hunting, 132
Horseman's Manual (1831), 196
Horserace Betting Levy Board, 116
Hounds of the World (Buchanan-Jardine), 74, 209
Hourihane, Bertie (West Carbery), 153
Hume Gardiner, Joe, of Virginia, 158
Hunt
  boundaries, 88
  committees, 88–9
  servants, 90
  jumps, 90, 93–4
  supporters clubs, 90, 93, 191
  secretaries, 93–4
  staff, 94–5
  Servants Benefit Society, 95
Hunter Trials, 230–1
Hunters, 109–16
  suitable for different countries, 109–10
  selection and buying of, 110–13
  conformation of, 111–13
  making of, 113
  feeding, 114
  protection from cold, 114
  shoeing of, 115
  hygiene of, 115
  ailments of, 115
  exercise of, 115

treatment of accidents in hunting field,
    129–30
  vertebrae fractures, 130
  when stuck in ditches, 130
  lameness out hunting, 130
Hunting by Scent (Budgett), 209
Huntsmen in U.S.A., 62
Hyland, Mrs J., M F H (Bermingham and
    North Galway), 154

Income, 90
Iredale, Major Ernest, M.F.H. (Melbreak), 141
Ireland, hunting in, 146–54
  country, 146–7
  history, 147–8
Irish M.F.H.A., 153
Irton, Lamphugh, of Eskdale, 143
Island Hunt, 151
Italy, foxhunting in, 176f
Ivester Lloyd, T., 211

Jackson, Roy, Master of Radnor,
    Pennsylvania, 58
James I, King, 20
James, David, 211
Jockey Club, 183, 184
John, King, 18
Jorrocks, John, Surtees character, 24, 195, 197
Jorrocks's Jaunts and Jollities (Surtees), 196
July, American foxhound and foxhound
    strain, 60, 164
  July-Trigg strain, 60, 63
Jumping, 122–3

Kelly, Dermot, 192
Kemp, Bob, huntsman in Portugal, 181
Kennels, organisation and management, 77f
Kennel
  management in U.S.A., 62
  'recognized' foxhound, 89
  huntsman, 92
  fox's, 99
Kerr, James, M.F.H. (Shillelagh and
    District), 149
Kerry beagles, 74–6
Kilbride, Patrick, M.F.H. (Shillelagh and
    District), 149
Kildare Hunt, 149
Kilkenny Hunt, 150–1
  Hunt Club, 150
  blood in Italy, 177
Kindersley, Major Charles, M.F.H. (Eglinton
    and Caledon, Canada), 172
Kirkham, John, huntsman in Portugal, 181
Knight, Dick (Pytchley), 24
Knowles, T. W., M.F.H. (South Union), 152
Knox, Flurry (Somerville and Ross character),
    204
Knutsford, Lord, 68
Kruger, G. H., M.F.H., 149
Kruger, Mrs G. H., M.F.H., 149

La Touche, John, M.F.H. (Kildare), 149
Lafayette, Marquis de, foxhunting friend of
    George Washington, 31, 159

Lake District weather, 140
Lake of Two Mountains Hunt (Canada), 173
Lalor, Desmond, M.F.H. (Leix), 150
Lambton, Capt. Hon. Claud, M.F.H. (College
    Valley), 67
Lambton, Ralph, friend of Surtees, 196
Land Commission, in Ireland, 148
Land League, in Ireland, 148, 150
Langrishe, Sir Hercules, M.F.H. (Kilkenny), 151
Larrabee, Sterling, M.F.H. (Old Dominion), 158
Lawrence, John, M.F.H. (Llangibby), 66
Leadenhall market and purchase of bagmen, 26
Ledburn Boswell, 73
Leix (Laios or Queen's County) Hunt, 150
Letts, Martin, M.F.H. (College Valley), 68
Leverhulme, Lord, 183
Levinge, Sir Richard, Founder of the
    Westmeath Hunt, 148
Lewis, Squire, of St Pierre, 65
Liége, Bishop of, 18
Lifting hounds, 102
Limerick Hunt, 153
Lismore, Lord, M.F.H. (Ormond), 150
Lisrenny, home of the Filgate Family, 149
Lloyd, Capt. Simon, 177
Lochaber and Sunart Farmers' Hunt, 141
Loder, Norman, M.F H. (Southdown), 206
Logan, Bruce, M.F.H. (Coniston), 142
London Hunt (Canada), 172, 173
Long, John, huntsman in Portugal, 181
Long, Thomas Fields, M.F.H. (Kildare), 149
Longford, 1st Earl of, 148
Lonsdale, 1st Earl of, Master of the
    Cottesmore, 26
Lonsdale, 5th Earl of, 144
Louis XIII, King of France, 20
Louth Hunt, 149
Loweswater, 137
Lowther, Capt. Hon. Anthony, M.F,H., 144
Lunesdale Hunt, 144

MacAndrew, Capt. Hon. Colin, 192
McCalmont, Mrs Dermot, M.F.H., 75
McCalmont, Major Dermot, M.F.H.
    (Kilkenny), 151
McCalmont, Major Victor M.F.H. (Kilkenny),
    151 177
McGowan, J. B. M.F.H. (Galway Blazers), 154
McIvor, S. H., M.F.H. (Dungannon), 154
McKeever, M., 149
McKeever, R. W., M.F.H., 149
McNeill, Charles, M.F.H., 107
Mackay-Smith, Alexander, M.F.H., 11, 35, 215
Macroom Hunt, 153
Maddux, Sid, 215
Maddux, Bob Lee, 215
Manheim, F. H., M.F.H. (Galway Blazers), 154
Mann, Major J. J., M F H., 11
    on size of pack, 97
    on scent, 44
    on kennel administration, 77–9
    on hound diet, 84
Maryland, red fox introduced into, in 1730,
    156
    early hunting in, 30

March Phillips, Gus, 212
Markham, Gervase, 19
Market Harborough (White Melville), 200
Marrane, Italian ditches, 178
Masefield, John (1878–1967), 193, 204–6, 212
Mason, Noel (Findon Harriers), 169
Masters, Miss Sylvia, M.F.H. (Tipperary), 150
Masters
    election and responsibilities of, 89
    qualifications of, 89–93
Masters of Foxhounds Association (M.F.H.A.),
    29, 89, 93, 184, 192
M.F.H.
    in America, 34, 60, 62, 127, 172
    in Australia, 170
Mather, Charles, M.F.H. (Radnor), 33
Meath Hunt, 148–9
Meade, J. O'M., M.F.H., 11
Melba, Nellie, 170
Melbourne Hunt (Australia), 169
Melbreak Hunt, 140, 141
Mellon, Mr Paul, M.F.H., of Tan-y-Bryn,
    Virginia, 159
Mells Hunt (Tennessee), 163
Melton Mowbray, becomes 'capital' of
    foxhunting, 25, 29
Memoirs of a Foxhunting Man (Sassoon), 206
Mendel, G. J., principles of, applied to
    breeding of foxhounds, 51–2
Mernagh, Jim (Bree), 151
Mernagh, John (Bree), 151
Meynell and South Staffs Hunt, 192
Meynell, Hugo
    co-pioneer of scientific foxhunting, 21
    succeeds Boothby as Master of the Quorn, 22
    breeds ancestor of modern foxhound, 23
    attitude to farmers, 28, 54
Meynell Stormer 1791, 54
Middlesex Hunt (Massachusetts), 160
Middleton, Capt. Bay, 28
Midland Hunt (Alabama and Georgia), 164–5
Midland Harlot '70, 164
Midland Hunt (Tasmania), 168
Milden, Denis, Sassoon character, 206
Miller, Richard, champion point-to-point
    rider, 185
Milnor, William, historian of the *Gloucester
    Foxhunting Club*, 31
Milton (Fitzwilliam) Hunt, 148
Milton Potent 01, 66
Molyneux, J., 212
Moniz, Galvao, or Senhor Ing, (Equipagem de
    Santo Huberto), 181
Monmouth, James Scott, Duke of, 21
Monsarez, Count of (Portugal), 182
Moore, Daphne, 212
Moore, Capt. J. D., M.F.H. (Avondhu), 152
Mooreland Hunt, Alabama, 163
Morgan, Mrs, M.F.H. (West Waterford), 152
Morpeth Hunt, 109
Morris, Samuel Jr, President of the Gloucester
    Foxhunting Club, 155
Mount Juliet, Kilkenny, kennels at, 151
Mount Vernon (Virginia), 159
Mountain, American foxhound, 60

Murphy, John, M.F.H. (North Kilkenny), 150
Murphy, John, M.F.H. (United Hunt Club),
    152
Murphy, Mrs R. P., M.F.H. (Muskerry),152
Muse, American foxhound, 60
Musgrave, Miss, M.F.H. (West Waterford), 152
Muskerry Hunt, 152
Musters, John, 22
Mytton, Squire John, 26

National Equestrian Centre, 230
National Hunt Committee, 183
Nelson, R. I., M.F.H. (Dulhallow), 153
Nettle-stings, 132
New South Wales, hunting in, 167
New Sporting Magazine, 196
Newcastle, William Cavendish, 1st Duke of,
    20
Nicholas, Harry, M.F.H., President of the
    American M.F.H.A., 156
Nicholson, John (Lunesdale), 144
Night-hunting in U.S.A., 32, 59, 124, 158, 162
Nimrod, see Apperley, C. J.
Noguiera, José (Equipagem de Santo
    Huberto), 180–1
Noonan, John (Avondhu), 152
North Kilkenny Hunt, 150
North Tipperary Hunt, 150
Northern hound, or beagle, 19, 23, 54
Nose-bleeds, equine, 137

Oak Spring (Virginia), 160
Oaklands Hunt Club (Australia), 169
O'Brien, Mary (Avondhu), 152
O'Brien, Thomas (Avondhu), 152
O'Driscoll, Barry (Carbery), 153
O'Driscoll, Edward, M.F.H. (Carbery), 153
O'Driscoll, Patrick, M.F.H. (Carbery), 153
O'Dwyer, Jack (Scarteen), 75
O'Dwyer, Tommy (Scarteen), 75
Ogilvie, Will, poet and author, 28
Old Dominion Hunt (Virginia), 31, 158–9
Old Huntsman, The (Sassoon), 206
Old Surrey and Burstow Hunt, 192
O'Neill, P. W. (Ballymacad), 148
Oppian, 17
Orange County Hunt (Virginia), 158
Orchard, Vincent, 214
Ordway, Mrs, M.F.H. (East Galway), 154
Ormond Hunt, 150
O'Reilly, Michael (North Kilkenny), 150
Osbaldeston, George, M.F.H., 26, 54, 212
Osbaldeston Furrier, 26, 54
Ottawa Valley Hunt Club, 173, 174

Pack, size of, 97
Page, Robin, 212
Paget, Major Guy
    on Lord Annaly, 92–3
    hunt biographer, 213
Paget, J. Otho, 212
    on qualifications of M.F.H., 90
Palava, Count (Portuguese Master), 181
Panels (hunt jumps) in U.S.A., 125
Parker, Bob (Rome Hunt), 180

Parker, J. P. N., M.F.H. (Kildare), 149
Parrington, Tom, founder of the hound show
    at Redcar, 54
Pattinson, Abe (Ullswater), 143
Pearson, William, of Bannockrout, M.F.H.
    (Melbreak), 141
Pearson, Ray (Old Dominion), 158
Peck, Alan, M.F.H. (Blencathra), 142
Peel, John, 142
Peel, Major R., M.F.H. (Galway Blazers and
    Ormond), 150
Penn-Marydel, American foxhound strain, 35,
    58, 60, 62, 156–7, 163
Persse, Robert, M.F.H. (Co. Galway), 153
Peterborough hound show, 54
Phipps, Mr Hubert, of Rockburn, Virginia,
    159
Phoebus, Gaston, Comte de Foix, 18
Pickering, John (Bermingham and North
    Galway), 154
Pickering Hunt (Pennsylvania), 156
Pickersgill, Joseph, M.F.H. (Scarteen)
    quoted, 76
    Master of the Galway Blazers, 153
Piedmont Hunt (Virginia), oldest in U.S.A., 32
Pine Lodge Hunt Club (Australia), 170
Pitt, Miss Frances, M.F.H. (Wheatland)
    on scent, 46
    on hunt terriers, 108
    author, 213
Pittman, Mr, Editor of the Sporting Magazine,
    198
Plato, 16
Point-to-point
    Secretaries Association, 183
    horses, 184
    sponsors, 186
Point-to-points
    compared with conventional race meetings,
        185
    dope testing at, 186
    as source of income for hunt funds, 186
    ladies riding in, 186
Pollard, Hugh B. C., author of The Mystery
    of Scent, 42f, 213
Pony Club, The, 123
    in Italy, 179
    in Australia, 171
Pooler, James, M.F.H. (East Down), 154
Popplewell, Newton, M.F.H. (Wexford), 151
Porcupines, hazard of in Canada, 175
Portarlington, 2nd Earl of, M.F.H. (Leix), 150
Porter, Edmund (Eskdale and Ennerdale), 143
Porter, Jack (Eskdale and Ennerdale), 143
Porter, Willie, M.F.H. (Eskdale and
    Ennerdale), 143
Portugal, Foxhunting in, 180f
Powell, Mrs (North Tipperary), 150
Power, John, M.F.H. (Kilkenny), 150
Power, Richard, M.F.H. (Kilkenny), 150
Preston, Major, M.F.H. (Ormond), 150
Profumo, Major Philip, M.F.H. (Galway
    Blazers), 153
Puckeridge and Thurlow Hunt, blood in
    Australia, 169

Puleston, Sir Richard, M.F.H., 21
Puppy Shows, 48
Pytchley hounds in Portugal, 181

Quarterly Review, 198
Queensberry, 7th Marquess of, M.F.H., 72
Quigley, Sylvester L., M.F.H. (Pickering), 156
Quorn Hunt, 27, 109, 198

Rabies, in Canada, 175
Racehorse Betting Levy Board, 184
Radcliffe, Delmé, 24, 42, 210
Radnor Hunt (Pennsylvania), 58, 156
Randolph, Mrs Archibald (Piedmont), 159
Rappahannock River, 158, 161
Rat-catcher, 121
Real Charlotte, The (Somerville and Ross), 203
Reeves, T. H. M. (Kildare), 149
Reynard the Fox, 193, 205–6
Reynell, Sam, M.F.H., 146, 148
Reynolds, Rev. E. M. (Coniston), 142
Rhett, Harry Moore Jr, M.F.H. (Mooreland), 163
Ribblesdale, Lord, quoted, 28
Richard I, King of England, 18
Richardson, John (Blencathra), 142
Richmond, 4th Duke of, 173
Richmond and Gordon, 9th Duke of, 213
Rideability of countries, 93–4
Riding to Hounds
    farmland and wild life, 117–18
    Masters and hunt staff, 19
    courtesy, 120–1
    saddlery and dress, 121
    getting to the meet, 123
    in the United States, 124–7
Ringwell and Bowood Hunt (Tasmania), 169
Riot, deer, in U.S.A., 63
Rivers Bulkeley, Col. Charles, 28
Robards, H., (Limerick), 153
Robinson, Ben, American hound breeder, 162
Robinson, Miss (Leix), 150
Robson, Jacob, M.F.H. (Border), 67
Roccagiovine, Marchese di, 177, 179
Roche, John (Mr Stewart's Cheshire), 157
Rohan, J. S., M.F.H. (Waterford), 152
Rolls, Eric, author, 166
Rome Hunt, 177–8
Ronald, Heather B., 11, 166
Rook, David, 213
Rose Tree Hunt (Pennsylvania), 155
Ross, Capt. Charles (Gloucester Foxhunting Club), 155
Ross, Martin (see also 'Somerville, Edith'), 203, 213–14
Rossell, Col. J. E., 216
Rostad, Thurston J., 216
Russell, Parson Jack, M.F.H., 10
Russell, Mrs J. A., M.F.H. (United Hunt Club), 152
Russell, Richard, (Irish M.F.H.A.), 11, 152, 154
Rutland, 4th Duke of, 21
Ryan, Clement, M.F.H. of Scarteen, 74
Ryan, John, M.F.H. of Scarteen, 74
Ryan, T. F., M.F.H. of Scarteen, 11, 75–6

Santo Estevao, 182
St Hubert hound, 18
    monastery of, 54
Saddlery, 121
Salisbury, Countess of, 18th century M.F.H., 27
Salkeld, Col., M.F.H. (Dumfriesshire), 72–3
Sassoon, Siegfried (1886–1967), 206, 213
Scarteen Hunt ('Black and Tans'), 74–6, 152
Scarth Dixon, William, 213
Scent
    sources of, functions of, 41
    Somerville and Beckford on, 41–2
    Budgett and Pollard on, 42f
    masking, 44
    M. F. Berry on, 45–6
    Major Mann on, 44–5
    Frances Pitt on, 46
Scott, Major W. W. B., M.F.H., 152
Scott Henderson Committee, 29, 189
'Scrutator', 213
Shanahan, Dr P. J. (Waterford), 152
Sharp, Vernon, M.F.H. (Hillsboro), 163
Shedden, Lady Diana, 213
Sheehy, J. R. (Limerick), 153
Sherston, George, Sassoon character, 206
Sherston's Progress (Sassoon), 206
Shillelagh and District Hunt, 149
Shirley, Mary (Louth), 149
Sidesaddle, 121
Sidney Hunt (New South Wales), 167
Sifton, Lt-Col. Clifford, M.F.H. (Toronto and North York), 172
Silver Fox, The (Somerville and Ross), 203
Silverton Hunt, 154
Silverton Woodman, 73
Skinner, Col. F. G., on red foxes in U.S.A., 162
'Skittles' (Miss Walters), 28
Skrine, C. J. (Island), 151
Sloan, George (Hillsboro), 163
Smith, John (Westmeath), 148
Smile and Tear, The (Somerville), 203
Smith, H. W., 216
Smith, Thomas ('Gentleman' or 'Craven'), M.F.H., 42, 213
Smith, Thomas Assheton, M.F.H., 42
Smith-Barry, John, of Cheshire, 22
Smyth, W. D., M.F.H. (Strabane and Donegal), 154
Snake-fences, in U.S.A., 158
Società Romana della Caccia alla Volpe (Rome Hunt), 177f
Somerville, Edith (1848–1949), 153, 203–4, 213–14
    first lady M.F.H. in Ireland, 203
Somerville and Ross, 203–4
Somerville, William, 22, 41, 214
South and West Wilts Hunt, 23, 157
South Union Hunt, 152
Southern Hound, 17, 18, 19, 54
    in U.S.A., 58, 158
Southern States of U.S.A., growth of sport in, 165
Spallete, Italian scrubland, 178
Sparling, C., M.F.H. (Co. Clare), 153

Sparrow, Walter Shaw, 214
Speid-Soote, Capt., M.F.H. (Ballymacad), 148
Spigot, Col. (Wexford), 151
Sport (Bromley Davenport), 202
Sporting Magazine, 196, 198
Spring, J. A., M.F.H. (Bree), 151
Spring, Judy (Bree), 151
Springfield Hunt (Canada), 173
Stacpoole, Mrs de (Meath), 149
Stafford, Mrs Eve, M.F.H. (Strabane and
      Donegal), 154
Stamford, Lord, M.F.H. (Quorn), 26, 28
Steel, Anthony, 214
Stephens, Wilson, 211
Stoney, R. D. V., Lt-Cdr (Galway Blazers), 154
Stormer, 1791, 23
Strabane and Donegal Hunt, 154
Style, Major David (Fell hunts committee), 11
Subscriptions in Australia, 171
Sullivan, D. (South Union), 152
Summerhays, R. S., 214
Surtees, R. S.
      co-founder of *New Sporting Magazine*, 196
      on point-to-points, 187
      on qualifications of M.F.H., 91
      on subscription packs, 27
      on the use of railways, 24
      biography, 196
      quoted, *Handley Cross*, 197-8
      books, 214
      swallowtails, 121
Swan, Capt. D., M.F.H. (Ormond), 150
Sydenham, Lord, 173

Tagus, River, 180
Talbot hounds, see Southern
Talbot-Ponsonby, Major, M.F.H. (Kildare), 149
Tandy, Major Patrick, M.F.H. (Westmeath), 148
Tanner, J. N., M.F.H. (Muskerry), 152
Taunton Vale Harriers, 70
Temple, Howard, M.F.H. (Strabane and
      Donegal), 154
Tennessee, development of as a hunting
      country, 161-2
Tennessee Lead, American foxhound, 60
Terriers, 107-8
Thallon, Wing Commander (West Carbery),
      153
Thomas, Joseph B.
      founder of American Foxhound Club, 35
      pioneer of hunting in Tennessee, 162
      author, 216
Thompson, Kevin (Duhallow), 153
Thoughts on Hunting (Beckford), 195-6
Times, The, hunting reports, 29
Tipperary Hunt, 150
Tiverton hounds, 70
Tiverton Whipcord, 73
Tonson Rye family (Muskerry), 152
Tor di Quinto Cavalry School, Rome, 179
Toronto Hunt, 172, 173, 174
Trigg, Haden C., of Kentucky, 60
Trollope, Anthony (1815-1882), 200-1, 214
Trotter, J. O., 28
Tulloch, John, of Tundergarth, 73

Twici, Guillaume, 18
Twigg, H. C., 216

Ullswater, 137
Ullswater Hunt, 140, 143-4
Umberto I, King of Italy, 179
Umberto II, King of Italy, 180
Underhill, G. F., writer, 28, 214
United Hunt Club (Ireland), 152
Urbanization and roads, Britain, 192

Vale of Aylesbury Hunt, 192
Vale of Lune Harriers, 163
Van Urk, J. Blan, 216
Vater, Van der, M.F.H. (United Hunt Club),
      153
Veterinary advice, 128-32
Victoria, main centre of Australian foxhunting,
      169
Vila Vocosa, Portuguese hunting centre, 181
Vine and Craven Hunt, 192
Viner, R. T., 214
Virginia, north
      pre-eminence of as a hunting country, 160
      deterioration of country, 161
Vischer, P., 216
Vitry, Marquis de, 20

Wadsworth, Major Austin
      founder of Genesee Valley Hunt, New York
          State, 33
      on qualifications of M.F.H., 91
Wadsworth, William P., author of *Riding to
      Hounds in America*, 127, 216
Walker hounds, 164
Walker, W., 216
Walker, John W., American breeder of
      hounds, 162
Walker-and-Fell bred hounds, 162, 163
Walker, family, of Kentucky, 59, 63
Wallace, Capt., R.E., as breeder of hounds, 30,
      56
Walters, Miss Robin (West Waterford), 152
Warrenton Hunt (Virginia), 160-1
Warwickshire Hunt, 109
Warde, John, of Squerreys, M.F.H., 22, 26
Washington, General George, first President
      of the U.S.A. and Virginian M.F.H., 31,
      59, 159
Wastwater, 137
Waterford, 3rd Marquis of, M.F.H.
      (Tipperary and Waterford), 150, 151
Waterford Hunt, 151
Watson, A. E. T., author, 214
Watson, Frederick, author, 213, 214
Watson, George, founder of the Melbourne
      Hunt, 169
Watson, Harold, Chairman of the Lunesdale
      Hunt, 144
Watson, John, M.F.H. (Carlow), 149, 169
Watson, John, M.F.H. (Meath), 148
Watson, Lavinia M., 11
Watson, Robert, M.F.H. (Carlow and Island),
      148
Webb, J. F., M.F.H. (Wicklow), 149

Webb, Mary (Wicklow), 149
Weir, Joe (Ullswater), 144
Welcome, John, 215
Wellington, 1st Duke of, hounds in the
    Peninsular War, 181
Wellington-Waterloo Hunt (Canada), 175
Welsh hounds, 193
West Australian Hunt Club, 170
West Carbery Hunt, 153, 203
West Kent Hunt, 192
West Waterford Hunt, 152, 164
Westmeath Hunt, 148
Wexford Hunt, 151
White, Justin, M.F.H. (Macroom), 153
Whitelands Hunt (Pennsylvania), 156
Whitetailed deer, hazard of, in U.S.A., 159
Whippers-in, 94–5, 96–103
    in Australia, 170
Whissendine brook (Cottesmore), 199–203
Whyte-Melville Major G. J., 146, 199–200
Wicklow Hunt, 149
Wiggin, Sir Charles, M.F.H., on hound
    breeding, 53
'Wild Geese', The, 74
William I, King of England, 17
Williams, Capt. Evan, M.F.H. (Tipperary),
    150
Williams, Tom, M.P., 189
Williams-Wynn, Sir Watkin, blood of hounds
    in Italy, 177
Willoughby de Broke, 18th Baron, 26, 28–9,
    51, 54, 215

on hound condition, 83
on qualifications of M.F.H., 90
Wilson, Mrs Tyler, M.F.H. (Warrenton), 160
Windermere, 137, 142
Wire, 93
    woven, in U.S.A., 126
Woods, Richard, M.F.H. (Shillelagh and
    District), 149
Woolridge, Sam, breeder of hounds in
    Kentucky, 59
Worcester Smith, Harry, M.F.H., President of
    American M.F.H.A., 33, 34, 160
Worth Newenham, W. P., M.F.H. (South
    Union), 152
Wrixod Becher, Sir William Bt., M.F.H.
    (Duhallow), 153
Wrixon, Henry, M.F.H., founder of the
    Duhallow, 153
Wyndham-Quinn, Col., 215

Xenophon, 16

Yarborough, 1st Baron, founds Brocklesby
    stock, 23
Yarra Glen and Lilydale Hunt (Australia), 170
Yates, Major Sinclair, Somerville and Ross
    character, 214
'Yoi-Over', 215
York, Edward, 2nd Duke of, 215
Young, J. R., 215

Zetland Hunt, 192